THE SOCIALIST IDEA

THE SOCIALIST IDEA

a reappraisal

edited by
Leszek Kolakowski
and Stuart Hampshire

Basic Books, Inc. Publishers
New York

© 1974 Graduate School of Contemporary European
Studies, University of Reading

Library of Congress Catalog Card Number: 74-14109
SBN: 465-07936-9
Printed in Great Britain
75 76 77 78   10 9 8 7 6 5 4 3 2 1

CONTENTS

114126

INTRODUCTION

Leszek Kolakowski

The papers in this volume* were presented at the April 1973 inter-
national meeting in Reading sponsored by the publishing house
Weidenfeld and Nicolson and the Graduate School of Contemporary
European Studies, Reading University. The organizing committee
(Robert Cecil, Reading University; Stuart Hampshire, Wadham College, Oxford; Leszek Kolakowski, All Souls' College, Oxford; Sir
George Weidenfeld, publisher) decided to change the title, originally
'What is Wrong with the Socialist Idea?', into a milder one, 'Is there
Anything Wrong with the Socialist Idea?' The first title, in fact, seemed
to take for granted that something actually *is* wrong with the socialist
idea. It was, however, the overwhelming – though apparently not
unanimous – opinion of those who participated in the meeting that the
deep crisis affecting both contemporary socialist thought and socialist
movements does not result only from contingent historical circumstances, but is also rooted in ambiguities and contradictions in the primordial socialist message.

The purpose of the meeting was not to criticize existing socialist
regimes or movements but to analyse again the basic traditional concepts and values which constitute the socialist idea, and to question their
validity in the light of both historical experience and of theoretical
criticism. It was obvious that the discussion could not ignore the experiences of so-called socialist countries, but this critique was intended
to help the analysis of the idea of socialism itself, rather than to express
direct political attitudes.

The original proposal for the meeting laid out its tasks as follows:

> The socialist idea has sustained so many blows – presented as great
> victories – that people who share traditional socialist values should

* Except for those by Richard Lowenthal, Steven Lukes and Gilles Martinet.

reflect upon some fundamental issues which this idea involves, and should not be satisfied with criticism of existing socialist systems as its 'imperfect' or 'distorted' embodiment. The idea itself seems to be dying in socialist countries and it is manipulated and used elsewhere as a slogan in so many and such different political groups that it is hardly possible to find any clear content common to all its variants. We should ask ourselves at what point the traditional idea of socialism, the basic assumptions of socialist ideology, became resistant to theoretical objections and to modification in the light of historical experience. Such fundamental concepts as 'social control', 'working class', 'revolution', 'ownership' and 'equality' still call for new analysis, free of prejudice. The difference between the socialist idea itself and comprehensive projects of social reform (such as health service, insurance, pensions, general education, progressive taxation, etc.) should be reconsidered ...

Here are proposals for the topics to be discussed:

1. *The concepts of economic self-management and social control of production*
It may be readily agreed that democracy in the productive process is the necessary condition for socialist development; and that, in particular, the influence of the working class on production, if limited to each productive unit separately, may coexist with despotic forms of government and leave to the ruling bureaucracy complete freedom in the application of the means of production, in investment policy and in the distribution of national product. On the other hand, contemporary technology itself – not to mention the complex nature of the modern economy – require very special competence at all levels in both economic and technical management of production. Is economic democracy possible and is it compatible with competent management? Or is the very concept of competence a 'bourgeois invention'? Is the alternative to bureaucratic despotism some system of free competition, based on co-operative property, with all that that entails? How far is the Yugoslav experience relevant to the question, and what may be learnt from it? Can society rid itself of bureaucracy and, if not, can it tame it? Or is bureaucracy perhaps not the product of technology at all but only of particular social conditions?

2. *The implications of modern technology for socialism*
In the traditional Marxist sense socialism was supposed to draw its historical strength from and demonstrate its superiority by abolishing the fetters which the capitalist mode of production imposed on tech-

2

nical and productive progress. It is obvious that social problems are by no means solved either by economic growth or by technical progress in itself either in the East or the West (the very concept of progress in this sense being more and more doubtful, considering the price paid for it by mankind). It may also be argued that societies based on capitalist modes of production have not lost the ability to stimulate technical development – rather the opposite seems to be true; it is also arguable that the traditional Marxist distinction between productive and non-productive labour, and consequently the very concept of surplus value, is more and more doubtful. How far can the socialist idea be defined in terms of productivity? What is valid and rational in the idea that socialism, as opposed to capitalism, promises more free time for cultural development and more satisfaction of material needs? What is the meaning of the often-repeated statement that technology itself (not only its application) is not 'neutral' in relation to social conflicts, and what would a specifically 'socialist' technology signify?

3. *Socialist planning and the market economy*
The productive anarchy of the capitalist economy was traditionally seen in socialist ideologies (beginning with the early utopians) as the opposite of socialist planning. This opposition raises doubts on both sides. What does the concept of socialist planning mean, as opposed to the economic activity of the state in industrial capitalist countries? And how far is there interdependence between 'rational' planning and the 'irrationality' of the market even within the socialist economy? Briefly: how far has the relationship changed between the two pairs of 'opposites', planning–market and socialism–capitalism (they have certainly ceased to be regarded as opposites nowadays)?

4. *Socialism and ownership*
It is often argued (1) that ownership of the means of production has lost its primordial importance in highly developed capitalist societies; and (2) that the abolition of private ownership of the means of production is in itself irrelevant to the problem of socialism since, as is well known from experience, extreme despotism, both political and economic, may be established where the ruling group has no formal title of ownership. How far is this true? Is tyranny, based on monopoly of command over the means of production, the only alternative to capitalist society? Does the freedom of the individual – as many claim – involve freedom of possession, at least to a certain degree?

Is a non-despotic society conceivable in which the ruling group keeps monopolist power over the means of production? Or does the socialist idea involve many forms of ownership?

5. Socialism and the nation

Most Marxists (including Marx himself) believed that the national question would be automatically solved as the unity of human culture progressed and that socialist development would naturally abolish national conflicts, since the latter were a by-product of class antagonism within capitalist society. It has turned out, however, not only that socialist states have miserably failed to provide any solution for national conflicts, while preserving national oppression intact; we have witnessed also in recent decades, against all expectations, the growth of nationalism throughout the world. National and tribal tensions and struggles seem to dominate the current political stage more than other conflicts. Does the very existence of such an entity as the nation necessarily limit the validity of the socialist idea, which apparently failed to take account (except in a tactical sense) of the reality of the nation? Are Jaurès' ideals on this point piously naïve? What does the concept itself of national sovereignty mean in a socialist perspective?

6. Socialism and the working class

What is left of Marx's fundamental idea that the industrial proletariat would carry out – by virtue of its peculiar class origin – the socialist transformation? Was Marxian social philosophy as a whole based on a false prediction concerning class polarization in the capitalist society and the inevitable impoverishment of the working class? Looking at the most developed industrial societies, what remains of the theory that the bourgeoisie–proletariat conflict dominates the historical development of our epoch? What is rational in the argument that the working class was 'integrated', gained middle class status and lost its interest in socialism? Let us imagine what the dictatorship of the proletariat would mean if the (real, not imaginary) working class took over exclusive political power now in the United States. Was the Marxist philosophy of history at this crucial point just an arbitrary fantasy? If so – is there any 'class content' in the socialist idea?

7. The meaning of equality

Equality belonged to the very core of all traditional socialist ideologies. Engels' statement that equality means nothing more than the

4

abolition of classes does not sufficiently clarify the concept; neither does the slogan adopted by Marx (for the 'first phase of' socialism) 'to everybody according to his work'. Equality of wages has proved from much convincing experience to be economically impracticable. On the other hand, an economy which is supposed to be entirely based on use-value (if conceivable) cannot provide any common measure for comparing different kinds of 'work' in order to apply the slogan just mentioned. Moreover, some people claim that a certain social stratification is a necessary condition for social stability. Are there serious arguments in favour of such a statement? The existing socialist societies are full of privileges of different kinds, not only in income, but in access to scarce goods, in education, in freedom, in prestige, in power. Which of them could, and which could not, conceivably be abolished? What does the idea of equality mean in the light of this experience?

8. Socialism, revolution and violence
It is obvious that the question of whether or not a socialist society is bound to be preceded by revolutionary upheaval depends on the meaning we give to the words 'socialism' and 'revolution'. The history of revolutions based on socialist ideologies in the twentieth century does not fit into Marxian predictions. On what basis can we claim today that socialist revolution is likely (or more likely than before) to break out in highly developed societies? Is there anything that makes the prospect of socialism impossible without a revolutionary collapse of the whole system (whatever that means)? What does the concept of revolutionary class mean today? How can we deny – after so much experience of it – that violence has a self-perpetuating tendency, and why should we expect that if violence is applied to existing capitalist societies it will not produce a society based entirely on institutionalized violence?

9. The ideal of unity of civil and political society
According to the Marxian idea, the socialist society would abolish the distinction between real life, i.e. the entire mass of conflicting individual interests, the informal social structure, the relations of production etc., and the political and legal order, which expresses and falsifies these relations while giving the society an illusory unity. What is valid in this 'organicist' ideal, bearing in mind that in existing socialist societies this apparent abolition means simply the attempt to replace all spontaneous social ties by the forms of

organization imposed by the state? What does this unity mean, if not simply the totalitarian state? In what sense is it conceivable that the mediatory functions of law and of state institutions could be abolished without the destruction of society? And why should we tend towards such a unity? Does the Marxian ideal simply involve the inadmissible prediction that all conflicts will be removed from social life once class antagonism disappears?

10. Socialism and Weltanschauung

Is the socialist idea necessarily bound to have a philosophical basis? To be sure, a kind of naturalistic, Promethean, anti-religious philosophy was to Marx an integral part of the socialist consciousness. This connection has remained in communist parties, which believe that they cannot dispense with some sort of philosophical background – in contrast to social democratic movements, which seem to be philosophically indifferent. Is there something in the very nature of the socialist idea that makes it imperfect without a proper philosophy? If so, of what does this connection consist, and why should a certain Weltanschauung be applied to the social programme or even to a certain method of analysing historical processes?

11. Education and 'Socialist Man'

Traditional socialist ideology (Marxian or not) involved a vision of the 'new man' who would emerge as a result of new social relations (abolition of the distinction between manual and intellectual labour; replacing egoistic motives by social ones etc.). The question arises, however, of how the kind of education predicated by this idea can be distinguished from sheer compulsion. It may be argued that, for example, the abolition of the distinction between manual and intellectual work can really only be carried out by compelling people to do a certain kind of work, which presupposes mass repression and turns the socialist idea into a caricature of itself. The traditional controversy over whether people should change themselves before they start building the socialist society or are only able to change themselves in building this society does not seem to have lost its relevance.

12. Socialism and the values of tradition

The socialist idea in the Marxian version (and in the Fabian version also) was deeply rooted in rationalist ideals of the Enlightment. It implied that the society of the future would throw off the burden of traditional values in all cultural matters, including in particular sex and family life, and bring about emancipation from all restrictions, institutions and sentiments allegedly incompatible with the rational life (whatever that means). Consequently, it seemed that the dissolution of the family and unrestricted sexual freedom naturally belonged to the socialist idea (this view seems to have prevailed in Russia for a certain period after the revolution, to be replaced later by the return to a strictly puritanical morality; both Soviet and Chinese societies are in this respect the most conservative in the world). It seemed to many people, moreover, that socialist culture would bring about a complete rupture with previous history in all respects except that of technology itself (and sometimes even technology was not spared). In the light of our experience this rationalist ideal may seem not only naïve but dangerous as well. Can we imagine a society which will start an entirely new culture in a cultural desert? If not, are the values imposed by tradition to be accepted simply as such, i.e. as imposed by the tradition, in defiance of rationalist slogans? What is right in the view that no social stability and no moral education can be assured without a certain respect for tradition as such (including some traditional values concerning sex and family)? In what sense does socialism mean a rupture with the preceding culture and in what sense may it be viewed as its continuation?

For a variety of reasons this plan could not be entirely fulfilled; some topics were absent, some papers did not fit exactly into the proposed schema. To fill, at least partially, these lacunae, we decided to add to the volume three papers which were not presented at the meeting. Two of them, by Richard Lowenthal and Gilles Martinet, were read at the International Seminar on 'Socialism in Changing Societies' held in Tokyo in April 1972 and sponsored by the Japan Cultural Forum in co-operation with the International Association for Cultural Freedom and two Japanese magazines. Another, by Steven Lukes, was specially written for this volume. Five papers presented at the Reading meeting (by Kolakowski, Ludz, Harrington, Sirc and Hirszowicz) were commented on by other participants (respectively, Hampshire, Kusin, Brus, Nuti and Marek) and these comments are included in the volume.

We do not reproduce here the discussion – usually very animated – that followed each paper. It may be useful, however, to point out some recurrent topics of the discussion and to mention the main points which divided the participants.

7

As could be expected, the discussion continually reverted to the meaning and validity of most traditional socialist values; in some cases the divergences and arguments followed patterns familiar in socialist thought for many decades or even centuries.

There was disagreement not only on how to define the concept of socialism but even on what approach to take in trying to define it. The Marxian tradition was usually the starting point in this debate. It was pointed out, however, that in some important issues Marxism itself tried to combine heterogeneous sources without removing their contradictions and achieving internal coherence. Thus, in conformity with the legacy of the Enlightenment, Marxism stressed the autonomy and free development of individuals as supreme values, while on the other hand it inherited a romantic nostalgia for the perfect unity of society. These two tendencies (as Taylor stated) run counter to one another and are reflected in two quite different conceptions of what a socialist society should be like. The rationalist and utilitarian side of Marxism produced visions of a socialism made up of individual happiness, abundance, leisure, creativity. The romantic side stressed the need for a return to the organic community and would tend to produce totalitarian socialist utopias – if it is true (as Kolakowski argued) that the ideal of perfect unity is unlikely to be carried into effect in any form other than totalitarian despotism. Another tension (stressed by Petrović) may be noticed between Marx's revolutionary humanism and his economic determinism. From the first point of view the movement towards socialism implies a permanent process of interdependence between the spiritual development of individuals and the changing material and institutional conditions of their lives; this means that socialist transformations cannot be defined in institutional terms. The other approach describes historical processes in purely 'objective' terms and leaves no room (as Raddatz pointed out) for reflection about how individual consciousness and personal values are affected by institutional transformations; consequently, it lets us conceive the socialist movement as a technical device destined to carry out certain institutional projects (in particular expropriation), and socialism as a condition where these projects are fulfilled, regardless of what happens otherwise to the human beings who make up the new society.

To define socialism merely in terms of public ownership and power negates the ideological concept of socialism – this point was not disputed among the participants. Neither was the belief that socialist theory cannot be a blueprint for universal salvation, removing all social conflicts and dissatisfactions. Such general agreement, however, did not pre-empt controversy on all the more specific issues. Should we define socialism as a certain desirable set of social relations, or rather (as Hampshire suggested) as a method of solving social problems according to the aspirations and needs of underprivileged classes? In the discussion two attitudes – the utopian and the pragmatic – constantly collided with one another. It was repeatedly stressed by some (Marek, Petrović) that we cannot dispense with utopias, i.e. with imaginary pictures of a 'disalienated' human community, even if we know that such an ideal is not within the reach of human potentialities; we need it as a kind of regulative idea, rather than as a real goal to be achieved; we need it to help us see a general direction to follow in all practical issues. However, a more pragmatic approach seemed to prevail in the discussion. Since it turned out that many social claims which in nineteenth-century capitalist society seemed hopeless were in fact satisfied, the radical 'either-or' in viewing social systems (capitalism–socialism) lost its persuasive force (Walter Kendall's opinion). The pressure of the organized labour movement has proved undeniably successful in employing the existing state institutions to improve the lot of the working class, and thus there is no reason to put any *a priori* limit to the efficiency of this pressure; on the other hand, the existing socialist systems have proved themselves incapable of resolving any social problems which, judging from experience, could not be solved within capitalist society. They solved, at incalculable human cost, the problems of industrialization in some underdeveloped countries and so they assumed the role of organizers of primitive accumulation, but they have been unable to cope with a single task which, according to the tradition of socialist thought, was supposed to fall to the specifically *socialist* form of social organization.

Whether the existing socialist societies can be considered as poor preliminary steps towards the socialist form of life, as defined in the Marxian tradition, or simply as instruments of rapid industrialization in countries which lay on the peripheries of capitalist development – the answers to this question varied according to the participants' views on the criteria for defining the socialist world. Harrington's opinion that material abundance is a precondition for socialist development and that we should measure progress by the reduction of necessary work and by the growth of leisure carried the obvious conclusion that the socialist revolution has never yet occurred, that no society remotely deserving the name of socialist is in existence and that socialist development is in principle inconceivable in underdeveloped societies, in particular in the

Third World. This opinion was not shared unanimously. There was, on the other hand, the rather isolated opinion that existing socialist systems, inefficient and oppressive though they are, should be considered as crucial steps beyond the class society since, although failing to destroy all sources of social antagonism, they succeeded in destroying one of them, that resulting from class division (Nuti). This question led automatically to another: how far is it true that the Soviet-type societies have produced a new class division? Another largely unshared view was that the deficiencies of socialist systems are to be explained by the incompetence of the ruling bureaucracy and not by class antagonism between this bureaucracy and society (Nuti). Most of those taking part (Hirszowicz, Walter Kendall, Kolakowski, Sirc) argued that the system of privileges instituted in these societies gave birth to a new clash of interests, different in some respects, but basically similar to class division (power without responsibility; exclusive control over the means of production by the ruling group; permanent conflict between the trend towards technological and economic progress and the monopolist position of the political bureaucracy).

Harrington's view of leisure as the basic criterion in evaluating socialist development was criticized for another reason. It was pointed out (Taylor) that the very idea of leisure is self-defeating, since the growth of leisure entails the growth of new demand for goods to fill the free time, with a consequent move towards new products and new forms of consumption. Taylor argued that the most urgent changes needed to allow the advanced industrial societies to escape the disastrous consequences of their economic growth (the endless spiral of mutually stimulating demand and production) imply a spiritual reorientation. To achieve a recycling technology and non-quantitative growth people would have to rearrange priorities in the personal needs, not only to reform their institutions.

No matter how important the divergences brought to light in the discussion, agreement seemed to prevail that any meaningful concept of socialism implies the ability of the working society to decide its own fate, which includes, in particular, control over the means of production. This topic was broached many times from different angles. Brus insisted upon the distinction between public and social ownership, the latter involving economic democracy (and consequently political democracy also, as the former is inconceivable without the latter). The experience of Eastern Europe proves that a system which achieves public ownership of the means of production makes none of the progress traditionally expected of a socialist society unless that ownership assumes a social character, i.e. unless the working society enjoys its rights to economic self-management. Marek stressed the demands for industrial democracy spreading throughout the industrial societies as a new phenomenon opening a fresh perspective both to Western socialism and to the people's democracies. A democracy which stops at the factory entrance does not deserve its name, nor does a democracy which stops at the factory exit. Hirszowicz made the distinction between different levels of industrial democracy (technological, managerial and social) while stating that industrial democracy is conceivable only as part of a participatory democracy encompassing all aspects of social life.

It was not difficult to reach agreement on the meaninglessness of economic self-management without political democracy. But more specific issues concerning the feasibility and the practical content of economic self-management provoked debate. It was argued that no institutional devices had yet been invented to reconcile the contradictions between efficient management and industrial democracy; if we want to have both, this is conceivable only by means of all sorts of compromise. And are not many aspects of the Yugoslav experiment discouraging? More often than not, real management and the real power of decision lie in the hands of professionals, whatever the formal rights of workers. On the one hand, the greater the autonomy of particular industrial units, the more room is left for the unrestricted operations of the normal laws of capitalist accumulation, with all its destructive aspects. On the other, highly centralized planning is both inefficient and anti-democratic, judging from the experience of the Soviet-type societies, and the more sophisticated the technology of a country, the more glaring does the inefficiency of its central planning appear. It is impossible (as Sirc argued against Nuti) to run the whole economy. But can we expect that the existing economic system of Western Europe and North American will prove susceptible to important changes which would bring about a piecemeal transformation, with more and more equality in the distribution of wealth, more and more democracy in industrial management, more and more participation of all in the joint results of production? It was argued (by G. A. Cohen) that the possibilities which the tremendous technological progress in capitalist society opened up for the growth of leisure cannot, and never could be, be employed for this purpose since, faced with the choice between more output and more leisure, capitalism must by its very nature invariably opt for the former. Thus reductions in working hours were so far negligible within this system. It was argued too (Nuti) that progressive taxation could lead, theoretically, to a more egalitarian redistribution of social wealth, but in fact it does not.

Generally speaking, there was no agreement about how far the experiences of the socialist countries are relevant both to the prospects of the socialist movement in Western Europe and to the validity of the very idea of socialism. Nobody denied this relevance but its limits were differently defined. Are we to explain the technological and economic inefficiency of these systems by contingent historical circumstances or rather is it built into the very foundations? How much is due to failures in operation and how much to the basic faultiness of the construction? How far do these experiences cast doubt on the feasibility of socialist ideals and on the possibility of achieving all their values jointly? It appeared that some of the values belonging to the very core of socialist tradition conflict with each other in practical application: very often the need for freedom and the need for equality prove to be incompatible; the ideal of full industrial democracy can hardly be harmoniously combined with competent management; we need both more leisure and more consumer goods and it is difficult to see how we can get more and more of both; we need both security and technological progress, but complete security seems to imply stagnation and technological progress means permanent disequilibrium (Sirc). There is no theory capable of supplying a system of reasonable compromises between the conflicting values, far less eradicating their contradictions. We need (Hampshire argued) more and more comprehensive planning, yet lack a reliable theory for it, since our knowledge of society is necessarily limited, and we are bound, in social engineering, to produce many unforeseen effects. Is it not therefore safer and more responsible to test the possibilities of the existing forms of social organization, instead of promising a great leap towards perfection with no guarantee at all that the results will not be much worse than the present situation?

It was repeatedly pointed out in the discussion that some important changes in socialist consciousness in the Western world resulted not only from the failures of Soviet-type socialism but from the transformation of capitalist societies, which made some inherited socialist values irrelevant, less important or doubtful. According to Marxian predictions, socialism was supposed to do away with the restrictions which the capitalist mode of production imposed on the progress of technology and it was here that socialist organization would prove its superiority. Not only did it turn out that the existing socialist societies are losing the 'technological competition' while clumsily imitating Western models, but the very value of technological progress has become less and less attractive as the main criterion of social progress in view of its notorious destructive aspects.

The second important point on which nineteenth-century socialist thought seemed, in the light of new experience, particularly vulnerable, was the role of the working class in the socialist movement. While criticizing the theory of the *embourgeoisement* of the working class and opposing the tendency to identify the welfare system with socialist development, Bottomore pointed out that the socialist movement lacks any reliable class theory applicable to contemporary changes. The tendency, popular among various leftist groups, to look for another revolutionary vanguard in marginal or merely underprivileged groups (immigrant workers, lumpenproletariat, racial and national minorities), none of which is the working class in the Marxian sense, was on frequent occasions depicted in the discussion as a reflex of despair, rather than being based on sociological analysis. It was pointed out, on the other hand, that the changes in the position of the working class in highly developed societies are not restricted to welfare benefits but include the negative control the unions are able to exert in many important social and economic matters, which could be described as a limitation on private ownership or as partial expropriation (Kendall).

The third aspect of socialism where the crisis of values is patent is the internationalist tradition. An analysis of the 'state' concept of the nation as opposed to its 'class' concept was made in the discussion by Ludz. Many phenomena were depicted to show how the hostility between nationalist and socialist ideologies has lost most of its force: it is normal, not exceptional, for leftist movements to support nationalist claims of the kind which surely deserve the label of 'reactionary' according to old Marxist theories, and in many conflicts it is almost inconceivable for the left not to espouse the nationalist cause (Taylor). Nostalgia for the tribal community is very strongly felt in many leftist groups (Hampshire); on the other hand, nationalism is encouraged by the growing economic function of the state and for this reason, too, it often coincides with socialist programmes (Brus). In some forms nationalism (especially in Eastern Europe) coincides with democratic claims for autonomy and participation (Kusin), while in the large socialist powers socialist ideology became indistinguishable from chauvinist or imperialist aspirations. Some of the participants stressed the validity of traditional Marxist tenets that conceive the nation as a transitory phenomenon, without any specific value from the point of view of the socialist movement (Eric Hobsbawm); others did not see any incompatibility between the internationalist attitude and national allegiances (Ludz). At least two points were not questioned: that the existing socialist states failed utterly to fulfil old promises to solve national problems, and that internationalist ideals had practically died out in the socialist movements. Great-power jingoism and claims for national independence both appear very often in socialist ideologies and nobody finds this unusual any longer.

To give a personal view of the Reading meeting I take the liberty of quoting my concluding remarks after the debates:

It was not the aim of our discussion to criticize existing political systems, movements or parties, socialist or communist. It is obvious, however, that one cannot discuss the socialist idea today as if the existing attempts to realize it were irrelevant to the discussion, as if nothing has happened since the idea was born. In organizing this meeting we wanted to avoid four categories of people, four kinds of mentality one often finds in discussion on the relationship of the socialist idea to its practical embodiments.

First, there are people who simply think that there is nothing wrong either with the idea or with the shape it has taken in socialist societies; the idea is coherent, consistent and splendid and was perfectly incarnated in the Soviet-type countries. This is the point of view of orthodox communists.

Second, there are people who think that the idea has proved utterly bankrupt in the light of existing experience and that there is therefore nothing to talk about; the communist system buried the socialist idea for ever.

Third, there is the approach typical of many Trotskyites and critical communists. It may be summarized as follows: one cannot deny that there is a bureaucratic distortion in communist countries, that many mistakes have been made, but the principle or the essence are sound; all right – if you insist, I concede that this system was built on several dozens of millions of victims, on invasions, on national oppression, on glaring inequalities, exploitation, cultural devastation, political despotism – but you cannot deny that the factories are state owned! And these state-owned factories in communist countries are of such priceless value to mankind that all other circumstances are irrelevant and secondary when faced with this achievement.

Fourth, there is the attitude which is quite common among the New Left and which can be expressed as follows: all right, I agree that the existing socialist states are all rubbish, but we are not interested either in their history or in their actual conditions because we are going to do better. How? That is very simple. We just have to make the global revolution that will destroy alienation, exploitation, inequality, slavery, discomfort, pollution, overpopulation and traffic jams. The blue-print is ready, all we have to do is make the global revolution.

If we look around we realize that there are few who would not fall into one of these four categories. We have succeeded at least in that these attitudes were absent here. This means that we take seriously both the socialist idea and the existing experience of socialist countries and we agree that this experience is very relevant to the discussion of the validity and the prospects of the idea. We must recognize, however, that within these narrow limits we turned out to be divided on all the issues raised in our discussion. This fact itself proves that almost 150 years after the word 'socialism' came into being we still have to go back to the beginning. I would not say, however, that this is a reason for despondency or despair. Even if it is true that we cannot ever abolish human misery, it may at the same time be true that the world would be even worse than it is if there were no people who thought that it could be better.

Where are we now? What we lack in our thinking about society in socialist terms is not general values which we want to see materialized, but rather knowledge about how these values can be prevented from clashing with each other when put into practice and more knowledge of the forces preventing us from achieving our ideals. We are *for* equality, but we realize that economic organization cannot be based on equality of wages, that cultural backwardness has a self-perpetuating mechanism that no institutional changes are likely to destroy rapidly, that some inequalities are accounted for by genetic factors and too little is known of their impact on social processes etc. We are for economic democracy, but we do not know how to harmonize it with the competent running of production. We have many arguments against bureaucracy and as many arguments for increasing public control over the means of production, i.e. for more bureaucracy. We bemoan the destructive effects of modern technology and the only safeguard against them that we know is more technology. We are for more automony for small communities and more planning on the global scale – as if no contradictions existed between these two slogans. We are for more learning in the schools and more freedom for pupils, i.e. in practice, less learning. We are for technical progress and complete security, i.e. immobility. We say that people should be free in their pursuit of happiness and we pretend to know the infallible criteria of happiness for everybody. We are against national hatred and national isolationism in a world where everybody is against national hatred, but there is more of it about than ever in human history. We maintain that people should be considered as material beings, but nothing shocks us as much as the idea that people have bodies: it means that they are genetically determined, that they are born, they die, they are young or old, men or women and that all these factors can play a role in social processes regardless of who owns the means of production, and thus that some important social forces are not products of historical conditions and do not depend on class division.

We were happy a hundred years ago. We knew that there were exploiters and exploited, wealthy and poor, and we had a perfect idea of how to get rid of injustice: we would expropriate the owners and turn the wealth over to the common good. We expropriated the owners and we created one of the most monstrous and oppressive social systems in world history. And we keep repeating that 'in principle' everything was all right, only some unfortunate accidents slipped in and slightly spoiled the good idea. Now let us start afresh.

Are we fools to try to keep thinking in socialist terms? I do not think so. Whatever has been done in Western Europe to bring about more justice, more security, more educational opportunities, more welfare and more state responsibility for the poor and helpless, could never have been achieved without the pressure of socialist ideologies and socialist movements, for all their naïveties and illusions. This does not mean that we are exculpated in advance and allowed to cherish these illusions endlessly, after so many defeats. It does mean, however, that past experience speaks in part for the socialist idea and in part against it. We are certainly not allowed to delude ourselves that we hold the secret of the conflict-free society or the key to perfection. Neither may we believe that we possess a consistent set of values which can in principle be carried out together unless some unpredictable accidents occur, since most of human history is made up of unpredictable accidents. We cannot continue believing in the whole set of traditional socialist values and retain a minimum of mental integrity unless we remember a number of trivial truths: that among these values there is none which would not conflict with another when put into practice; that we never know all the results of the social changes we set in motion; that both the sedimentation of past history and the perennial features of human biology set limits to social planning and that these limits are only vaguely known to us. There is nothing surprising in the fact that we strongly resist the implications of many banal truths; this happens in all fields of knowledge simply because most truisms about human life are unpleasant.

THE MYTH OF HUMAN SELF-IDENTITY:
Unity of Civil and Political Society in Socialist Thought

Leszek Kolakowski

These remarks are not historical. Their aim is to point out a soterio-logical myth hidden in the traditional Marxist anticipation of socialism as based on the identity of civil and political society. I will try to reveal a continuity (though not identity) between this soteriology and con-temporary totalitarian variants of socialism and to say why the Marxian ideal of unity is in my opinion impracticable. A short historical remark may be useful, nevertheless, to bring into relief the background against which Marxian thought seems to have developed.

Marx's ideas on the relationship of civil society to the state took shape in his criticism of four doctrines which differed widely in the negative in-fluence they exerted on his thought. They are: (1) Hegel's and then Las-salle's theory of the state; (2) the classical liberal concept; (3) anarchist (mostly Bakuninist) criticism of the state; (4) totalitarian communism.

The first two of them may be called liberal in the sense that they both involved a separation of the political from the civil society as a per-manent feature of human life and both rejected the idea that the state could ever replace the civil society or, at the other extreme, become superfluous; in other words, they were neither totalitarian nor anar-chist. Both Hegel and Lassalle, however, differed from classical liberal tenets in that they went beyond a purely utilitarian concept of the state and attributed an autonomous value to it as the highest form of human community. The classical liberal doctrine envisaged the state in strictly utilitarian terms as a necessary device which societies had to apply in order to keep inevitable conflicts of particular interests within well-defined legal limits and thus prevent society from turning into an unrestricted war of all against all, i.e. from eventually falling prey to the tyranny of the strongest.

When we confront the Marxian strictures on Bakunin we may sometimes feel it difficult to square them with his criticism of Lassalle; the former is attacked for blaming the state as the main source of all social evil, the latter for worshipping it as the most splendid achievement of the human spirit. We may state, however, that Marx's basic conception of the relationship between political and civil society, as expounded in 1843 in the unfinished *Critique of the Hegelian Philosophy of Right* and in the *Jewish Question*, had persisted intact throughout his intellectual development, and there is no reason to maintain that it was ever denied in later writings.

To be sure, Marx started in Feuerbachian fashion by blaming Hegel for his 'inversion' of the relation of 'subject' to 'predicate' in dealing with the question. For Hegel, he says, the real human subjects become predicates of the universal substance embodied in the state. Real priorities are thus reversed since 'the universal' may be only a property of an individual being and the genuine subject is always finite. It is not the state that creates 'real individuals'; the state, on the contrary, is an 'objectified man'. The stated aim of democracy is to restore the state to its real human creators. When stating that 'the universal' needs human subjectivity to reach its own perfection, Hegel not only makes the separation of the state from human beings eternal but sanctions the illusion of the state as the embodiment of the universal interest. Hegel believed indeed that the spirit of the state, its superiority over all particular interests, is incorporated in the consciousness of functionaries, since only they can identify their particular interest with the universal one and make possible the synthesis of general good with the aspirations of particular layers of society. Consequently, Hegelian philosophy supports the ideological illusion of the Prussian bureaucracy that considers itself the incarnation of the universal interest. Marx stresses, however, that when bureaucracy becomes an autonomous principle and when the interest of the state gains independence as the interest of the bureaucracy – and is thus a 'real' interest – bureaucracy must fight against the aspirations of other particular orders which gave it birth.

Marx thus took over the Hegelian distinction of civil society and the state, while denying their permanence and the necessity of their separation. The civil society is a whole mass of conflicting individual and group aspirations, empirical daily life with all its conflicts and struggles, the realm of private desires and private endeavours. To

Hegel, its conflicts are rationally moderated, kept in check and synthesized in the superior will of the state, this will being independent of any particular interest. To Marx the state, at least in its present form, far from being a neutral mediator, is the tool of some particular interests disguised as the illusory universal will. Man as citizen and as private person is two different and separated beings, but only the latter, the member of the civil society, is the 'real' concrete being; as a citizen he participates in the abstract community owing its reality to ideological mystification. This mystification was unknown in mediaeval society where class division was directly expressed in the political order, i.e. the segmentation of the civil society was reflected in the political organism. Modern societies, having abrogated the direct political validity of class stratification, split social life into two realms and this division is carried over into each individual existence; it became a contradiction within every human being, torn between his status as a private person and his role as a citizen. Consequently political emancipation – in defiance of Bruno Bauer's philosophy – must not be confused with human emancipation. The former may politically cancel the differences between people in ownership or in religion, i.e. make the differences politically insignificant and thus liberate the state from religious or class distinctions (by, for example, the abolition of ownership qualifications in political activities or of legal privileges for certain denominations). This change, important though it may be, does not abrogate either religious or class division in society and allows them to keep working. It leaves untouched the separation of civil from political society; the former is still a realm of real life, egoistic and isolated for every individual, the latter provides life with collective character but only in an abstract illusory form. The aim of human – as opposed to political – emancipation is to restore to collective life its real character, or to restore the collective character to civil society. At the end of the *Jewish Question* we find the important sentence which expresses – still in philosophical and embryonic form and not yet in class terms – the great Marxian hope for universal human emancipation; a hope that was to continue determining all his further efforts to outline his vision of a society abolishing for ever the dichotomy between man's personal and his collective existence:

> Only when the real individual man will absorb back the abstract citizen of the state and – as individual man, in his empirical life, in his individual work, in his individual relationships – will become the

species being, only when man will recognize and will organize his 'forces propres' as *social* forces and, consequently, will not separate from himself the social force in form of *political* force any more, only then the emancipation of man will be accomplished.

Nobody can pretend to find in this sentence everything that Marx would say later about the meaning of the future kingdom of freedom. But everything he said grew out of this primordial hope. In the quoted sentence the concept of 'human emancipation' lacks any mention of class struggle and the mission of the proletariat. And yet, the same vision of man returning to perfect unity, experiencing directly his personal life as a social force, makes up the philosophical background of Marxian socialism. In all later writings which were to define his position in contrast to liberal, anarchist and communist totalitarian doctrines, the same eschatological concept of the unified man remains.

What is wrong with this hope? Is there any historical connection between the Marxian vision of the unified man and the fact that real communism appears only in totalitarian form, i.e. as the tendency to *replace* all crystallizations of the civil society by coercive organs of the state? How can this connection be grasped?

While we cannot examine in detail the intricacies of the problems in the chronicles of Marxist doctrine here, I must summarize, however crudely, the paramount points of Marxian criticism of the four approaches just mentioned.

Anarchism, i.e. Stirner and Bakunin. Bakunin's concept was based on three premises. First, that state institutions are the main sources of all social evil. Second, that people left to themselves and free from the burden of political machinery will develop their natural ability for friendly co-operation within loosely organized small communities. Third, that any attempt to rebuild the state, once the existing one has been crushed, will end with another and still worse version of the same tyranny; a new apparatus made up of the former workers cannot but refurbish or reinforce eternal slavery and the upstarts who run it will be instantly converted into turncoats from their class and will guard their freshly acquired privileges against that class. To Marx the first two arguments were obviously wrong and based on ignorance of well-proved historical facts. Since the origin of the state is to be looked for in civil society, and not conversely, Bakunin's demand for the demolition of the state amounts to putting the carriage before the horse. The existing political bodies do not produce inequality and exploitation but

express them; briefly, the alienation of labour precedes political alienation. To dissolve the political framework of the capitalist order, while
retaining the relations of production unaltered, would be to preserve conditions which would be bound to create soon the same framework again.
As to the third point, Marx never dealt with it. It remained open for his
followers. His comment on the Paris Commune, in particular his saying
that the working class cannot take over the ready made state machinery
but has to smash it, was welcomed, to be sure, by Bakunin's acolyte
Guillaume as a shift towards the anarchist standpoint. Wrongly so, as later
writings (especially the *Critique of the Gotha Programme*) would reveal.

The classical liberal concept corresponded to the idealized model of
capitalist society as analysed in *Capital*. Marx was aware, of course, that
the real patterns of capitalist economy do not coincide perfectly with
this model, which presupposes that the state is utterly inactive in economic life and allows the laws of free competition to work unbridled.
Still, this was the model he was dealing with in his major work. The
liberal concept – the state limited to the role of watchman and for-
bearing to interfere in the 'free contract' relations between entrepreneurs and wage earners (not to speak of other aspects of industrial
activity) – was not, strictly speaking, 'wrong' in Marx's eyes, as far as it
matched the genuine tendency of capital. What was wrong was the
ideological delusion that this kind of separation met the inalterable
requirements of human nature or that, once laid down, it would last
indefinitely. According to this concept the maximum productive
efficiency and consequently the optimum general good is secured within a political framework based on the minimum interference in economic relations. The state has to care about security; welfare and wealth
will look after themselves. Marx's anticipated organization of society
was exactly the opposite: political government would become superfluous while economic management, 'the administration of things',
would exhaust the functions of the public organs. The expression
'withering away of the state' comes from Engels but it fits into Marxian
predictions. The question arises: what premises do we have to admit
in order to believe that a social organization free from any mediating
and coercive power and from any political bodies is practicable? What
conditions would make conceivable a society which can 'administer
things' without 'governing people'?

Hegel's and Lassalle's cult of the state was attacked by Marx from
another point of view. Lassalle did not share, of course, the ideal of the
economic neutrality of the state. On the contrary, he believed that the

workers, through the parliamentary system, could influence the state and compel it to help in organizing independent productive co-operatives which would eventually dominate economic life. For Marx, Lassalle utterly neglected the class character of the existing state and cherished a utopian fancy that the state, which is in fact a self-defensive device of the privileged classes, may be employed as an organ of socialist transformation. By considering the state as a value in itself and overlooking its class function Lassalle reveals his historical ignorance.

Marx did not deny that the state apparatus may play an independent role in the class struggle; this happens, he thought, in exceptional circumstances which he analysed in the case of 'Bonapartism'. Moments of temporary autonomy of the state occur as a result of stalemate in a sharp class war. Marx did not try to synthesize his general view on the state as an organ of class domination and his remarks on these exceptional conditions. Nor did he lay down any theoretical view about how the socially indispensable functions of the state can coexist with its role as the oppressive instrument of the propertied classes. No wonder that what the Marxist movement took over from its founder was the crude idea that the state is 'nothing more' than an organ of class rule, the fist of the owners held over the head of the exploited, and that, since the basic class antagonisms are irreconcilable, the 'capitalist state' can never be at the service of workers' welfare.

Marx's criticism of totalitarian utopias takes up much less space in his writings. It does appear in the '44 Manuscripts' as criticism of primitive egalitarian communism, willing to destroy anything that cannot become the private property of all, i.e. everything that distinguishes individuals from each other, and to abolish talents and all personal qualities which make cultural creativity possible. Far from promising the assimilation of the alienated world, this communism pushes alienation to the extreme when it tries to debase the whole society into the present position of workers. To this Marx opposes what he calls 'the positive abolition of private property', an expression he did not explain and which it seems, he did not use subsequently. Its meaning may be guessed from the context, dealing with religious alienation and the anticipated abolition of atheism. The latter loses any meaning once human self-affirmation no longer depends on negation of God to become positive self-affirmation. One may guess that his analogy suggests a meaning for the 'positive' abolition of private property: a society which no longer depends on the negation of private property is probably a society in which the very question of private property has moved out of people's consciousness and stopped troubling their minds. Nor does this explanation give us any plain clue to the meaning of communism, except that Marxian criticism bears out what we can easily gather from elsewhere: that the 'man of communism' was modelled in Marx's imagination (in contrast to many utopias of the Enlightment) on pictures of universal giants of the Hellenic and Renaissance worlds, rather than on the patterns of barracks and monasteries. This last point cannot be disputed. What remains obscure is the relation of this buoyant perspective to the structure of the imaginary communist world and to the gloomy reality of the real one.

A pattern of Marxian thought on the question may be expressed as follows:

1. The alienation of labour can be accounted for by the division of labour resulting from technical development.

2. The alienation of labour induced class division and gave birth to special apparatus intended chiefly to protect by coercive measures the vested interests of the privileged strata.

3. In mediaeval European societies the fabric of this apparatus reflected directly the class structure and its function was obvious.

4. In industrial societies the political superstructure and civil society became separated, not in the sense that the former stopped serving the latter, but in the sense that the true nature of political society has been concealed behind legal equality and personal freedom. Consequently, the image of the relations between the two was bound to become mystified in the minds of those involved.

5. At the same time, traditional social ties and loyalties have been utterly shattered in a society where the profit motive rules economic activity unchallenged. As a result, the political society – distorted though its picture may be in the social perception – makes up the only form of (apparent) community, the only place where individuals recognize (in the abstract) the social character of their existence.

6. This results in the almost perfect split of every individual into his real but self-centred life in civil society, on the one hand, and his communal but abstract existence as state member on the other. Social functions (especially work) are perceived as private matters and particular interests (in political functions) wear the mask of social service.

7. The state may emerge as an autonomous social force only in the exceptional circumstances of a temporary equilibrium in the fierce class combat. Nor is the state likely to take over important economic functions within the capitalist order.

8. The task of communism is to reunite the two aspects of human life which have fallen apart, the personal and the collective, not by destroying the former (as primitive communism would) nor by simply removing the latter while leaving civil society to itself (as anarchist dreams would have it), but by organizing a society organically incapable of producing separate political organisms.

9. This restoration of human unity will be brought about by the violent smashing of the protective shell of the existing state, expropriating the exploiting classes and handing over the means of production to the producers. Once the latter are in a position to command all the accumulated forces of production, they will abolish naturally the profit motive in their economic activity and subordinate it to social needs only.

10. Given these conditions, class antagonisms will no longer emerge and, consequently, no organs of political rule will be needed. The public organs will be entirely devoted to the 'administration of things,' education and the welfare of the people.

11. As a result, not only will the split between the social and personal functions of individuals be healed, but so will the division between subject and object of the historical process (transparence of social relations, control of associated individuals over their life-processes, etc.), between man and his natural setting, between desires and duties, and between essence and existence.

What became of this scheme and, in particular, of its forward perspectives? Among socialists hardly anybody before the October Revolution seriously doubted its validity. Lenin's *State and Revolution*, written a couple of months before October, may appear like a daydream today, but it must have looked the same on the very day after the seizure of power. The totalitarian development of post-revolutionary Russian society is often accounted for not only by the exceptional conditions (non-exceptional ones, alas, are not found) at the moment of revolution (overwhelmingly agrarian society, isolation and the collapse of hopes of revolution in the West, economic devastation, political exhaustion), but also by the peculiar tradition of this country in the relation between civil society and the state. According to some Russian historians of the nineteenth century, the predominance of the state over civil society went so far that, far from being a product of class division, the state itself produced social classes by a series of measures imposed from above; the very size of the underpopulated territory and the need for constant military protection from invasions compelled the state to build up a larger and larger apparatus of administration and war and to harness the whole economic activity of the country in the service of the state. All important economic changes were due to the initiative of the state. As a result, the main features of what we today call a totalitarian system were virtually existent in the pre-revolutionary tradition: the predominance of the principle that all citizens' activities (including economic) have to have aims which coincide with those of the state; that no spontaneous crystallizations of social life may be allowed to grow unless they conform to the aims of the state; that each citizen is the property of the state. The unusual autonomy of the Russian state in relation to civil society was not denied by Russian Marxists (Plechanov, Trotsky), even if they did not go as far as those who devolved on the former the entire responsibility for the construction of the latter, including the very formation of social classes.

But this is not the question we are dealing with. The question is whether, apart from peculiar circumstances and the peculiar tradition of the country where the first attempt was made to found a social organization on Marxian premises, any suspicion may be justified as to the connection between these very premises and the real results of this attempt. To ask this does not amount to putting the frivolous and unanswerable question: 'What would Marx say if he saw the work of his followers?', since it is obvious that he could not see it without surviving for many decades longer than he did, i.e. without changing himself in a way that we cannot possibly guess. Nor do we ask if the patterns of contemporary communism have been, as it were, fully preordained by, or prefigured in, the Marxian scheme. It is plain, if not notorious, that an ideology is always weaker than the social forces which happen to be its vehicle and try to carry its values. Consequently, since no real interests involved in social struggles are reducible to the simplicity of an ideological value system, we may be certain in advance that no political organism will be the perfect embodiment of its ideology. To state this of Marxism, as of any other ideology, we can dispense with historical knowledge. To those who think about the prospects of socialist development the real question is: does inquiry into the Marxian idea of the unity of civil and political society lead us to presume that any attempt to set up such a unity will be likely to produce an order with strongly pronounced totalitarian traits?

It should be stressed that we, in 1973, are not the first to broach this topic. Otherwise we could be suspected of looking for a *harmonie préétablie* between an idea and its subsequent embodiment just to resolve intellectual anomalies and to put the contingency of history into apparent order. Actually the same question had been repeatedly raised – mostly by anarchists and syndicalists, but by some Marxists as well – long before the answer could be found in the empirical realities of the socialist state.

The main reason advanced for putting it was that Marx was deluding himself in predicting a socialist organization with centralized economic management but without political power and social oppression. Such a system – according to Bakunin's criticism – is bound to engender a new class of rulers either from working-class renegades or from the intelligentsia. Waclaw Machajski even maintained that Marxian socialism is an ideological device of the intelligentsia trying to replace the then privileged classes and to seize power in order to profit from their socially inherited cultural and intellectual superiority. Sorel insisted that all leaders who expected the socialist revolution to be carried through by political parties were just the new would-be revolutionary despots and that, no matter how democratic the phraseology they used, people like Jaurès or Turati announced only another form of oppression over the working class. Similar utterances can be quoted from French syndicalists and Proudhonists. Sorel expected a new oppressive society to emerge from any programme of political (i.e. party sponsored) revolution, as opposed to the movement of real workers. The latter could win only if they managed to get rid of the supremacy of intellectuals and to become masters of production directly and not through political functionaries or managers.

Socialists did not, of course, accept this line of reasoning. Some of them, however, pointed out the dangers of a new despotism which could emerge if either the revolution occurred in 'immature' conditions or the leaders failed to interpret the meaning of Marxian socialism properly. Jaurès wrote that if socialism resulted in a group of rulers controlling the right to all economic decisions in addition to their political power, this would mean delivering up to a handful of people an omnipotence before which the might of Asiatic despots would turn pale. Plechanov, in his polemics against revolutionary populism, noted that if by chance a conspiratory movement succeeded in seizing power in economically backward conditions, it would only establish a kind of oriental satrapy or renew Tsarist despotism on a communist basis. He repeated similar warnings against Bolsheviks who were, in his opinion, heirs of narodnik conspiracy, rather than Marxists.

There were others who emphasized the moral rather than the

27

economic preconditions of socialist society, if this society were not to degenerate into a new oppressive class system. I quote Edward Abramowski, a theorist of anarcho-cooperatism, who is less known in the West, being a Pole. He wrote in 1897:

> May we venture an opinion that the rise of the socialist system could omit its previous stage of moral revolution? That one could organize communist institutions without finding in human souls the corresponding needs, without having the foundation in the consciousness of people? ... Let us suppose for a moment that a revolutionary Providence, a conspiratorial group professing socialist ideals, happily succeeds in mastering the state machinery and establishes communist institutions with the help of the police disguised in new colours. Let us suppose that the consciousness of the people takes no part in this process and that everything is carried out by the force of sheer bureaucratism. What happens? ... The new institutions have removed the fact of legal ownership, but ownership as a moral need of people has remained; they have banned official exploitation from production, but have preserved all the external factors out of which injustice arises and which would always have a field large enough to operate in – if not in the economic sphere, then in all other fields of human relations. To stifle aspirations to ownership the organization of communism would have to apply extensive state power; the police would replace those natural needs out of which social institutions grew and by virtue of which they freely develop. Moreover the defence of new institutions would only be possible for a state founded on principles of absolutism, since any effective democracy in a society beset by violence under the new system would threaten that system with rapid decay and would bring back all the social laws which would have survived in human souls untouched by revolution. Thus, communism would not only be extremely superficial and impotent, but would turn into a state power oppressing individual freedom; instead of the former classes two new classes would emerge – citizens and functionaries – and their antagonism would necessarily appear in all domains of social life. Consequently, if communism in such artificial form, without moral transformation of people, could even survive, it would contradict itself and it would be a social monster such as no oppressed class ever dreamt about, least of all the proletariat that is fighting for human rights and is called upon by History itself to achieve the liberation of man.[1]

Thus the concept of the rise of a socialist 'new class' had not waited for Burnham. It had been anticipated long before people were able to find it in experience (after the October Revolution Kautsky seemed to have been the first to apply this concept to the new society, in 1919). We must, however, make the distinction between critics who warned against the new communist class society, which would result if the revolution failed to find appropriate economic or moral conditions, and those who claimed to have found the germ of a totalitarian order in the very concept of socialism as elaborated by Marx. The two kinds of arguments are logically independent.

Let us turn to the latter way of arguing, as we know it from anarchist writers. I think that there is considerable justification for this criticism. To say so I do not need to share anarchist ideals or to consider them either feasible or consistent. I will try to repeat in modified form those critiques which are noteworthy, and to adduce some other remarks on the subject, not necessarily taken from the same sources.

1. The crucial point in the Marxian ideal of unity is his distinction – inherited from the 'utopian' socialists – between the administration of things and governing the people. This distinction is vague, since we cannot imagine how things can be administered without people being used, controlled and organized for this purpose. Management of the economy involves control over people and it is not prima facie clear what is meant by saying that this would be not a 'political' but a purely 'economic' control. It is self-evident that economic planning involves the planning of the labour force and labour organization. In effective planning and management three kinds of instruments can be employed: material incentives, moral motivations and physical coercion. The first presupposes a free labour market (economic activity depending on private motives, striving after personal profit, competition between working individuals) and is hardly compatible with the Marxian image of the unity of social and personal life. The second presupposes a for-midable moral revolution in men's minds; what reason is there to believe that such a revolution is likely or possible? The experience of socialist countries speaks clearly against any hope of using moral in-centives as a lasting and efficient basis for production; most phraseology intended to arouse 'enthusiasm for work' was used rather to cover various means of pressure and violence. It seems hardly necessary to stress the incompatibility of the third kind of instrument with the Marxian programme. If, however, we read the notorious attacks of Trotsky on Kautsky from 1920, we notice that to him the system of

compulsory labour was not a transitory necessity of the civil war period but a permanent feature of socialist society.

> The principle itself of *compulsory labour* service has just as radically and *permanently replaced* the principle of free hiring as the socialization of the means of production has replaced capitalist property. . . .[2] The only solution of economic difficulties that is correct from the point of view *both of principle and of practice* is to *treat the population of the whole country as the reservoir of the necessary labour power* . . . .[3] The foundation of the militarization of labour are those forms of state compulsion without which the replacement of capitalist economy by the socialist will for ever remain an empty sound. . . . No social organization except the army has ever considered itself justified in subordinating citizens to itself in such a measure, and controlling them by its will on all sides to such a degree, as the state of the proletarian dictatorship considers itself justified in doing, and does. . . .[4] For we have no way to socialism except by the authoritative regulation of the economic forces and resources of the country, and the centralized distribution of labour-power in harmony with the general state plan. The labour state considers itself empowered to send every worker to the place where his work is necessary[5] [*emphasis added*].

Trotsky mentions, to be sure, the 'enthusiasm for work' residing in the working class, but he is aware that the planned economy cannot rely upon this factor. His idea, roughly speaking, is: 'Let the workers work – for almost nothing – and go where we want them to go, out of revolutionary enthusiasm. If they fail to do so, they will do the same anyway under the persuasion of the policeman's gun.' In other words, Trotsky promised us socialism conceived of as a permanent concentration camp. He did not seem to be worried about the possible incompatibility of this programme with Marxian doctrine. Two circumstances may none the less be adduced in his favour. First, a free market for the labour force seems indeed to run against the Marxian concept of socialism. Second, he offered a practicable solution to a question which Marx left unanswered. Indeed, if we set aside the free market, then coercion and moral motivations are left as the only possible stimuli for work; and the second proved to be utterly unreliable. In fact, all three factors have been applied, in differing proportions, in the history of socialist states. Material incentives seem now to be on the way towards prevailing in economic organization.

2. Following on the question of stimuli for work the question arises

of the stimuli for production itself. Marx recognized that civil society is ruled by private interest and that, left to themselves, people will produce and trade anyway; however, they are unable to master the global results of their joint productive activity and the latter turn against them in the form of quasi-natural catastrophic laws. However, if the motives of private profit in production are eradicated, the organizational body of production – i.e. the state – becomes the only possible subject of economic activity and the only remaining source of economic initiative. This must, not by bureaucratic ambition but by necessity, lead to a tremendous growth in the tasks of the state and its bureaucracy. This is what really happened. The civil society– as opposed to the state apparatus – has to be left economically passive and deprived of any reasons for, or possibilities of, taking the economic initiative. Without impulses from the state apparatus no economic activity arises in the society, except on the insignificant fringe of small private producers considered as relics of the past. What is not planned by state organs is simply not produced, whatever the social needs may be. Some changes, slowly and reluctantly initiated in socialist countries to restore the influence of the market on production prove economically efficient to a certain degree, but in the same degree run counter to the Marxian version of unity.

These two circumstances may justify the suspicion that, far from promising the fusion of civil with political society, the Marxian perspective of unified man is more likely to engender, if put into practice, a cancerous growth of quasi-omnipotent bureaucracy, trying to shatter and paralyse civil society and leading the (rightly blamed) anonymity of public life to its extreme consequences.

3. This trend becomes still more likely if we consider the third point: the question of the autonomy of political bodies as distinct from social classes. It is in fact difficult to imagine what reasons could be advanced in favour of the belief that, once social classes (in Marx's sense, i.e. based on the criteria of the ownership of the means of production and the appropriation of surplus value) have been abolished, the conflict of private interests will stop. The class struggle in capitalist society is a historical form of the struggle for the distribution of surplus product. Why should we presume that the same struggle for surplus product will not go on within an economy based on public ownership (whether that means an authoritarian or a democratic system)? And since public ownership must inevitably beget social layers endowed with privileges in controlling the means of production, the labour force and the

instruments of coercion, what reasons could we possibly have to deny that all devices will be employed to safeguard the position of these layers and increase their privileges? (Unless, of course, we predict a sudden restoration of the angelic nature in the human race.)

It is arguable that, in dealing with these questions and in predicting the return of man to the lost unity of his social and personal existence, Marx admitted, among others, two very common false premises: that all human evil is rooted in social (as distinct from biological) circumstances and that all important human conflicts are ultimately reducible to class antagonisms. Thus he entirely overlooked the possibility that some sources of conflict and aggression may be inherent in the permanent characteristics of the species and are unlikely to be eradicated by institutional changes. In this sense he really remained a Rousseauist. He also overlooked the formidable force of human aspirations for power for its own sake and the extreme antagonisms arising from the relations of power as such, i.e. irrespective of the social origin of given ruling bodies. Of all the famous sentences which have had a dizzy career in history, this is one of the most striking in its falsity: that the history of all hitherto existing societies is the history of class struggles. That political bodies are nothing more than instruments of classes; that their interests may always be identified with the interests of the classes they are supposed to represent; that they do not produce interests of their own of any noteworthy importance; that people delude themselves if they imagine they struggle for other values (for freedom or for power, for equality or for national goals) as values in themselves, since these values are only vehicles for class interests – all these beliefs are consequences of this one sentence. They gave to Marxism its stupendous efficiency and its catechismal simplicity. Needless to say, Marx's work shows convincingly that in all detailed analyses his thought was much subtler and more differentiated than this sentence would suggest. And yet without basically taking this belief he would not be able to nourish his hope for a unified man.

Let us conclude:

1. There is no reason to believe that the restoration of the perfect unity of the personal and communal life of every individual (i.e. the perfect, internalized identity of each person with the social totality, lack of tension between his personal aspirations and his various social loyalties) is possible, and, least of all, that it could be secured by institutional means. Marx believed such an identity had been achieved in stagnant

primitive communities. However, even if this romantic image is well founded, nothing substantiates the hope that it can be resuscitated in the predictable future: it would presuppose an unprecedented moral revolution running against the whole course of the past history of culture. To believe that a basis for such a unity may be laid down first in coercive form (i.e. the violent destruction of civil society and its replacement by the omnipotence of an oppressive state) and will grow subsequently into an internalized voluntary unity, amounts to believing that people who have been compelled to do something by fear are likely later to do the same thing willingly and cheerfully. From everything we know about human behaviour the opposite is more probable.

2. The social equivalent of this unity of person was thought of as the unity of civil and political society. This in its turn was conceived of as a community in which political power had become unnecessary. Such a community is inconceivable unless one of two conditions is fulfilled. The first: that no conflicts of interest arise between groups or individuals, so that economic management does not need to be associated with political power and public instruments of mediation or moderation are not necessary. Only if all conflicts of human interests were rooted in class division (in the Marxian sense of the word) – which is obviously not the case – could we expect this condition to be satisfied in the future. The second condition: that all decisions in public matters, however insignificant, are taken directly by the community as a whole in a democratic manner. Such a system, if practicable, would not abolish conflicts of interest (and thus would not comply with the requirements of perfect unity) but would be capable of moderating them without creating separate political bodies for this purpose. This ideal was patterned in anarchist thought upon mediaeval Swiss villages and, of course, cannot be attributed to Marx. If not for historical, then for technical reasons it is obviously impracticable in any community larger than a mediaeval Swiss village. Societies based on a universal – and still spreading – interdependence of all elements of the technological and economic structures are bound to produce separate bodies both for economic management and for mediating the conflicting aspirations of different sections, and these bodies will in turn always produce their own particular interests and loyalties.

3. The growth of the economic responsibilities of central powers is an undeniable tendency which may be noticed in different political systems. Not only is the trend towards nationalizing larger and larger segments of production, transport, trade and exchange system

inevitably accompanied by the rise of bureaucracy. The same may be said about all tasks which, it is widely acknowledged should rest on the shoulders of central powers: the welfare, health and education systems, the control of wages, prices, investment and banking, the protection of the natural environment and the exploitation of natural resources and land. It is not impossible, but it is difficult to be consistent when one fulminates at the same time against both the growth of bureaucracy and the uncontrolled wastefulness of the operation of private industry; more often than not, increasing control over private business means increasing bureaucracy. The urgent question is how society can tame its expanding bureaucracy and not how it can dispense with it. Representative democracy presupposes separate bodies with special privileges in deciding on public matters, and thus it cannot secure the ideal of the perfect unity of civil and political society. It may be said in general that representative democracy carries a great number of vices and only one virtue. All its blemishes and dangers are easily found in the Marxist literature. And its only virtue is that nobody as yet has invented anything better.

★   ★   ★

I believe that socialist thinking which is centred on its traditional topics (how to ensure for the working society more equality, more security, more welfare, more justice, more freedom, more participation in economic decision) cannot at the same time be infatuated with prospects of the perfect unity of social life. The two kinds of preoccupation run against each other. The dream of perfect unity may come true only in the form of a caricature which denies its original intention: as an artificial unity imposed by coercion from above, in that the political body prevents real conflicts and real segmentation of the civil society from expressing themselves. This body is almost mechanically compelled to crush all spontaneous forms of economic, political and cultural life and thus deepens the rift between civil and political society instead of bringing them closer to each other.

If it is asked whether this result was somehow inscribed in the original Marxian thought, the answer is certainly 'no' if 'inscribed' means 'intended'. All evidences are there to show that the primordial intention was the opposite of what grew out of it. But this primordial intention is not, as it were, innocent. It could scarcely be brought to life in a basically different form, not because of contingent historical circumstances but because of its very content.

34

The dream of a perfectly unified human community is probably as old as human thought about society; romantic nostalgia was only a later incarnation. This dream has been philosophically reinforced by that element in European culture which arose from neoplatonic sources. There is no reason to expect that this dream will ever be eradicated in our culture, since it has strong roots in the awareness of a split which humanity has suffered apparently from the very beginning of its existence after leaving animal innocence. And there is no reason to expect that this dream can ever become true except in the cruel form of despotism; and despotism is a desperate simulation of paradise.

3

UNITY OF CIVIL AND POLITICAL SOCIETY: Reply to Leszek Kolakowski

Stuart Hampshire

I certainly agree with Mr Kolakowski's negative conclusion about the myth of human self-identity, as this is proclaimed or implied in some of Marx's writings and, even more, as it is proclaimed in later Marxist theory. No such final liberation of man is any longer to be expected from any likely socialist transformation of the social order, whether this transformation is achieved suddenly and by violence, or gradually and without violence. I also think that the quasi-philosophical theory, on which the expectation was founded, is illusory. But I think it may be possible to say something more about the sources of the illusion: and it may be possible to infer some more positive conclusions about the future of socialist theory and its philosophical foundations.

I will start from the Hegelian, and, later, the Marxist, contrast, recalled by Kolakowski, between civil society and the state in terms of which Marxist utopianism has been expressed. In his monistic enthusiasm, Hegel had been determined to overcome every one of the dualisms in Kant's philosophy, and, most of all, the surviving contrast between the intelligible natural order and the unknowable supernatural order. In order to do this, Hegel had to abandon the Humean and Kantian conception of philosophy as marking the boundaries of human understanding and as distinguishing powers of mind: philosophy was no longer to be a non-empirical anthropology, supplementing the natural sciences and putting each of them into its proper place. Philosophy was not to be any kind of anthropology at all; the powers of individual minds in relation to the natural order, or to the supernatural order, were not to be its primary concern. The subject of study was to be the World Spirit and its phases of developments. The World Spirit is neither the knower nor the known, neither the human mind nor the natural order, and its development is not merely the development of human knowledge; nor is it the natural evolution of things. It is, mysteriously, a higher synthesis of the two. This idealism requires that we do not, and cannot, raise questions about the possible limits of human knowledge of a reality which is altogether independent of human knowledge. It also requires that there should be no distinction between reality as it is constituted by the human mind and the supernatural reality that exceeds our understanding.

The principal motive behind this suppression of all the dualisms of traditional philosophy was more a final settling of accounts with religion in all its forms than with politics and the nation state, though of course it was both. The claims of religion, which had dominated European thought for centuries, were to be finally trimmed and contained by a philosophical scepticism that acknowledged no limits. Rousseau and Kant, and many sceptics of the Enlightenment, had left a residuary place for religion, alongside the demands of citizenship and of rational morality, as one principal human interest among others, though no longer an absolutely overriding interest. Those sceptics of the Enlightenment who had dismissed religion as total illusion still looked to new moral sciences, and to new schemes of education, to liberate men from their inherited superstitions and oppression. After the Revolution and the Terror, and after the career of Napoleon and the Restoration had effectively destroyed immediate hopes of a new autonomy and rational liberation, Hegel's scepticism was more thorough-going. It was his ambition that philosophy, his philosophy, should absorb religion as part of itself, and it would exhibit Christianity, both as a set of doctrines and as a set of institutions, as one necessary and intelligible phase in the development of the Spirit towards final reconciliation with itself in philosophy. The Enlightenment was just another necessary stage, in which philosophers were still projecting the salvation of men into an ideal world, which was now a future utopia; now the ideal was a future state of society, a community of intelligence, not a supernatural and other-worldly blessedness. We had left the ages of religion behind and entered the age of politics, because philosophers had now realized that they had been cultivating their salvation only as a fantasy of another world, while they could through the nation state bring the ideal and the actual into agreement. Thought, speculation about the ideal, should be embodied in institutions and so become, in the Hegelian sense, concrete.

For Marx, the young Hegelian philosopher and journalist, this overweening philosophy was not to be rejected because of its pretensions to completeness, but rather because it was a spiritualist philosophy, and also because it was still abstract, in spite of its claim that philosophy must become concrete. This spiritualist philosophy gave no explanation of the fierce laws by which those who stole wood in the forests were punished. The existence of such laws as these, and of the other institutions that cripple men's lives at particular times and places, are not to be explained by the adventures of the Idea or of Spirit. The level of abstraction is too high to touch the actual living conditions of men. The conditions of actual lives are to be explained, in the spirit of Feuerbach, by material interests, generalized and systematized. Marx's reversal of philosophy was to make philosophy scientific not by changing its methods of argument, but by changing the subject-matter. Philosophy would be scientific if it explained social facts and social change as functions of material realities.

Three features of Marx's scientific socialism are inherited from this past, particularly the Hegelian past. First, Marxism is to be all-embracing, a totality that allots all human interests, and all the human sciences, their due place. Marx may have retreated a little way from the all-embracing philosophy of his early years while writing *Das Kapital*; but his socialism still did not allow that diverse and disputable philosophies of mind might be open to socialists without inconsistency. Second, Marxism pointed the way to the liberation of man, in a traditional sense, just as Spinoza's *Ethics* had: the philosophy of socialism was a philosophy of human salvation and all the essential problems of man in society have their answer within it, not only in modern societies, or in societies of a particular kind, or with a particular history, but in any society. The theory was entirely general, covering all human history, economics, sociology, and the rest of the moral sciences, within its general framework. Third, Marx's theory of man and of the social order did not start from any theory of human knowledge, explicitly worked out and defended; nowhere are the presumed limits of human knowledge and of the sciences marked out in an argumentative way; nor is the implication accepted that men may in future generations know vastly more about their own nature, and about the workings of society, than Marx or any of his contemporaries could know. That positive knowledge in the human sciences develops and is accelerating, and yet that it is at an early stage in its development still, and that the moral sciences have scarcely begun their career – these are not propositions that are emphasized in Marx's thought; and they are only with difficulty acceptable in the Marxism that has succeeded it. There is little place for really surprising discoveries in individual psychology or in social anthropology, and no sense of these open-ended empirical disciplines. The various kinds of oppression, which socialism is expected to remove, are taken to have causes that are already known; at least there is no suggestion that the classless society, which will be the outcome of the dictatorship of the proletariat, will need help from any new body of knowledge to meet surviving evils. On the contrary, the administration of things will under communism replace the administration of persons: and this provision implies that all social problems, and problems of an individual's fulfilment, as far as they are dependent on social organization, will have been solved.

Such a theory of knowledge is scarcely a theory of knowledge at all; and rational socialism, it seems to me, must have another and more critical theory of knowledge as its foundation. Kolakowski mentions the consequences in policy of this doctrine of social salvation. The consequences are likely to include not only a naïve attitude to possibilities in the arts and to literature, but also a philistine and dogmatic attitude to experiments and theories in clinical psychology, social anthropology and in other human sciences. The Marxist response, clearly indicated in Kolakowski's paper, is that the empiricist theory of knowledge, which I have been implicitly advocating, is linked historically to the Civil Society, the bourgeois society, of early and middle capitalism: that it is an appropriate and progressive philosophy in the phase of liberal thought, and of liberal policies, which private enterprise in its heyday needed: that all empiricist theory of knowledge, with its typical respect for piecemeal discoveries in the social sciences, is out of place, and relatively inapplicable, in the late stages of monopoly capitalism and when the state is a powerful planning authority: that classical liberalism, best expressed by J. S. Mill, still stresses the need for the experimental social sciences, and for a free market in ideas, at a time when central government and the big corporations between them in effect allocate the resources for the various sciences, arts and technologies. There is a measure of false consciousness in making these claims for uncertainty, and for the piecemeal social sciences, when forms of life are determined by economic organization quite independently of any such theories, and in pursuit of separate interests. One cannot, I think, deny some force to this reply; certainly there is a contrast between the ideal civil society, with its area of experimental private life and of respect for individual preferences, and the planned economies, the planned education and social order, of the highly industrialized nation states.

I am certainly not proposing a return to classical empiricism, of the type represented by Mill, as the basis for socialists' thinking: much, though not all, of Marx's criticism of classical liberalism, as also of the utopias of the Enlightenment, seems to me convincing. And, even apart from Marx's implicit criticism, Mill belongs with Marx to the age of philosophical anthropology, which begins with Rousseau and which ended, or which should have ended, with the rise to power of the Nazis: I say 'should have ended', because the prevailing theories of social change, whether liberal or Marxist, had proved so inadequate to the facts of national socialism and of fascism. What kind of theory might take the place of the philosophical anthropologies of Rousseau and of Marx, which have so far guided socialist thought? Whether we are socialists or not, we now know enough to know that we still have very little knowledge of the kind that a social planner needs to have, if central planning by the government is to be a rational, responsible procedure. Those socialists who in the natural course have been in-fluenced by Marx, certainly the great majority, look for some signifi-cant relation between the economic and social changes in society and the growth of the scientific knowledge that purports to explain these changes. The relation must be one of interaction between changes in theory and changes in actual organization; and not only that, but also between social theories and the planned social changes that are the consequence of believing these theories to be true.

The loop, or playback relation, that links social theories and social policies is a complicated one; and we have no reason to assume it to be constant at different periods. To take relatively straightforward ex-amples: it may be necessary, because of modern technology and eco-nomic organization, to plan on a very large scale land-use, house-building, architectural methods and styles in new towns, the clearing of derelict urban areas and so on, at a time when the sociological and psychological knowledge that would rationally justify any particular plans just does not exist. We have to tamper with forms of life in a very direct way at a time when we are still learning by these tamperings what the effect will be; and the 'we' refers here to governing circles, who have inherited or acquired some social theory, however rudimentary and untested, which implicitly guides their choices. The technologies, and new operations of central government and of subsidiary corpora-tions, seem to impose a necessity of comprehensive planning at a time when the relevant theory which might guide the planning is far from comprehensive: on the contrary, it is fragmentary, uncertain, and there is only enough of it to justify small experiments in planning, not a large irreversible commitment that will alter many lives. The public agencies and the bureaucracies who do the planning are staffed principally by people who generally subscribe to liberal ideals of consumer choice and of the free experiments of the individual. Just as the new technologies and consequent social organizations of the Industrial Revolution seemed to classical liberal empiricists to require as a necessity the removal of barriers to freedoms of thought and discussion, free experiments in living, and to require private initiative by the private citizen in inventing new customs and habits, so the new and contrary necessities are mediated by social theories, and by an ideology, which present a contrasting picture of rationality. The rational social process now is a set of related changes which are planned and controlled by a single authority over a considerable period of time; it largely excludes the occurrence of unpredicted factors of individual preference that might destroy the plan. The liberal doctrine of the hidden hand, which leads to optimum results by the blind intersections of egoisms, rested on the assurance that the preferences of individuals are reliably known only by the subjects themselves, and that they are revealed by choices under free competition.

Self-knowledge in liberal theory was, and is, a comparatively unproblematical notion, and there is no suggestion, as in Marx, that there are illusions of consciousness and that apparent wants and interests may mask the real ones: and that the unmasking calls for a scientific enquiry. The goodness or badness of the social order is a function of individual satisfaction, freely discovered and easily recognized. Therefore no comprehensive theory of human needs, or of the conditions of liberation, was required: neither a philosophical and historical theory, as Marx's, nor one founded upon the social sciences. But the rational social process, which is operated by the open and visible hand of the planner, not only seems to require a comprehensive theory of human needs to justify the chosen outcome: it requires a theory of how the various needs can best be combined, what the offsetting costs of one desired end against another are. And yet not only do we not have such a comprehensive theory; we are not even sure that there could be such a theory, or what it would be like. There are philosophical doubts about the possibility of any such theory, and about its objectivity. From the point of view of social anthropology, the most intelligently presented of the social sciences other than economics, the idea of a comprehensive theory belongs to the pre-history of social science: it now seems naïve to measure social costs in terms that are not to be found in the particular vocabulary of the society to which the measurement is applied. The very idea of a comprehensive theory of needs and of social costs has also generally been represented in popular thought, and at a pre-theoretical level, as either sinister or absurd. In the *Brave New World* or *1984* fantasies, the comprehensiveness of a theory of social need that guides planners is precisely the sinister or absurdly inhuman element. It seems that we cannot imagine social theory, or the social sciences, as comprehensive guides to action: precisely in proportion as they are scientific, they must not be comprehensive, as a supernatural doctrine of salvation can be, or as Marxist theory was.

There are various ways of understanding the relation between organized social theory and social planning. The first has already been mentioned: that past comprehensive theories, whether religious or enlightenment theory or Marxist, have been theories of salvation after some Fall of man, some distortion, or alienation. The myth of alienation is no less a myth in its secular form. The second explanation is that the planned utopias, sinister or ridiculous, are simple-minded extensions of individual needs and interests to a whole society, itself represented as an accumulation of individuals each seeking only, or mainly, satisfaction for themselves. There is no vision, first, of community nor, second, of spontaneity and this makes the utopias also like hells. I think Charles Taylor will speak about the idea of community, a strong element certainly of traditional socialism. The utopias of modern social science, whether of Huxley or Skinner, simply prolong the demand-satisfaction of bourgeois theory without the experimenting, and the uncertainty and ignorance, upon which freedom in bourgeois democracies depend. The third explanation of the horror of the comprehensive social plan is to be found in the following argument: first, there is the premise that diversity and independence of forms of life, and of life styles, are both a justification and an outcome of the liberation, and of the autonomy, which socialism will bring: and diversity and independence of forms of life are incompatible with any comprehensive and shared vision of a desirable social order: therefore any vision of a desired social order must either be incomplete and uncertain, or it must not be shared by all or most members of society. I think I discern this moral view in both Kolakowski's and Taylor's contributions. I believe that this view has a rational basis in the nature of knowledge.

Organized knowledge of any kind, and particularly scientific knowledge, is cumulative, and, in this sense, it is progressive. There is a continuing acceleration in the rate at which it is acquired, unless a social catastrophe interrupts the process. Secondly, the accelerating advance of knowledge is subject to the division of labour: increasing specialization, and subdividing of subject matters, is to be expected as part of the advance of knowledge, and even as part of the meaning of the concept of the advance of knowledge. It is an intrinsic feature of knowledge that it should subdivide and subdivide rather as cells do when they multiply. Unless the original problems and questions that brought the science into existence have been divided into a host of different questions, it is most unlikely that real progress has been made. Theorists of progress supposed that these features of advancing knowledge would be features of social advance also. But this was an illusion. It remains true that the social sciences, like the natural sciences, will become more specialized, less comprehensive as they advance; and it remains true also that comprehensive visions of desirable futures to be reached by clearly marked routes will seem less and less credible. The vision of the conflict-free future in a classless society was a vision of redemption: if there was no Fall in historical time, and therefore no redemption, and if the whole myth is replaced by an empirical anthropology, socialist and radical thought ought not to take its immediate goals to be ultimate goals; it ought to be ready to revise them as more is learnt in the human sciences about interdependencies of desires and interests and sources of suffering.

Socialism ought to be more a definite method of social change than a definite goal of change, in the sense that it takes rationality in planning seriously, and consequently takes the slow, questionable development of the social sciences seriously. To take these sciences seriously involves critically examining the balance of sheer ignorance, mere guess-work and real knowledge that lies behind any particular planning decision. The overwhelming need, from the standpoint of philosophy, is to explore the reasons for our ignorance in the social and human sciences. A more critical, and half empirical, theory of knowledge is needed to decide which human sciences, and which lines of enquiry within them, are likely to lead to substantial results if pressed, and which are hopeless, in spite of *a priori* expectations. And one reliable mark of progress in a science, or line of inquiry, is precisely that its results are exact, narrow in scope, and unexpected: one knows the science is genuinely launched in a path of progress in proportion as it disappoints the comparatively simple expectations with which it began. That this has not happened to the science of society foreseen by Durkheim and Weber could not itself have been foreseen even twenty years ago. But the comparative failure, so far, of sociology as a source of accurate and useful general truths has implications for social planning: it at least implies that we do not have grounds for confidence about causes and effects on a large scale, the scale of sociological analysis. This is an outcome that was not foreseen and is intrinsically surprising.

My conclusion is that a period has ended for political theory generally, and for socialist theory in particular. The period began with Rousseau and the Enlightenment and ended at about the same time as the supression of dissent in Hungary and Czechoslovakia and the Sino–Soviet dispute. This was the period in which the advent of total salvation through politics, backed by a philosophy of history, was still a possible and not unreasonable creed for socialists and radicals: the period before social anthropology had made its mark, and when theories of human nature and of its development were usually based on the known history of Europe alone.

We know how little we know about the conditions under which, given our present knowledge, the moral ideals of socialism can best be realized, with the least possible compromise. I have not thought it part of my topic to say what these ideals are, nor how independent they may be of their conditions of realization.

—— 4 ——

SOCIALISM AND
WELTANSCHAUUNG

Charles Taylor

Is the socialist idea bound to any particular philosophical basis? The best
way to begin this discussion would be to start from the most widespread
view that socialism is tied to a particular Weltanschauung, Marxism,
and see what is being claimed here.

Marxism never claimed that the only societies which exhibit some of
the key features of socialism, like common property, would have a
materialist basis. For Marx recognized that there had been a 'primitive'
communism, associations like the early Christian church etc. Nor does
it claim that the only philosophical basis which can animate a socialist
movement in our day is historical materialism. Obviously there are
others, such as Fabianism and Christian socialism. These make up the
so-called utopian socialisms, against which Marxism defines itself.

The claim rather is something of this kind: the only kind of philosophical basis which can animate a socialist movement in our day which
could actually win through to revolution and the founding of a new
society is historical materialism (or dialectical materialism, if one takes
the later variant). The various earlier, historical 'socialist' societies are
irrelevant, since socialism must have an entirely different aspect coming
at the culmination of the industrial revolution and the ensuing transformation of human life than it did before. And the non-Marxist
socialist movements of today are inadequate, because they fail to understand what is really going on in society; they lack a 'scientific' base, and
therefore cannot know how to go about transforming this society.

This is one way of expressing their inadequacy, which is rather that
of an engineer with the wrong blue-print, or faulty stress-tables, who
in consequence can never build the bridge. But there is another side to
the Marxist claim. Not only the revolution, but the building of a
socialist society, requires a certain philosophical base. Socialism requires

45

a new kind of man, freed from the irrational myths of the past (religion), scientific in spirit, creative, and at one with his fellows in this dedication to the great common enterprise. It is a picture suspiciously without shadows, and which has received its most vulgar statement in the socialist realism of an earlier epoch of Soviet literature. But some great positive tranformation was also essential to Marx's vision as well, even if this was not as shallow as Zhdanov's. Marxism claims to be the only world-outlook compatible with such a transformation. The kind of man capable of building socialist society must have an outlook of this kind. For if he has a religious outlook, or a vulgar materialist (and hence atomist) one, or a Romantic, nostalgic one, he will in one way or an-other be incapable of constructing and becoming part of a socialist commonwealth. The religious man cannot face the task at hand without illusions. He lacks the Promethean dimension essential to socialist man, as does the Romantic. The atomist cannot give himself to the collective enterprise, and so on.

All these different requirements hold together in the tight philoso-phical synthesis of Marxism. Materialism is seen as essential, ultimately because it is the only possible *terrain d'entente*. Socialism means and requires the rediscovery of a certain unanimity of purpose among men after class-divided society. This unanimity is regained by abolishing class society. Achieving this abolition requires a correct understanding of this society, as we have seen. But the unanimity gained in the revo-lution has to have a philosophical expression as well. The only possible basis for this unanimity will be the correct view of man's true situation, i.e. historical materialism. The Babel of illusory views today, religious, utilitarian, etc., is simply the obverse side of a class-divided society.

After this brief sketch of the affirmative Marxist answer to our question, we might be tempted to respond with a resounding 'no'. In fact the Marxist belief in the necessity of their Weltanschauung is bound up with two connected features of Marx's vision that probably none of us here share: the belief that political conflict could really be put behind us, which means of course that the required extraordinary convergence in men's goals and life-situations could be achieved; and the belief that this unanimity would coincide with their maximum creativity.

Probably none of us believes in such a happy ending to the human story. Perhaps none of us believes that illusion, conflict, ill will, division can be definitively overcome. And therefore we react to any claim to achieve unanimity of purpose, to overcome political conflict, by reaching for our pistols, as it were. But our desire to oppose the senseless attempt to suppress human diversity should not make us jump to conclusions. Even if there is not just one correct socialist Weltanschauung, perhaps socialism in our day must go along with one of a restricted number of views about man and the world. Perhaps the kind of social and economic changes socialism calls for require one orientation from a relatively restricted list if they are to be carried through successfully.

For the purposes of this discussion we might start off thinking of socialism simply as the condition of common ownership and control of the means of production, or at least an important part of the means of production, exercised at least putatively on behalf of the whole people without respect for special privileges, and at least putatively in compliance with their decisions. This is a far cry from what many of us would recognize as the socialism we would like to see in effect. Socialists naturally strive to reach a society from whose description the words 'at least putatively' could be dropped, that is, which would really be egalitarian and democratic. And many would want to add further conditions, for example concerning decentralization. But I have merely tried to offer the minimum description of a society which could call itself socialist. There are, of course, many societies in the world today which meet this minimum description, very few, if any, of which could be held up as ideals.

There is, of course, an influential strand of social democrats whose conception of socialism does not meet the above description, those who hold that ownership is irrelevant and that socialist goals can be attained exclusively by control through a planned mixed economy. But in this case, the claims made for control without ownership are very far-reaching. The above definition could be modified to meet this view, if we spoke of 'ownership and/or control'.

Now is there an affinity between socialism, so defined, and any given philosophical outlook(s) today, such that the conditions of success of one are tied up with the other? Certainly one could plausibly argue that there is such an affinity in many developing societies today between a drive for modernization and at least an obeisance to socialist forms. Hence the vogue of the name, served up in all kinds of sauce, including 'Arab socialism', 'African socialism', and so on.

A plausible account of this connection can readily be given in rough fashion. The economic changes sought by the leaders of these societies involve industrialization, the adoption of new techniques, the acquisition of new social disciplines, the acceptance of new social groupings, very often at the expense of old ones (for example urbanization at the expense of village life), the acceptance of new modes of organization, a different kind of education, etc. Not all these changes are involved in each case, but at least some selection from this list is always at stake.

Now whereas England and America and other 'Atlantic' countries went through these changes under the leadership of an entrepreneurial class which used government only in a supporting role, and certainly did not require it to plan the change, and whereas the next generation of developing societies such as Germany and Japan, although their development was orchestrated from the top, leaned heavily on traditional social allegiances to revolutionize the relations on which these ultimately depended, present-day developing societies have neither of these options, in the main. They mostly lack an entrepreneurial class; and traditional allegiances are either too eroded, or else in some way unsuitable (too opposed to the changes to be introduced, for example).

So 'socialism' steps in to fill the breach. It justifies the orchestration of the whole set of changes by the state, which in any case is usually a necessity. But the government acts not in the name of some restored former greatness alone, or even mainly (as with the Meiji restoration), but with an eye to goals which are billed (correctly) as unprecedented: equality, freedom, control over destiny. The inspiring models tend to be the Soviet Union, China, Cuba (itself modelled on the earlier communist societies) with a greater or lesser degree of free variation.

There is a kind of affinity between socialism and 'modernization' in these contexts, if I can use this slippery and much-abused word. The set of goals I outlined earlier dictate fairly well the adoption of a 'socialist' ideology, and the socialist measures in fact adopted can generally only be sustained and justified by the highly 'modern' goals mentioned in the last paragraph.

Now this affinity with what I have referred to by the vague coverword 'modernization' has been fundamental to modern socialism since the beginning, that is, for the last century and a half. It would therefore be useful to try to examine a little more closely what lies behind this word. To have an adequate conception of this would be, of course, to have an insight into contemporary society which would make most of the social science written to date superfluous. This is a worthy goal, but one which no one can yet claim to have achieved. But in order to discuss this question, one has to press ahead with one's highly inadequate formulations, and this is what I propose to do.

The nub of the concept for our purposes here is perhaps this: since the seventeenth century men – first in 'Atlantic' countries, then elsewhere – have tended more and more to define themselves as agents who derive their purposes from themselves. Philosophically speaking, most earlier notions of man defined his 'normal' or optimal condition at least partly in terms of his relation to a larger cosmic order, with which he had to be in tune. The 'modern' view sees him rather as an agent who optimally would use the surrounding world as a set of instruments and enabling conditions with which to effect the purposes which he either found within himself (as 'drives' or desires) or chose freely.

This philosophical view of man, which reaches one of its paradigm expressions in the Enlightenment, has been of tremendous practical import. The industrial revolution is the expression in a way of living, and of treating nature and human relations, of this Promethean, self-defining stance. And the attendant transformations have made this way of looking at ourselves almost as 'normal' and inescapable for contemporary men, as the notion of cosmic order must have been for those who lived in closed hierarchical societies in the past. I say 'almost' as normal, because there has remained a horizon of nostalgia around the consciousness of modern man which has prevented him really giving himself whole-heartedly to this view of himself.

The nostalgia begins almost immediately. If we find the full statement of the 'modern' notion of man in the age of the Enlightenment, the same age sees the various movements which fed into European Romanticism, and which were characterized by a deep nostalgia for the irrecoverable past, either the heroic primitive age of Ossian or Homer, or the idyllic harmony of Polynesia, or the age of Pericles, or the great age of faith. But the relation to earlier ages never got beyond one of nostalgia. The best minds of the Romantic period recognized that one could not go back, and should not want to. What they protested against was the atomistic, manipulative bent of the Enlightenment.

Against the notion of man as the individual subject of desire, manipulating the surrounding world with the goal of fulfilment, the Romantic period developed a view of man which I would like to call (following an expression used by Isaiah Berlin) 'expressivist'. Human life is seen as the external expression of a man's potential. This view, which we see developing in Rousseau, Herder, into Romanticism, Hegel, Marx, eventually infecting even the utilitarian tradition, through Mill, does not return to pre-modern models of man. The potential which a man expresses is very much his own; it develops out of him, and is not

49

defined by some relation of harmony with a larger order. But at the same time, the expressivist view does not restrict itself to the consequentialist calculus of desire and its fulfilment. Life is seen also under the categories of expression, as being a true embodiment of potential, or a distorted, compressed travesty of what men truly are.

By the same token, men's relation to the surrounding world is not simply seen as manipulative. The expressivist view developed an ideal of communion between men, and between men and nature, which became one of the great themes of the Romantic period. Men sought to recover a relation with nature where they sense it, too, as expression – of spirit, life-force, or whatever – with which their lives, as expression, were in tune. So that we get with the Romantic period something which resembles the pre-modern notions of man as part of a larger order; with this vital difference, that on the earlier views man could only come to himself by finding his right relation to the larger order, whereas now men reach communion with nature by discovering what they really have it in them to express.

Now the relevance of all this to our question is that socialism from its beginnings as a modern political movement has been deeply involved with both the Enlightenment and expressivist currents. On one side, socialism as a doctrine, whether with Babeuf, Saint-Simon, or Marx, to name three stages, has been heavily committed on the modern side in the battle against older definitions of man. There has been a recurrent struggle of modernization around an issue of the following form: traditionalists following older forms of thought tended to see certain social structures as embodiments of a cosmic order; modernizers tended to see all structures as serving or disserving human happiness or effective action. Monarchy, aristocracy, the role of the clergy, have all been defended as the embodiments of an order that commanded men's allegiance in an unconditional way, and attacked as dysfunctional, bastions of privilege and special interest. And the fight continues right into our day. The battles over women's liberation are the lineal descendants of these struggles over the articulations of traditional society. One side would justify a differentiation of role through its supposed anchoring in nature; the other denounces this view as a screen for exploitation, and demands the abolition of the distinction in the name of liberty and equality.

Now on this issue, socialist movements have been fairly consistently on the modernizing side; and this right up to the present day, where one finds them generally espousing such causes as women's liberation. But at the same time, they have generally, though perhaps not quite so consistently, taken up the expressivist critique of modernization. That is, they have tended to reject an atomistic picture of society, a manipulative view of man's relation to nature, and even a reading of the ends of life in terms simply of desire-fulfilment.

I do not believe anyone can doubt the debt of Marx, certainly the young Marx, to Romanticism in general, and what I have called expressivism in particular. The picture which one finds in the young Marx of liberated man, who has made himself over by labour, and whose work ceases to be a travail and becomes free creativity, this surely is a quintessentially expressivist picture. And even those who hold the most hard-nosed interpretation of the evolution of the mature Marx can hardly believe that this quite disappeared from the purview of the author of *Capital*.

But the evolution of Marx, on one interpretation at any rate, and certainly the evolution of Marxism under the impetus of Engels, illustrates the tension and ambivalence in the socialist tradition which is implicit in its attitude to modernization from the beginning. On one hand many socialists have had profound sympathy with the Romantic experience of modern society as a desert in which everything has been levelled, and all beauty has been stamped out to create a mundane, serviceable world of use-objects. On the other, socialists have been among the most uncompromising modernizers, tearing asunder traditional societies, institutions, customs with a savage dedication unmatched by the great nineteenth-century utilitarians, for instance. Traditional Russia was more brutally operated on by its Bolshevik surgeons than ever India was by the James Mills and MacCaulays.

Because of this ambivalence, it is not surprising that Marxism should present two faces, and be the source of endless dispute between two kinds of claimants to its heritage. On one side there are those who see Marx as the great critic of alienation and who see the revolution as built on and leading to a great leap in human culture, and a recovery of unity between man and man, and between the sundered aspects of human life, work and play, economy and politics, and so on. On the other are those who see Marx above all as the author of a scientific theory of capitalism, its insoluble contradictions and necessary demise. The former focus on the young Marx's penetrating study of the atomist, manipulative, compartmentalizing bent of capitalist society; the latter on the mature Marx's proof that capitalism, as an engine for delivering the goods, stood condemned by its own contradictions, that it had to be superceded by socialism in order to do what it itself had set out to do, and most effectively had done up to now, namely to increase men's control over nature.

This second line has of course become the dominant line in Marxism. This was already so at the end of the nineteenth century, for a variety of reasons, one of which was undoubtedly the intellectual climate of that period in which Marxism could appear to best advantage under its guise as 'scientific socialism'. But this orientation was sealed by the success of a Marxist revolutionary party in a 'backward' country. Marxism in fact had to take the role of a modernizing ideology. Socialism = Soviet power + electrification, to quote Lenin's equation. But both of these required that the ruling *élite* adopt the stance of engineers relative to the at best inert, often refractory, social matter they had to deal with. Both to hold power, and to build what were considered to be the economic 'preconditions' of socialism, the *élite* had to enforce the list of changes in social grouping, mode of organization, work discipline, etc., which we lumped above under the title 'modernization', and to encompass this by a practice which was itself highly manipulative. Small wonder that the Soviet variant of Marxism has been a tough Engelsian one. The expressivist elements are still there, of course, in the vision of the new Soviet man, and in the fundamental notions of collective will of the proletariat. But they have taken second place, and the vision of Soviet man is heavily weighted towards the dominator of nature, rather than the subject of creative activity. This Soviet model has been the one which has been seized upon (with sizeable modifications) by developing countries in the way mentioned above.

But in the West, socialism has not been a monolithic movement, and the ambivalence has had free reign. The modernizing emphasis in socialism has frequently come to the fore – for instance, in the 1930s when the Marxist predictions about the total incapacitation and breakdown of capitalism seemed to be coming true; but also more recently. One has only to think of the great election pitch of the British Labour Party before 1964, centred around the new frontiers of science policy. But in the very fact that it would not be possible today to be so unambiguously affirmative about the beneficent effects of science and technology, we can measure the ambivalent nature of the socialist tradition. For since those balmy days of 1964 our world has suffered a severe failure of nerve, or at least of confidence in modernization. This is not without precedent, as we see when we contemplate the Romantic period, but this wave of doubt has its own peculiarities, and seems above all to be of uncommon depth and social breadth. And the nature of the socialist tradition is such that it cannot just combat this failure of nerve as a retrograde step. For we recognize in the implied critique of the direction of our society too much that is integral to the socialist line of thought from the beginning.

How does this help to answer our question: is the socialist idea bound to any particular philosophical basis? Presumably, it suggests that socialism is bound up with two rather incompatible such bases, and that one or the other tends to predominate depending on the historical situation. But while this might be a roughly valid historical answer, there is a more particular answer which is germane to our situation.

In fact modern socialism starts as an attempt to combine two things, the drive to modernization, i.e. to make a society of free agents, and the expressivist critique of capitalist society and the attendant aspirations. In one sense, subsequent socialist movements have had all sorts of philosophical bases; they have been Marxist, Christian, Hegelian, vaguely utilitarian, or a mixture of all these at once, such as the British Labour Party. But in another sense, they have generally been in one way or another concerned with these two aspirations and the problem of combining them. There has been a spectrum within socialism in this respect, in that some have been far more concerned with one goal than the other. William Morris might be put in this respect at the 'expressivist' extreme against, say, the Webbs, who were not very much more than utilitarians who had discovered the superior efficacy of collective instruments. But in general the two concerns have been at work.

Thus although their ontologies may differ greatly, and in this sense the illusions of Marxist communism must be set aside, the philosophical anthropology of socialists and socialist movements is likely to converge around certain themes. And applied to the particular predicament of present-day Western societies, this is likely to entail an even closer convergence.

For in a sense our world has come to a pass in which the original preoccupation of socialism has become everybody's problem: how to create a 'modern' society, that is, one in which men are maximally free agents, capable of choosing their own ends and acting effectively towards them, while preserving what are more and more seen to be man's essential relations to other men, to the past, and to nature. The problems and crises of modern society seem to be conspiring to force these 'Romantic' concerns on us.

The various ecological crises, actual and threatened, have thrust the problem of our balance with nature to the fore. What seems to many the increasing distance and unresponsiveness of great bureaucratic structures is forcing us to reconsider the drive to size and large-scale interdependence. This is being called even more into question by the results of galloping urbanization. The ills of large-scale, unresponsive structures and the attendant decline in the quality of urban life lead to an increasing privatization and fragmentation of social discipline which makes these problems harder to solve.

And along with all this, whether cause or effect, there is an undoubted loss of faith in many Atlantic countries in what were unquestioned goals yesterday, such as endless growth, a focus on rising consumer standards, the liquidation of traditional modes of life in favour of one large, urban civilization. The anxious questioning about the pace of change, which accompanies the vogue of a book like *Culture Shock*, for instance, probably does not correspond to any increase in the pace of change by any objective measure – at least for large numbers of Americans – so much as it reflects a waning confidence in the goals of a greater collective command over nature and individual command over goods and services for the sake of which this perpetual change was once happily undertaken. It is the same collapse of faith in the goals that underpinned the 'Atlantic way of life' and its attendant disciplines which at least partly lies at the root of the present wave of 'permissiveness', which is the kind of 'change', if it really deserves the name, which really causes anguish among a goodly section of the population.

In the face of this crisis, a socialist with a knowledge of the tradition cannot help feeling that 'this is where we came in'. In a sense, the major problem of our society is to find a new formula for an industrial, technological, 'modern' civilization (in the sense outlined above), which is not committed to endless accumulation, constantly rising consumer standards (as against other forms of improvement of life-situation), continued resource-exhaustion, ever-greater agglomerations. This is much more difficult than it sounds. For there is a close link between a 'modern' society, that is, one in which men are free agents, and increasing production and consumer standards. For during the whole modern era, one of the paradigm ways in which men have expressed their freedom and agency has been in self-betterment through production. There are other vaunted dimensions of freedom, which are in a sense of incomparably greater importance, freedom of thought, of religious confession, of expression, organization, self-government, and so on. Their lack would be sensed as a great deprivation by most citizens of an advanced Atlantic society today. But as long as they are not threatened, they go unnoticed. We do not experience freedom daily in choosing our religious confession, for we do not choose this daily, if indeed we ever chose it. Where the members of a modern Atlantic society experience free agency on a daily basis is as consumers, and sometimes to a more limited degree as producers or bargainers. A certain number also experience this through their participation in the political process, and this is not to be discounted. But it has always been a minority, and nowadays the proportion of those who experience politics in this way seems to be declining dangerously. This is not to say that fewer people are participating in politics, but that a growing number of those who do at one time or another come away with a sense of impotence and frustration.

It thus promises to be extremely difficult, if not impossible, to move our societies off the track of rising consumption and GNP to a set of goals which touch the cadre of our collective existence, the design of our cities, our balance with nature, an equitable distribution of resources, the decentralization of power. At times it seems much more likely that we shall remain fixed on the present course, but that the failure of confidence in our goals will lead to increasing fragmentation, and violent challenges by minorities in the name of every conceivable variety of neo-Romantic *Schwärmerei*, which will in turn call into being a much more repressive society, a society run by the Agnews in order to suppress the Abbey Hoffmanns. Quite a depressing prospect.

Our taking another road requires among other things that another view of man, other paradigm images of free agency, become widespread. Now there is an affinity between this hoped-for shift in philosophy and socialism; not only because socialism as a doctrine has been talking of other images of agency from the beginning, such as creativity and self-management, but also for the much more immediate reason that the kind of institutional changes which would have to accompany this shift in perspective as its vehicle would be socialist in direction.

One of the principal entrenchments of the present course of our societies is the large corporation dedicated to the continued extension of its operations. For this extension mainly depends on an expanding consumer society. The large corporation in Atlantic societies, and substantial parts of the Third World where they have implanted themselves, fosters the expansion of this society with all its considerable means. And these do not simply include advertising and powerful leverage with government. Much more important is the fact that the large corporation is the major channel for investment funds in many Western societies. Governments and societies bend themselves to its priorities in order to receive the precious manna of investment and employment-creation. The only way the large corporation can be displaced as the principal engine of economic development and the direction of investment is through greater collective control of the means of production and the channels of investment, that is, by moving in a socialist direction. Until the hegemony of the major corporation is challenged, a new direction will be utterly out of the question for many Western societies, not to speak of Third World ones.

The shift in orientation which our civilization now needs thus seems to require an adoption of socialist structures. But the dependence may be reciprocal as well: that is, a brace of what we might consider socialist goals will require a new orientation critical of the 'modernization' of rising GNP and consumer standards. Ask any socialist in a Western country today what his goals are, and his answer will at least include the following: greater equality in conditions of life, in particular the alleviation of the greatest conditions of need, a shift in priorities towards collective goals and needs, rendering the decision-making structures of society more responsive to citizens (though there is wide difference over the means to this).

Now it is arguable that these goals can never be met in anything but the most exiguous and limited fashion without a change in generally-held priorities away from the rising consumer standard. It used to be thought that poverty would be abolished by going all out for growth, since rising GNP was bound to trickle down, and richer tax-payers would be more generous in their provision for collective need. But this hope now seems illusory. In part we have discovered that the culture of poverty is more intractable. But in addition, we find that growth for the sake of rising consumer standards has its own dynamic, that the ever-increasing expectations of consumers outrun the rise in production with relative ease, and there is probably more resentment today against the tax dollar spent for welfare, benefit payments, and other collective enterprises than there was a few years ago, at least in the societies with which I am familiar. The present obsession with inflation in many Western countries is becoming an incitement to income scramble, where the devil will take the hindmost.

We probably cannot alter our public priorities away from private consumption towards the meeting of crying public need unless we manage to alter widespread philosophical priorities about the importance of growth and ever-rising consumer standards. And it is arguable that we will never be able to cope properly with poverty and deprivation, or move substantially towards equality, until we do so alter our public priorities. In a society in which the principal accepted goal is continued improvement of living standards as measured by goods and services, public measures in the direction of equality or to alleviate deprivation take on the aspect of robbing Peter to pay Paul. They will be resisted not only by the well-to-do, but by the affluent majority who thus align themselves against change. In a society which gave greater importance to the design of its cities as decent places to live, for instance, many of the programmes which today we look on as 'give-aways' to benefit a deprived minority, for example low-cost housing, would be seen in a different light, as in pursuance of a general goal.

Hence it is possible that many of the accepted goals of socialists today, greater equality, the alleviation of need, a shift in priorities to collective goals, can only be attained in company with a mutation in commonly held definitions of the good life; and that this will have to be defined less emphatically in terms of rising consumer standards, and more in terms of a more humanly satisfying collective environment, cultural growth, the acquistition of objects which last (as against the quick-turnover, disposable goods of today), other kinds of scientific achievement (such as a recycling economy that would not push us towards resource exhaustion). I think that the same point could be made in connection with the fourth goal mentioned above, rendering the decision-making structures more responsive, but there is no space to draw the connection here. If this is so, then there is an affinity in our particular historical situation between a programme which can be called socialist on one hand, and certain philosophical views about man, the ends of life, and man's relation to nature. This convergence is peculiar in a way to our historical situation, but the roots of it are to be found in the modern socialist tradition, as I tried to argue above. This does not mean that contemporary socialism is tied to a particular global Weltanschauung, for there are many philosophical positions which can underpin the positions concerning man and the ends of life referred to above. Marxists, Christians, neo-Romantics and others might come to some agreement on the kind of shift in aspiration and ideal we need today.

But without being linked to some such view of man and the ends of life, I doubt that a socialist movement can generate the power to make the changes it aims to encompass. And since some basic philosophical positions cannot support this view about the ends of life, they will be in a sense incompatible with a relevant socialism which can really be in contention.

I think this is the case, for instance, with utilitarianism (of the straight, not watered-down, J. S. Mill variety). No one will want to say that utilitarians cannot espouse socialist goals, as these are defined here. On the contrary, lots of Fabians did. But the way of defining the goal in terms of individual consumption is so bound up with utilitarianism that this philosophy cannot even formulate the changes in aspiration and ideal that are necessary. Utilitarians, in other words, must conceive their socialist objectives in the very atomist, growth-orientated, redistributive terms which ensure their failure today.

Thus a relevant socialism in our day is restricted, as it were, in its choice, not of ontology indeed, but of philosophical anthropology. A much more modest result than the seamless garment of orthodox Marxism. But one that has a parallel bent. For Marxism, as we saw, did not deny that there can be an indefinite number of socialist *doctrines*. Its claim was that only one could animate a movement which would have contemporary bite. The Marxist claim for a total Weltanschauung turns out to be untenable. But something of the same claim can be made for a certain view of man today, although this will admit of many underpinnings, and many interpretations.

— 5 —

REFLECTIONS ON EQUALITY

J. P. Mayer

If I am not mistaken, the last important book entitled *Equality* was written by R. H. Tawney. It was published in 1931 and appeared in a fourth revised edition with a new chapter in 1952. A few years later Tawney came to see us in Stoke Poges, where I live, and we were sitting on the porch of my house – it was a beautiful summer day – and as always during the long years of our friendship we were exchanging views on the perennial problems of socialism. Tawney, as you all know, was a close friend of the Webbs and the teacher of the generation of Attlee, Cole, Sir Stafford Cripps and Herbert Morrison. I remember that I criticized, during this converstaion, the preoccupation of the British labour leaders with economic problems and their conspicuous lack of ethical ideas. After all, I said, the welfare state, however imperfect it may be, is in full swing: you have fulfilled the aims of your generation and you ought to write a new book on equality. (I had at that time completely withdrawn from any party political affiliation, though I had not broken – how could one? – with such a man as Tawney.) He listened attentively – Tawney was always a good listener – and remarked: 'If I understand you rightly, you want me to write a new sermon on the mount?' 'Precisely,' I replied.

No one has written this new sermon on the mount, though nearly twenty years have passed since this memorable conversation. No doubt the tendency towards a more egalitarian society has continued. The middle wealth groups have dramatically increased and the upper wealth stratum of English society has considerably decreased. Wages too have increased, even if we take inflationary processes into account, but there are still socially significant and unsolved wage differentials. Probably the problem of a new approach towards national wage and salary differentials is one of the most crucial and urgent problems of our society. However, I regard it not as my task to enter into these problems. I must leave the discussion of these questions to my economist colleagues, though they may be well advised to call in sociologists if they formulate their blue-prints for governments.

What I intend to do here is to sketch briefly the history of the meaning of equality in the European tradition and then, perhaps, to confront two social philosophies with which I have been mostly concerned over the last two or three decades, and consider whether they can help us to understand the needs and urgencies of our own time.

Athenian ideas on equality (*isonomia*, equality before the law, *isotimia*, equal respect for all and *isegoria*, equal freedom of speech and hence of political action) as Crane Brinton has pointed out,[1] came only to full fruition in Stoic philosophy, in Roman law and then in Christianity. The sociological conditions for cosmopolitan concepts at that time are so obvious that they need not be elaborated here. Men as reasoning beings, so the Stoics taught us, are identical, equal. Here the Stoic ideas on state and society have their roots, as Troeltsch and Pohlenz have so beautifully demonstrated.[2] If we add to this St Paul's exhortation to the Galatians (in 3:28): 'There is neither Jew nor Greek, there is neither bond nor free, there is neither male nor female, for you are all one in Christ Jesus' – we have nearly all the elements which enter into the slogan of *Liberté, Egalité* and *Fraternité* of the first phase of the French Revolution. But perhaps the religious element of the concept of equality should be further illustrated. Thus we read in St Luke (in 18:18–25):

> And a certain ruler asked him, saying, Good Master, what shall I do to inherit eternal life? And Jesus said unto him, Why callest thou me good? None is good, save one, that is, God. Thou knowest the commandments, Do not commit adultery, Do not kill, Do not steal, Do not bear false witness, Honour thy father and thy mother. And he said, All these have I kept from my youth up. Now when Jesus heard these things, he said unto him, Yet lackest thou one thing: sell all that thou hast, and distribute unto the poor and thou shalt have treasure in heaven; and come, follow me. And when he heard this, he was very sorrowful: for he was very rich. And when Jesus saw that he was very sorrowful, he said, How hardly shall they that have riches enter into the kingdom of God! For it is easier for a camel to go through a needle's eye, than for a rich man to enter into the kingdom of God.[3]

It is of course not my intention to introduce a religious note into our discussion, though I think the political sociologist must be *religiös-musi-kalisch* (the term is Max Weber's, who claimed to be *religiös-unmusika-lisch*). The egalitarian idea has a fundamentally religious accent and it is up to us to transpose this religious element into a modern, predominantly secularized, world.

I will only remind you of St Augustine, who taught us that men in the state of innocence were equal and free, but that the fall of man altered all this: 'The prime cause of servitude is sin.'[4]

Again it is not possible to retrace here the revival of the 'Law of Nature' philosophy, which the Stoics first formulated (from the sixteenth century in Europe onwards). With the breakdown of the mediaeval world order (though of course there were 'Law of Nature' elements in St Thomas), the rise of capitalism, the 'discovery of the individual' during the Renaissance and above all with the breakthrough of modern sciences – from Kepler to Newton – natural law becomes increasingly secularized. Through Thomas Aquinas the Aristotelian ideas on the laws of nature were transmitted to the West towards the end of the thirteenth century. Thomas conceived 'the state primarily in terms of law, not law in terms of the state. The foundation of his political theory must there be sought in the conceptions of the nature and source of law'. Thus writes McIlwain.[5] As the world is governed by God's providence, the whole community of the universe is governed by divine reason which is law eternal. And this law eternal (*lex aeterna*) is the true law on earth. Man as a rational being participates with God in eternal reason. Natural law (*lex naturalis*) is, consequently, the participation of a rational creature in the eternal law; by the light of natural reason (*lumen rationis naturalis*) man can discern evil and good. Jean Bodin, Hobbes, Spinoza, Locke, Rousseau, Puffendorf and Montesquieu are all intimately linked together, however great and important their differences with regard to the interpretation of the 'Law of Nature'. Yet perhaps one exception should be underlined here. With Thomas Hobbes a new period in the 'Law of Nature' philosophy begins. I quote from Heinrich Rommen's important book, *The Natural Law*:

Hobbes altered the meaning of the words 'nature' and 'natural', a process that characterizes the entire period of modern philosophy from the time of Descartes. 'Nature' and 'natural' become the opposite of *civitas*, 'reason', and 'order'. In the philosophy of Hobbes and Baruch Spinoza (1632–77) human nature is at bottom governed by the passions and not by reason. The *status naturalis* is a condition without any obligation or duty. It is a state in which, as Spinoza repeatedly asserts, might is right. This natural state of man is ruled by two things: fear of the might of others and power to instil fear into others. Hobbes denied that man has a natural inclination towards mutual help and love, which St Thomas speaks of so frequently. Hence law and the order of law cannot be derived from human nature; they become the work of the sovereign. What remains of the older conception of human nature as the source of natural law is the contention that the state originated in the fear of violent death and in the urge to render life and property secure.[6]

Finally, equality, freedom and fraternity appear codified in the *Déclaration des droits de l'homme* of 1789.[7] But it would be unhistorical to explain the *déclaration des droits de l'homme* merely as the culmination of some fundamental European political ideas. Georg Jellinek, in his masterly essay *Die Erklärung der Menschen und Bürgerrechte*,[8] has convincingly shown that the twelve North American colonies resolved in Congress in October 1774 that they should have rights which are theirs according to the inviolable rights of nature, the principles of the British Constitution and their own constitutions. Yet Jellinek also points out that the Philadelphia document was a protest, whereas the Constitution of Virginia, influenced by Jefferson, was a law.

I turn now to the two social philosophies which during recent decades have exerted considerable impact in clarifying our ideas about the sociological meaning of equality – I mean the sociologies of Karl Marx and Alexis de Tocqueville.

It is obvious that both thinkers have been profoundly influenced by the French Revolution. Equally, both thinkers realized that 1789 to 1815 was only the beginning of a long revolutionary process.

Marx has read the *Démocratie en Amérique*, but Tocqueville was already world-famous in 1844 when Marx, as an obscure German refugee in Paris, scribbled down his manuscripts, which in recent years have been so much discussed although I had discovered and edited them as far back as 1932. I feel it is necessary that I should quote here at least one page of these Paris manuscripts, in which Marx attempts to elucidate the problem of equality:

Equality is nothing but a translation of the German 'Ich = Ich' into the French, i.e. political form. Equality as the *groundwork of* communism is its *political* justification, and it is the same as when the German justifies it by conceiving man as *universal self-consciousness*. Naturally, the transcendence of the estrangement always proceeds from that form of the estrangement which is the *dominant* power: in Germany, *self-consciousness*; in France, *equality*, because politics; in England, real, material, *practical* need taking only itself as its standard. It is from this standpoint that Proudhon is to be criticized and appreciated.

If we characterize *communism* itself because of its character as negation, as the appropriation of the human essence which mediates itself with itself through the negation of private property – as being not yet the *true*, self-originating position but rather a position originating from private property . . .

Since in that case the real estrangement of the life of man remains, and remains all the more, the more one is conscious of it as such, it may be accomplished solely by putting communism into operation.

In order to abolish the *idea* of private property, the *idea* of communism is completely sufficient. It takes *actual* communist action to abolish actual private property. History will come to it; and this movement, which in *theory* we already know to be a self-transcending movement, will constitute in *actual fact* a very severe and protracted process. But we must regard it as a real advance to have gained beforehand a consciousness of the limited character as well as of the goal of this historical movement – and a consciousness which reaches out beyond it.

When communist workmen associate with one another, theory, propaganda, etc., is their first end. But at the same time, as a result of this association, they acquire a new need – the need for society – and what appears as a means becomes an end. You can observe this practical process in its most splendid results whenever you see French socialist workers together. Such things as smoking, drinking, eating, etc., are no longer means of contact or means that bring together. Company, association, and conversation, which again has society as its end, are enough for them; the brotherhood of man shines upon us from their work-hardened bodies.[9]

No doubt Marx regards the final removal of alienation as the establishment of equality; but it is an 'equality' which is identical with freedom in the Stoic or even in the religious sense, though I am quite aware of the fact that the mature Marx would have disputed this interpretation. In this context it is perhaps important to read again Marx's observations in his *Critique of the Gotha Programme*, which he wrote in 1875:

> In a higher phase of communist society, after the enslaving subordination of individuals under division of labour, and therewith also the antithesis between mental and physical labour, has vanished, after labour has become not merely a means to live but has become itself the primary necessity of life, after the productive forces have also increased with the all-round development of the individual, and all the springs of co-operative wealth flow more abundantly – only then can the narrow horizon of bourgeois right be fully left behind and society inscribe on its banners: from each according to his ability, to each according to his needs.[10]

It is evident if one thinks through these sentences that Marx, even at his mature age, conceives the free individual – the all-round developed individual – not in a strictly economic, egalitarian sense. I have often wondered whether Marx's idea of the 'all-round developed individual' is not connected with the fact that Marx failed to see the problem of *Vermassung*, the loss of individuality – a problem which grips and threatens us all. Moreover, if one reads Chapters 6 and 8, Book I, of the *Contrat Social*, and Book II, Chapter 4, of the same work, from which Marx made extracts in 1843, one has all the elements of this revealing statement. But I shall return to Marx's note-books presently.

We should perhaps add here these well-known phrases from the *Communist Manifesto*: 'In place of the old bourgeois society, with its classes and class antagonism, we shall have an association in which the free development of each is the condition of the free development of all.'[11]

At this point it might be opportune to say a few words about Max Weber, who in a speech on socialism to Austrian officers in Vienna in 1918 asked, too, what precisely does the Marxian term 'association of individuals' imply?[12] Weber deals at some length in this speech with the *Communist Manifesto* and with the meaning of the comment on association just quoted, which, of course, should be read together with the passage from the *Critique of the Gotha Programme* to which I have already referred.

Weber sees neither in the social-democratic parties, nor in the trade unions of his time the *Keimzelle* (germinating cell) for such an association which could transform bourgeois society into a socialist one. Though Weber gives a penetrating and objective analysis of the prophetic power of the *Communist Manifesto*, he rightly doubts its political validity in view of the evolution of capitalism as he saw it in his own lifetime. Weber sees the growth of vast employee groups, the resistance of the peasantry to socialism, and, above all, the immense bureaucracy in state and industry – with their different value and status aspirations – as effective brakes on 'socialism'. However universally Weber's sociology was conceived, we need only remind ourselves of his studies on religions of the eastern world to recall that he never abandoned his fundamentally 'liberal' orientation. The following sentences which Weber wrote as early as 1906 are significant:

> Everywhere the framework of a new bondage is ready, waiting only for the slowing down of technical 'progress', and for the victory of 'interest' over 'profit', in combination with exhaustion of as yet 'free' territory and 'free' markets, to make the masses tractable to its compulsion. At the same time the increasing complexity of the economic system, its partial nationalization or 'municipalization', and the territorial magnitude of national organisms, is creating ever more clerical work, an increasing specialization of labour and professional training in administration – and this means the creation of a bureaucratic caste ... Whatever spheres of 'inalienable' personality and freedom are still unwon by the common people in the course of the next few generations, and while the economic and intellectual 'revolution', the much-maligned 'anarchy' of production, and the equally maligned 'subjectivism' (by which, and *by which alone*, the individual has been made self-dependent) still remain unbroken, may *perhaps* – once the world has become economically 'full' and intellectually 'sated' – remain unachieved by them, for as far as our weak eyes can pierce the impenetrable mists of the future of mankind ...[13]

No doubt this liberalism which Weber himself attempted to overcome by his concept of the political charismatic leader defines the limitations of his political sociology. All the same, it must be stressed that Weber has clearly seen the economic and social consequences of the modern mass state: 'Die moderne Demokratie wird überall, wo sie Grossstadtdemokratie ist, eine bürokratische Demokratie.'[14] Yet Weber failed to see the conformist powers which such a 'bureaucratic democracy' could have, and has, brought into play. This is my reason for concentrating on a confrontation between the political sociologies of Marx and Tocqueville.

After this digression on Weber, we can now return to the *Critique of the Gotha Programme* from which we have already quoted. Prior to that quotation, Marx writes:

> In spite of this advance, this *equal right* is still stigmatized by a bourgeois limitation. The right of the producers is *proportional* to the labour they supply; the equality consists in the fact that measurement is made with an *equal standard*, labour.
>
> But one man is superior to another physically or mentally and so supplies more labour in the same time, or can labour for a longer time; and labour, to serve as a measure, must be defined by its duration or intensity, otherwise it ceases to be a standard of measurement. This *equal right* is an unequal right for unequal labour. It recognizes no class differences, because everyone is only a worker like everyone else; but it tacitly recognizes unequal individual endowment and thus productive capacity as natural privileges. *It is therefore a right of inequality in its content, like every right.* Right by its very nature can only consist in the application of an equal standard; but unequal individuals (and they would not be different individuals if they were not unequal) are only measurable by an equal standard in so far as they are brought under an equal point of view, are taken from one *definite* side only, e.g. in the present case are regarded *only as workers*, and nothing more seen in them, everything else being ignored. Further, one worker is married, another not; one has more children than another and so on and so forth. Thus with an equal output, and hence an equal share in the social consumption fund, one will in fact receive more than another, one will be richer than another, and so on. To avoid all these defects, right instead of being equal would have to be unequal.
>
> But these defects are inevitable in the first phase of communist society as it is when it has just emerged after prolonged birth pangs from capitalist society. Right can never be higher than the economic structure of society and the cultural development thereby determined.[15]

If we examine Marx's notebooks, which surely offer the most exact picture of his intellectual development, we hit upon the extracts from Spinoza and Rousseau,[16] both of whom certainly had a profound influence upon his conception of the state; and both thinkers studied democracy on the model of the small state. I have often wondered whether we cannot spot in this fact one of the causes of Marx's blindness to the phenomenon of *Vermassung*, as I have just indicated. A notebook of Marx's containing excerpts from *L'Esprit des Lois* has also come down to us (cf. MEGA I. 2, pp. 121ff). The following two passages which are fundamental to the political sociology of Tocqueville – Montesquieu was alway present in Tocqueville's mind – were ignored by Marx however; he simply read over them:

> When Sulla wished to restore freedom to Rome, she could no longer receive it; only a feeble vestige of virtue remained in her . . . all the blows were aimed at the tyrants, none at tyranny . . . Greek men of politics who lived under a government of the people recognized no other force that could sustain them than that of virtue. Today's men of politics talk to us only of factories, commerce, finance, wealth and even luxury (Book III, Chapter 3).

Or we read in Book XI, Chapter 4: 'By their very nature, democracy and aristocracy cannot be free states.' I wish I had time to compare Marx and Tocqueville as readers of Montesquieu, as Brunschvicg compared Descartes and Pascal as readers of Montaigne. Perhaps a younger scholar will some day go into this problem more thoroughly.

It is evident that Marx projects 'equality' into the future when 'the higher phase of communism' is established. It is also evident from these lines that the 'economic structure' determines, according to Marx, the 'cultural development'. As the state is part of this supposed superstructure, it seemed important to indicate some of the sources from which Marx has drawn his idea of the state.

Moreover we should perhaps add here that the institutional problems of democracy are structurally linked. I quote here a few lines by Ernst Fraenkel, which I have taken (admittedly without his permission) from his eassay 'The Representative and Plebiscitary Components in the Democratic Constitutional State' (Tübingen, 1958). Here we read: 'Burke and Fox, Madison and Hamilton, Mirabeau and Sieyès laid the foundations for the understanding of modern thought about representation.' (Many passages in Tocqueville's writings show how familiar he was with the writings of these men. I would supplement Fraenkel's list of names only with Royer-Collard.) 'Should there be,' Fraenkel continues, 'among the theoretical forerunners and political ancestors of the representative system any German state-thinkers and statesmen who are their peers, I have remained ignorant of them.' And then Fraenkel turns to Hegel. 'We can scarcely include Hegel in their number, for in *The Philosophy of History* he sees representation merely as a modification of democracy resultant upon the size of the sprawling modern state (*Flächenstaat*) . . .' It was this element of direct democracy which, I believe, hampered Marx's understanding of the structure of the modern mass state. Fraenkel goes on: 'In Germany, the dynamics contained in the representative-plebiscitary tension have not been consciously experienced on the basis of personal observation, but have been felt through the shared experience of the French Revolution or read up through study of it.' Thus far Fraenkel. Let us not forget that Malesherbes and other relatives of Tocqueville ended up on the scaffold, and that his father had white hair when Robespierre's death freed him from prison, although he was only in his twenties. The Great Revolution with its end-product Napoleon I, was Tocqueville's fundamental political experience.

But I doubt whether there has been or will be any society which could achieve the 'all-round developed individual 'by unfree institutions. Neither Russia nor modern China have realized Marx's predictions, though I am convinced that communist China is much nearer to the higher phase of communism, because the new Chineae society could fall back on thousands of years of communal traditions. I am also convinced that Chairman Mao has been predominantly shaped by Confucian traditions, though he had equally read at an early age Marx's *Communist Manifesto*.[17] Freedom and equality are interlocked, but it is by no means self-evident that the socialization of the means of production results in the establishment of the realm of freedom which Marx assumed in the third volume of *Das Kapital*.

It is certainly not accidental that Tocqueville has in recent years assumed the role of Marx's counterpart. I do not think that the many volumes by Tocqueville I have published in France and other countries are the primary reason for this. Tocqueville is not a utopian. He had practical experience of state affairs and came from a long line of jurists and administrators. Tocqueville too saw that equality and liberty were entwined. Though he admitted the tendency towards equality (he preferred the term *égalité des conditions*) he was by no means sure that the more egalitarian social process would produce a 'free' society. He differentiated two kinds of democracy: a free and an unfree one. The latter he characterized as 'despotism', towards which modern centralization is leading unless we are able to revive communal decentralization in all its many forms. Perhaps I should quote here a passage from

Tocqueville's *Recollections*, which shows a much more pliable thought-structure than Marx's in respect of social processes:

> Will socialism remain buried in the contempt that so justly covers the socialists of 1848? I ask the question without answering it. I am sure that in the long run the constituent laws of our modern society will be drastically modified; many of the main parts of them have already been substantially modified. But will they ever be abolished and replaced by others? That seems impracticable to me. I say no more, for the more I study the former state of the world, and indeed even when I see the modern world in greater detail, when I consider the prodigious diversity found there, not just in the laws but in the principles of the laws and the different forms that the right of property has taken and, whatever anybody says, still takes on this earth, I am tempted to the belief that what are called necessary institutions are only institutions to which one is accustomed, and that in matters of social constitution the field of possibilities is much wider than people living within each society imagine.[18]

It is evident, to me at least, that Tocqueville saw the relationship between equality and freedom much more as tension than Marx ever did. The structure of this tension becomes evident if one thinks through the following quotation:

> As long as the democratic revolution was at its height, people were concerned to destroy the aristocratic forces which fought against them, and a strong spirit of independence inspired them; however, to the extent that the victory of equality became more complete, the same people gave themselves over more and more to their natural instincts which such equality allows to arise, and so they strengthened and centralized social power. They wanted to be free, to be able to make themselves equal, and in the same measure that equality is consolidated with the help of freedom, freedom itself is brought into question.[19]

Perhaps the following text, taken from the continuation of Tocqueville's *Ancien Régime* will illustrate still further this tension between the processes towards equality and liberty. Comparing the English Revolution of 1640 with the French which began in 1789, Tocqueville writes:

Ressemblances:

1. Effort instinctif et en même temps théorique et systématique vers

la liberté, l'affranchissement civil et intellectuel réclamé comme un droit absolu. Par là, non seulement elles se tiennaent, mais elles se rattachent l'une et l'autre au grand mouvement de l'esprit humain moderne et en tant qu'elles sont l'effet des mêmes causes.

2. Effort, mais à un degré extrêmement inégal, vers l'égalité.

Différences:

1. Bien que les deux révolutions aient été en vue de la liberté et de l'égalité, il y a entre elles cette immense différence que la Révolution d'Angleterre a été faite presque uniquement en vue de la liberté, tandis que celle de France a été faite principalement en vue de l'égalité.

2. La multitude, le peuple proprement dit, n'a pas joué le même rôle dans les deux Révolutions: son rôle a été principal dans celle de France. Il a presque toujours été secondaire dans celle d'Angleterre qui a été non seulement commencée, mais conduite par une grande partie des hautes classes ou des classes moyennes, aidée par la puissance organisée de l'armée. Elle s'est servie des anciens pouvoirs en les étendant, plutôt qu'elle n'en a créé de nouveaux.

3. La troisième différence, c'est que la Révolution française a été antireligieuse, tandis qu'à la bien regarder, la Révolution d'Angleterre a été plus religieuse que politique. Quand on voit l'espèce de facilité avec laquelle Charles Ier a tenu tête à ses ennemis tant qu'il n'a eu en face de lui que des passions politiques, la rudesse et l'intermittence de ces passions qui, plus générales que les autres, étaient en même temps moins vives et moins tenaces, la nécessité où ont été les chefs des partis politiques, pour lutter, d'appeler à leur aide et contre leur gré l'appui des passions religieuses, on se sent plein de doutes sur le point de savoir si, sans la complication religieuse, l'Angleterre ne se fût pas laissé entraîner par le courant qui à cette époque menait toute l'Europe vers le pouvoir absolu.[20]

Another decisive difference between Tocqueville and Marx must be noted here, without which their social philosophies can hardly be understood.

Both thinkers speak about the abolition of classes (*Abschaffung der Klassen: abolition des classes*); and yet they mean something completely different. A comment in the last volume of *Democracy in America* (vol. I. 2, p. 266 of my French edition) – until now scarcely considered – gives us the opportunity to define the difference between the two thinkers rather more exactly. Tocqueville writes here:

Under the caste-regime generations follow each other without people changing places; the ones expect no more and the others nothing better. Imagination falls asleep amid such peacefulness and in such universal immobility, and even the idea of motion no longer presents itself to the human spirit. *If classes have been abolished* (emphasis added) and conditions have become almost equal, people are constantly astir, but everyone is isolated, detached and weak. The latter situation is astoundingly different from the former; nonetheless it is analogous at one point. Great revolutions of the human spirit are very rare in this situation.

These remarks must be supplemented by another comment of Tocqueville's; it occurs a few pages later (*ibid.* p. 288):

If a nation has achieved a social democratic condition, i.e. if neither castes nor classes exist within it, and if all citizens are roughly equal in education and possessions, the human spirit moves in the opposite direction. People resemble each other, and beyond this they somehow suffer from the fact that they resemble each other. Far from preserving whatever might still distinguish each one of them, they long only to lose themselves, to be absorbed in the common mass which alone represents right and might in their eyes. The spirit of individuality is all but destroyed.

For Marx, however, the abolition of classes means that 'leap into freedom' (*Sprung in die Freiheit*). That has always appeared a very dangerous utopia to me, and our experience of history has surely confirmed it.

I have spoken at some length of Marx's and Tocqueville's political sociologies *not* because they have in recent years become so fashionable, but because I think the revival of these last two great social philosophies is to some extent due to the fact that we have not been able to formulate a systematic political philosophy of our own; thus one takes refuge in Marx or Tocqueville and projects one's own problems into their time-bound concepts. I have tried to base my observations on what Marx and Tocqueville meant. It would be a fascinating task to discuss the misinterpretations of their writings and the influence of these misinterpretations, or in many cases simplifications, on history. In respect of Marx, I have only met one Western politician, Rudolf Hilferding, the author of *Das Finanz Kapital*, who had read *Das Kapital* thoroughly. Yet when he became Minister of Finance in the Weimar Republic, all his immense theoretical knowledge did not make him a better minister. Political theory does not always imply skill in political practice, as Tocqueville well knew. Let me add here another example of Marx mythology: when I had completed – in 1932 – my two volumes of Marx's *Frühschriften*, I brought a copy to the Chairman of the Social Democratic Party who was then Otto Wels. Wels was a real Berlin cockney, of working-class origin, blunt and rather clever. He looked at the volumes and said: 'They are impressive, but I suppose I should never be able to understand them. But perhaps,' he continued, 'I shall tell you a little story: as a young man I travelled with August Bebel to the Party Congress in Jena. During the train journey I confessed to August that I could not understand *Das Kapital*. I stopped on those pages where Marx uses some mathematic symbols to illustrate the concept of commodities (they are very near to the beginning of the volume). "Never mind, Otto," August Bebel replied, "I have not read further myself."' This leads us to Marx's own time, for Bebel was a party friend of Marx.

Tocqueville too was long enough misinterpreted. The constitution-makers of the French Constitution of 1875 took Tocqueville for a constitutional specialist, his weakest side, no doubt, and only later generations discovered him as one of the greatest political analysts since Aristotle and Machiavelli.

As I indicated earlier on we should free ourselves from taking refuge in Marx or Tocqueville and attempt to formulate our own problems and their solutions. What we require is a new political anthropology.[21] By which I mean an anthropology which answers questions like these: what are values in East and West, how have they been historically formulated, how have they been transmitted, and why and how have they been thinned out? What is their content and how is their hierarchy constituted, for there *is* a hierarchy of values. I am sure it is by now obvious that I find concepts like dialectics and alienation thin and useless. There are deeper layers in our historico-social structures, either in the East or in the West, be they mythical, linguistic, anthropological or psychological, and these cannot be reached by such vague concepts.

If the sociologist has to assume that Christian beliefs have become either meaningless or conventional – except for an ardently believing minority – what replaces them as a *catalyst* for the notions I have been discussing? It is here that we, as educationalists, academic teachers in the humanities, must work together and convince our political leaders that man does not live by bread alone. New values must be taught and, above all, *lived*. What we require are not always higher wages or higher salaries, or new and more refined luxuries. What we need is a kind of secular puritanism, simplicity, humility, daily service in communities of all kinds. Only then can we in the West escape the 'unfree' democratic society with its unbearable vulgarity, if not obscenity, and its stifling conformism, so effectively sustained by the mass media, in particular by films and television.

— 6 —

SOCIALISM AND EQUALITY

Steven Lukes

'. . . there is now, with the existence of a large amount of sociological research on inequality of opportunity and inequality of result, and with the resurgence of interest among moral philosophers in inequality, as manifested in John Rawls's work, the possibility of serious examination of social ideals and social reality in this area.' – James S. Coleman[1]

Professor Coleman's remarks raise three questions. First, what are the 'social ideals' of equality? What forms of inequality are undesirable and what forms of equality desirable, and on what grounds? Second, what are the 'social realities' of inequality? What is the upshot of all the research into inequality in contemporary societies? And third, what bearing does the answer to the second question have on that to the first? How does social reality affect social ideals? What is desirable, in the light of the actual and what appears possible? The relevance of these questions to the subject of this book needs no explanation. The ideal of equality has always been central to the socialist tradition: thus Professor Taylor specifies 'greater equality in the conditions of life' as the first goal of 'any socialist in a Western country today'.[2] In assessing the contemporary viability of the socialist idea, then, the three questions raised above demand to be faced: first, why is 'greater equality in the conditions of life' desirable?[3] Second, how unequal are such conditions in contemporary industrial societies, capitalist and state socialist, and what explains these inequalities? And third, are these inequalities ineradicable, or eradicable only at an unacceptable cost? Clearly, I cannot begin to answer these momentous questions here. What I shall try to do

74

is to offer some suggestions as to how they might be answered. Concerning the first (philosophical) question, I shall seek to suggest a modified Kantian ethical basis for the social, political and economic equalities that socialists have traditionally sought to establish. As for the second (sociological) question, I shall briefly sketch some of the evidence about actual inequalities and the range of explanations for them. And with regard to the third question I shall briefly consider a number of arguments for the inevitability of inequality. Having done these things, it will be clear to even the most sympathetic reader that everything remains to be done.

The Social Ideals of Equality

The ideal of equality has been made to seem absurd in either of two opposing ways. It has been interpreted as based either on the principle of absolute and unconditional equality – 'treat everyone equally in every respect' – or else on the empty formal principle, 'treat people equally unless there are relevant or sufficient reasons for treating them unequally'. In fact, few serious thinkers, let alone socialists, have advocated the former,[4] and all the interesting forms of egalitarianism have put content into the latter in two ways: negatively, by ruling out certain sorts of reasons as justifications for treating people unequally; and positively, by advancing, or presupposing, a set of reasons for treating them equally.

Historically, the fight for equality has taken the form of attacking specific inequalities and their alleged justifications: inequalities of privilege and power – legal and political, then social and economic – have been attacked as unjustifiable, because arbitrary, capricious or irrational. For example, it has been suggested that inequalities are unjustifiable unless they can be shown to satisfy one or more of the following criteria: (1) merit or deserts; (2) need; (3) social benefit (and on such a basis it would be hard to justify the present extreme inequality of in-inherited wealth in Britain).[5] But, quite apart from the difficulty of interpreting these criteria, especially the last, such an approach always presupposes a view of what is justifiable, that is, what are relevant and sufficient sorts of reasons for unequal treatment, and over this individuals, classes and cultures conflict. What, then, of the positive way?

One influential argument for treating people equally – and in particular for according them equal income and wealth – is the utilitarian argument for attaining the maximum aggregate satisfaction, on the assumption of diminishing marginal utility: as Dalton put it, an 'unequal distribution of a given amount of purchasing power among a given number of people is . . . likely to be a wasteful distribution from the point of view of economic welfare'.[6] In their recent important study of inequality, Christopher Jencks and his associates state their position as follows:

> We begin with the premise that every individual's happiness is of equal value. From this it is a short step to Bentham's dictum that society should be organized so as to provide the greatest good for the greatest number. In addition, we assume that the law of diminishing returns applies to most of the good things in life. In economic terms this means that people with low incomes value extra income more than people with high incomes. It follows that if we want to maximize the satisfaction of the population, the best way to divide any given amount of money is to make everyone's income the same. Income disparities (except those based on variations in 'need') will always reduce overall satisfaction, because individuals with low incomes will lose more than individuals with high incomes gain.[7]

But this assumption is questionable. Why assume that a given amount of purchasing power yields equal utility for everyone (assuming one could make the interpersonal comparison), and why assume that it diminishes as income or wealth increases?

In any case, egalitarians and socialists have not rested their case on this precarious basis alone: there is an alternative tradition of thought on the subject, of which Rousseau is the classical figure and Rawls the major contemporary exponent, which offers an alternative interpretation of equality and which appeals to deeper values than the utilitarian. This interpretation may be called the principle of equality of consideration or respect. On this view, all human beings have certain basic features which entitle them to be considered or respected as equals, and this is seen as implying practical policies for implementing substantial political, social and economic equality.[8]

What, then, are the basic features of human beings which command equal consideration or respect? For Christians the answer is that they are all children of God, for Kant that they are rational wills and thus members of the Kingdom of Ends, for classical liberals that they share 'common rights to which they are called by nature',[9] for many socialists and anarchists that they share a 'common humanity'. These are all transcendental answers, whether religious or secular. Others speak of man's 'inherent dignity', 'intrinsic or infinite value,' or 'human worth'.

But in all these cases, no *independent* reasons are given for respecting people equally – or at least none that would convince a sceptic disposed to do so unequally, according to, say, birth or merit. But it is arguable that there are a number of empirical features which could provide such reasons, to which, throughout their history, egalitarian doctrines have, implicitly or explicitly, appealed. On the one hand, there are basic human needs – minimally, the means to life and health – without which they could not function in a recognizably human manner. On the other hand, there are certain basic capacities (of which more below), characteristic of human beings, whose realization is essential to their enjoyment of freedom. It may be objected that, since people have these needs and capacities to different degrees, they are therefore worthy of unequal respect. But to this it may be replied that it is the existence of the needs and capacities, not the degree to which the former are met and the latter realized or realizable, that elicits the respect, and that respecting persons precisely consists in doing all that is necessary and possible to satisfy their basic needs and to maintain and enhance their basic capacities (and to discriminate between them in this regard is to fail to show them equal respect).

The principle of equal respect for needs tells against all humanly alterable economic and social arrangements which discriminate between individuals' access to the means of sustenance and health (and it is not irrelevant in contemporary Britain, where there are still marked class differences in the risks of death and infant mortality). But 'need' is a concept to which appeal cannot be made beyond this basic (if rising) minimum level: beyond that point, it becomes a question of individuals' entitlement to the means of realizing certain basic capacities. Three such capacities appear to be of particular significance.

There is, first, the capacity of human beings to form intentions and purposes, to become aware of alternatives and choose between them, and to acquire control over their own behaviour by becoming conscious of the forces determining it, both internally, as with unconscious desires and motives, and externally, as with the pressures exerted by the norms they follow or the roles they fill. In other words, human beings have the capacity to act with relative autonomy and to be or become relatively self-determining, to become conscious of the forces determining or affecting them, and either consciously to submit to them or become independent of them. Obviously, not all exercise this capacity to an equal degree, but all, except the mentally defective or deranged, possess it.

Secondly, human beings have the capacity to think thoughts, perform actions, develop involvements and engage in relationships to which they attach value but which require a certain area of non-interference in order to have that value. Enjoyments and delights of all kinds, intellectual and artistic activities, love and friendship are examples: all these require a space free and secure from external invasion or surveillance in order to flourish. There is, of course, considerable room for differences about which of these activities and relationships are of most value and about what kind of value they have, and indeed about which of them people should be left alone to engage in. But what seems indisputable is that there is a range of such activities and relationships in some of which all persons have the capacity to engage and to which they attach value.

Thirdly, human beings have the capacity for self-development. By this I mean that everyone has the capacity to develop in himself some characteristic human excellence or excellences – whether intellectual, aesthetic or moral, theoretical or practical, personal or public, and so on. Obviously, not everyone will be able to develop any given excellence to the same degree – and perhaps, *pace* Marx, not all will be able to develop them in a many sided, all-round fashion. But all human beings share the capacity to realize potentialities that are worthy of admiration. What counts as worthy of admiration will be subject to moral disagreement and cultural variation, but it is arguable that there is a delimited range of human excellences which are intrinsically admirable, though the forms they take differ from society to society, and that all human beings are capable of achieving some of them to some degree.

I have argued that these three characteristics of persons are at least part of the ground on which we accord them respect. What, then, does that respect consist in? The unsurprising answer is that, whatever else it involves, respecting them involves treating them as (actually or potentially) autonomous, as requiring a free and secure space for the pursuit of valued activities and relationships, and as capable of self-development. That answer has, given certain further assumptions, far-reaching social, economic and political implications, and points towards a society with substantially reduced inequalities, both of material and symbolic rewards and of political power.

What, we may ask, constitutes a denial of such respect? We fail to respect someone by denying his autonomy not only when we control or dominate his will, but also when we unreasonably restrict the range of alternatives between which he can choose. Such control and restriction is as likely to be social and economic as political, and as typical of the work situation and the family and of opportunities for education and employment as of the relation between the state and the citizen. In this sense, Tawney saw a central aim of 'measures correcting inequalities or neutralizing their effects' as increasing 'the range of alternatives open to ordinary men, and the capacity of the latter to follow their own preferences in choosing between them'.[10] But we also cease to respect someone when we fail to treat him as an agent and a chooser, as a self from which actions and choices emanate, when we see him and consequently treat him not as a person but as merely the bearer of a title or the occupant of a role, or as merely a means to securing a certain end, or, worst of all, as merely an object. We deny his status as an autonomous person to the extent that we allow our attitudes to him to be dictated solely by some contingent and socially defined attribute of him, such as his 'merit' or success or occupational role or place in the social order – or what Tawney called 'the tedious vulgarities of income and social position'.[11] This denial of autonomy was what William Godwin had in mind when he urged universal and equal political participation on the grounds that 'Each man will thus be inspired with a consciousness of his own importance, and the slavish feelings that shrink up the soul in the presence of an imagined superior, will be unknown.'[12] It is what William Morris meant when he wrote of socialism as a 'condition of equality' in which a man 'would no longer take his position as the dweller in such and such a place, or the filler of such and such an office, or (as now) the owner of such and such property, but as being such and such a man'.[13] It is what Tawney intended when he wrote of an egalitarian society as one in which 'money and position count for less, and the quality of human personalities for more',[14] and what George Orwell was thinking of when he wrote of 'breathing the air of equality' in revolutionary Spain, with 'no boss-class, no menial-class, no beggars, no prostitutes, no lawyers, no priests, no boot-licking, no cap-touching'.[15] Respecting persons in this way, as Bernard Williams has well put it, implies that they be 'abstracted from certain conspicuous structures of inequality' in which they are found and seen, 'not merely under professional, social or technical titles, but with consideration of their own views and purposes', as 'conscious beings who necessarily have intentions and purposes and see what they are doing in a certain light'.[16] But more is involved in respecting autonomy than looking behind the surface of socially defined titles or labels and seeing the world (and the labels) from the agent's point of view. Social existence in part determines consciousness; and the most insidious and decisive way of denying the autonomy of persons is to diminish, or restrict their opportunity to increase, their consciousness of their situation and activities. It is for this reason that respecting autonomy points towards a 'single status society' and away from the ideal of a stable hierarchy, since

> what keeps stable hierarchies together is the idea of necessity, that it is somehow foreordained or inevitable that there should be these orders; and this idea of necessity must be eventually undermined by the growth of people's reflective consciousness about their role, still more when it is combined with the thought that what they and others have always thought about their roles in the social system was the product of the social system itself.[17]

Secondly, one manifestly fails to respect someone if one invades his private space and interferes, without good reason, with his valued activities and relationships (and above all with his inner self). Examples of where it can be justifiable so to interfere are in cases, say, of imprisonment or conscription during wartime – where it may be claimed that there is 'good reason' for interference and thus no denial of respect in so far as they are necessary infringements of a person's freedom, either to preserve the freedom of others, or his own and others' in the long run, or as the only way of realizing other cherished values. But, in the absence of these justifications, such an invasion or interference is clearly a denial of human respect. It is easy to think of extreme forms of such a denial, as in the prison camps described by Solzhenitsyn or total institutions described by Erving Goffman. But less extreme forms result from inequalities of power and privilege in all contemporary societies. Liberals characteristically attack such invasions of liberty, especially in non-liberal societies, when they take the form of political authoritarianism, bureaucratic tyranny, social pressures to conformity, religious and racial discrimination. But interference with valued activities and relationships occurs in other ways to which liberals are less sensitive – through class discrimination, remediable economic deprivation and insecurity, and what Hayek has called the 'hard discipline of the market',[18] where nominally equal economic and social rights are unequally operative because of unequal but equalizable conditions and opportunities.

Finally, one also importantly fails to respect someone if one limits or restricts his opportunities to realize his capacities of self-development. It is the systematic and cumulative denial of such opportunities to the less favoured citizens of stratified societies, both capitalist and state socialist, that constitutes perhaps the strongest argument against the structured inequalities they exhibit. That argument really has two parts. The first part is simply an argument against discrimination, against the failure to 'bring the means of a good life within the reach of all'.[19] Thus the principal argument against a discriminatory educational system is not that it creates social inequality (which, as Jencks shows, it scarcely does, serving 'primarily to legitimize inequality, not to create it'),[20] but rather that it blocks the self-development of the less favoured and thereby fails to respect them. Again, where it is possible to make certain types of work more challenging and require a greater development of skill or talent or responsibility, it is a denial of human respect to confine workers within menial, one-sided and tedious tasks. Furthermore, workers – and citizens in political society as a whole – are denied respect to the degree to which they are denied possibilities of real participation in the formulation and taking of major decisions affecting them, for they are thereby denied the opportunity to develop the human excellence of active self-government celebrated by Rousseau and John Stuart Mill and central to the various forms of classical democratic theory. The second part of this argument against structured inequalities is that they provide an unfavourable climate for the self-development of ordinary people. The assumption that this is so was well expressed by Matthew Arnold, who claimed that for 'the common bulk of mankind', 'to live in a society of equals tends in general to make a man's spirits expand, and his faculties work easily and actively; while, to live in a society of superiors, although it may occasionally be a very good discipline, yet in general tends to tame the spirits and to make the play of the faculties less secure and active'.[21] Tawney made the same assumption, arguing that 'individual differences, which are a source of social energy, are more likely to ripen and find expression if social inequalities are, as far as practicable, diminished'.[22] Individuals, Tawney argued 'differ profoundly . . . in capacity and character' but 'they are equally entitled as human beings to consideration and respect, and . . . the well-being of a society is likely to be increased if it so plans its organization that, whether their powers are great or small, all its members may be equally enabled to make the best of such powers as they possess'.[23] His case was that establishing 'the largest possible measure of equality of environment, and circumstance, and opportunity' was a precondition for ensuring 'that these diversities of gifts may come to fruition'.[24]

I have argued, then, that certain basic human needs and capacities provide at least part of the ground for equality of respect, and give some content to that notion of 'respect', and I have further suggested that a society practising equal respect would be one in which there were no barriers to reciprocal relations between relatively autonomous persons, who see each other and themselves as such, who are equally free from political control, social pressure and economic deprivation and insecurity to engage in valued pursuits, and who have equal access to the means of self-development. Such a society would not be marked by inequalities of power and privilege (which is not to say that a society without such inequalities would necessarily practise equal respect).

However, I should conclude this section by noting an important tension between the notion of equality of respect, as discussed here, and that of 'equality of opportunity', as normally understood. In the context of public debate, especially about education, this latter principle is *not* generally taken to refer to equality of opportunity to develop individual powers or gifts, but rather equality of opportunity to achieve scarce social rewards. Thus understood, it comes into conflict with equal respect, since it focuses attention upon forms of differentiation and grading which carry status and prestige. It endorses and serves to perpetuate those very structures of inequality, characterized by competition and emulation, of which equality of respect makes light – and, practised seriously, would abolish. This distinction was well drawn by Tawney when he contrasted 'the claim for an open road to individual advancement' with the desire 'to narrow the space between valley and peak'.[25] The former aspiration has, of course, a central place in the history of socialism: it represents the meritocratic policy of widening the social base of recruitment to privileged positions, which has always been the central plank of social democracy. Thus C. A. R. Crosland wrote:

> The essential thing is that every citizen should have an equal chance – that is his basic democratic right; but provided the start is fair, let there be the maximum scope for individual self-advancement. There would then be nothing improper in either a high continuous status ladder . . . or even a distinct class stratification . . . since opportunities for attaining the highest status or the topmost stratum would be

genuinely equal. Indeed the continuous traffic up and down would inevitably make society more mobile and dynamic, and so less class-bound.[26]

By contrast, the egalitarian socialist focuses on equalizing the rewards and privileges attached to different positions, not on widening the competition for them. In fact, of course, these two strands are often intertwined in socialist theory and practice. But, although there are well-known arguments (an example of which we shall consider) to the effect that unequal rewards, together with equal opportunity to reap them, have essential economic and social functions, they are in tension with the social, political and economic implications of the principle of equal respect, which, as we have seen, points towards greater equality in the conditions of life, that is, of wealth, income, status and power.

The Realities of Inequality

Contemporary industrial societies manifest structured inequalities of such conditions, and of much else besides, such as access to education, social services and other public benefits, economic security, promotion prospects, etc. Some patterns of inequality appear to be common to all such societies, both capitalist and state socialist, others to the one system or the other, yet others to particular countries. But three myths, prevalent in recent times, are belied by the evidence. The first is that of 'convergence', according to 'the logic of industrialism'. This is misleading in so far as it suggests a continuing trend in the development of industrial societies towards greater overall economic equality, towards an ever-increasing consistency of stratification systems around the occupational order (e.g. towards the congruence of middle incomes and middle-class life style and status), and towards a uniform pattern of social mobility.[27] The second is that 'affluence' in capitalist societies has eroded inequalities of income, wealth and security of life and that the power of private capital has been tamed, from within by the 'managerial revolution' and the divorce between ownership and control, and from without by the growth of the state and/or a pluralistic diffusion of power among competing interest groups. The third myth is the official communist (especially Soviet) interpretation of state socialist societies, which, while acknowledging the existence of non-antagonistic classes (working class and peasantry) and the stratum of the intelligentsia, and the existence of inequalities of income, consumption

83

goods, education, etc., between rural and urban population and between occupational strata, maintains that these inequalities are in process of continuing decline (the so-called process of *sblizhenie*, or 'drawing together') denies that there is a hierarchy of status and is silent about the hierarchy of power.

Of the patterns of inequality common to industrial societies, it appears broadly true to say that, in contrast with traditional or nonindustrial societies, 'the occupational order comes increasingly to be the primary source of symbolic as well as material advantages'[28]: thus

> The occupational structure in modern industrial scoiety not only constitutes an important foundation for the main dimensions of social stratification, but also serves as the connecting link between different institutions and spheres of social life, and therein lies its great significance. The hierarchy of prestige strata and the hierarchy of economic classes have their roots in the occupational structure; so does the hierarchy of political power and authority, for political authority in modern society is largely exercised as a full-time occupation . . .[29]

As for income, there appears to be a remarkable similarity in capitalist and communist societies in the structure of earnings – more precisely, in the distribution of pre-tax money wages or salaries of fully employed male adult workers in all industries but farming.[30] There is a broad relationship between the hierarchy of skills and knowledge demanded by occupations on the one hand, and the hierarchy of material rewards on the other (though there is a narrower range of differentials under command than market economies), and, related to this, there are certain more specific trends: high rewards accruing to those in management and to the technically highly qualified and skilled, and a relative decline in the rewards of clerical work. As for status inequality (allowing for the 'softness' of the data and their paucity for socialist systems, except Poland), various studies suggest a common structure of occupational prestige. For example, according to Sarapata, the correlation between the occupational prestige hierarchies of Poland and the USA is 0·882, Poland and England 0·862 and Poland and West Germany 0·879.[31] As for inequalities of power, apart from the obvious differences, parallels can be seen in the differential distribution of power and authority (whether in the form of legal ownership or directive control) within 'imperatively co-ordinated associations', such as the industrial enterprise; conversely, a tendency towards political pluralism, albeit of a highly restricted and managed type, has been observed in communist systems.[32]

Of the inequalities characteristic of capitalism, the most obvious is that of wealth. It has been justly said that 'capitalism produces extremely rich people with a great deal of capital, and this is the most striking difference between the two systems'.[33] Moreover, such capital 'means so much more than the income it provides: security, diminished pressure to save and (in very large quantities) political power'.[34] The most recent study of the subject in Britain[35] estimates that the top 5 per cent of wealth holders own between one-half and three-quarters of the total personal wealth. There has, it is true, been a long-term trend towards a greater spread of such wealth, but this has mainly been from the top 1 per cent to the next 2–5 per cent (i.e. to relatives and others), as a defence against taxation.[36] It has been estimated that, equally divided, the yield from private property would substantially change the overall income distribution, providing a married couple with something over £9.00 a week.[37] Similar (though less extreme) concentrations of property ownership are found in other capitalist countries. Its impact is considerable because it 'leads to unequal incomes, and concentrates control over the economy in a few hands':[38] this is

accentuated by the fact that the very rich tend to hold their wealth in the form of company shares and real property yielding a higher return than the assets typically owned by small savers. The concentration of share ownership is even greater than that in the distribution of wealth as a whole, which is important since shares convey not only income but also rights of control, and even allowing for the increasing power of corporation managers these still remain of considerable significance.[39]

As for income inequality, after a temporary narrowing in the 1940s, it has remained relatively fixed and in some cases somewhat widened – both before direct taxation and (as far as one can estimate) after it. Overall taxation appears to be almost neutral in relation to income and in certain cases (the USA, West Germany) directly regressive, while redistribution through the Welfare State, although it obviously aids the poor more than the rich in relative terms, is paid for by wage-earners themselves, and is mainly 'horizontal' rather than 'vertical' – i.e. it takes the form of a 'life-cycle' transfer *within* social classes; moreover, these welfare facilities often tend to favour more privileged groups.[40] In general, the social democratic 'welfare approach' brings about little disturbance of the stratification system[41] – and some have claimed that there is increasing inequality at its base, with the growth of an underclass of unemployed and unemployables.[42] In capitalist societies that stratification system exhibits a cleavage between the manual and non-manual categories of occupation – not merely with respect to income (here, indeed, there is substantial overlap) but with respect to a whole range of privileges and advantages: white collar workers have strikingly better sick pay and pension schemes, holidays and other fringe benefits, life-cycle promotion and career opportunities, long-term economic stability (including for many guaranteed salary increases), working environment, freedom of movement and from supervision, etc. Non-manual workers 'even when they diverge are more like one another than they are like manual workers' and 'the big divide still comes between manual workers on the one hand and non-manual grades on the other'.[43] As for status inequality, such evidence as exists appears to point away from the thesis of an accommodative *embourgeoisement* of affluent workers and increasingly towards different forms of polarization between what Kerr terms 'the managers' and the 'managed'.[44] Inequalities of political power in capitalist societies are of course manifest in the inequalities already considered, since these represent the power of the dominant class to command a disproportionate share of rewards and privileges *vis-à-vis* the subordinate class. A full consideration of this topic would also involve an examination of all the means available to the former to preserve its rewards and privileges, not only within governmental institutions, but within the administrative service, the educational system, industry, the law, mass communications, etc., not only through coercive power but also through 'the mobilization of bias', operating anonymously through the structure of institutions (especially private property and the market), the rituals of social and political life, and ideological assumptions.[45]

The inequalities typical of state socialist societies display a different pattern. Property, in the sense of legal ownership, is, of course, largely absent: as Lane writes, 'the really significant difference in the system of social stratification compared to Western industrial societies is the absence of a private propertied class possessing great concentrations of wealth'.[46] On the other hand, following Djilas, one can argue that the white collar intelligentsia, and the *apparatchiki* above all, exercise rights of control over the use and products of collective property and expropriate surplus value from the subordinate class. On the other hand, there is no direct inheritance of such rights, as with private property, although there is evidence of *de facto* inheritance of educational privileges. The analogy between 'legal' and 'sociological' ownership cannot be taken too far, but clearly there is a considerable hierarchy of monetary privilege and power based upon such authority roles and above all upon party membership. With respect to income inequality, this has gone through a number of phases in all socialist regimes. The general pattern is this: a highly egalitarian stage of 'socialist reconstruction', followed by a substantial widening of differentials (most pronounced in the USSR with Stalin's attacks on 'equality mongering') in order to increase material incentives, followed by a subsequent move towards greater equality.[47] The current picture is one of a substantially narrower range of money incomes in socialist than in capitalist societies: thus, for example, the ratio of the lowest wage to the average in the USSR is 60:112. 6. and even the most extreme estimate of the total range is substantially less than what is widely accepted as true of the USA.[48] Moreover, apart from Yugoslavia, there is no structural unemployment. The stratification system has a different pattern from that in capitalist systems: social strata are distinguished by money incomes, consumption patterns, styles of life, education, use of the social services, housing, 'cultural level', but there appears to be no major 'break' or 'big divide', as under capitalism, between the manual and the non-manual strata. As Parkin suggests, in many state socialist societies highly skilled or craft manual workers enjoy a higher position in the scale of material and status rewards, and promotion prospects, than do lower white-collar employees.[49] Thus, for example, in both Poland and Yugoslavia skilled manual positions have higher occupational prestige than do lower routine white-collar positions. Parkin suggests that the overall reward hierarchy is as follows: '(1) White-collar intelligentsia (i.e. professional, managerial and administrative positions), (2) Skilled manual positions, (3) Lower or unqualified white collar positions, (4) Unskilled manual positions', and that the major break lies between the skilled and the unskilled.[50] Thus 'the most obvious break in the reward hierarchy occurs along the line separating the qualified professional, managerial and technical positions from the rest of the occupational order'.[51] Thus the status hierarchy does not appear to reflect and reinforce a dichotomous class structure on the Western capitalist model (though Machonin provides conflicting evidence on this point from Czechoslovakia).[52] Clearly, however, the most significant contrast between the systems lies in the hierarchy of political power. Here, despite the pluralistic tendencies identified by certain Western observers, the explicitly hierarchical, monistic and all-pervasive structure of party control, increasingly manned by the white-collar intelligentsia, is altogether distinctive.

Finally, brief mention should be made of inequalities characteristic of particular societies within these two broad systems. Thus, with respect to income inequality, the UK is more equal than the USA[53] and Norway is substantially more equal still, while the USSR has carried income equalization very far within the socialist bloc, especially through the redistributive effects of collective consumption,[54] whereas Yugoslavia has seen a marked widening of the span of incomes and life-chances, with the introduction of 'market socialism', as to a lesser extent did Czechoslovakia in the later 1960s. Other peculiarities relate to racial, religious and linguistic factors (USA, Northern Ireland, Canada), where inconsistencies between income and status hierarchies are to be seen, and long-range historical factors, as for example in Britain, where the stratification takes a distinctive form and the concentration of wealth is especially high.[55]

The explanation of inequality can be approached in either of two ways. On the one hand, one may seek to explain why individuals attain different positions, rewards and privileges; on the other hand, one may seek to account for the allocation of rewards and privileges to different social positions. The first approach implies a focus upon inequality of opportunity among persons; the second upon inequality of reward among occupational positions. In the foregoing, I have implicitly concentrated on the second question and I have also implicitly suggested a range of explanations for inequality at different levels. Some such explanations will be historically and geographically specific. Examples are, say, the particular circumstances explaining the exceptionally high status of Poland's intelligentsia,[56] or the cultural factors in ethnically or religiously divided communities or the long-range historical factors referred to above. Other factors explaining the differences between income distributions in different countries, and in the same country over time, are the activities of the central government and local authorities in allocating taxes and distributing benefits, the control of entry into occupations by professional associations and unions, national rates of economic growth, level of unemployment, etc. Other explanations will be at the level of the economic system, and will focus primarily on the institution of private property, and all that protects and legitimates it, under capitalism; and on political intervention, allocating rewards and privileges, in accordance with the ruling élite's policy objectives, under state socialism. However, at the next level, the constraints operating on both systems come into view: the division of labour under advanced industrialism, it has been argued, creates a certain role structure inevitably accompanied by differentials of material reward, status and power, which are in turn perpetuated by the nuclear family.[57] Some writers have sought explanations of inequality at a higher level still: according to them social inequalities arise from the functional prerequisites or basic features of all human societies, or, more universally still, from the genetic, biological or psychological differentiation of human nature itself.

The Realizability of Equality

This leads us naturally to the question of the alleged inevitability of inequality. There are a number of such arguments (of which I shall cite some typical contemporary examples), ranging from the 'hard' to the 'soft'. The hardest are those which appeal to biological and psychological data which, it is argued, set sharp limits to the possibility of implementing egalitarian social ideals: 'biology', writes Eysenck, 'sets an absolute barrier to egalitarianism'.[58] Then there are sociological arguments which maintain that inequalities are functional to, or inherent in, all possible social systems – or less strongly, in all industrial societies. And finally, there are arguments of a different order, which seek to show that the cost of implementing equality in contemporary societies are unacceptably high, because they conflict with other values.

The hard-line approach to the realizability of equality is currently taken by various participants in the contemporary debate about genetics, environment and intelligence. Professors Jensen, Herrnstein and Eysenck assert that 'intelligence' is mainly determined by heredity – specifically that about 80 per cent of the variance in IQ scores is genetically determined. Eysenck urges 'recognition of man's biological nature, and the genetically determined inequality inevitably associated with his derivation'.[59] Social class is 'determined quite strongly by IQ', and educational attainment depends 'closely' on IQ: 'talent, merit, ability' are 'largely innate factors'.[60] Eysenck maintains that 'regression to the mean' through social mobility and the redistribution of genes prevents social classes from calcifying into hereditary castes, and he concludes that a 'society which would come as near to our egalitarian desires as is biologically attainable would give the greatest scope possible to this social mobility'.[61] Herrnstein,[62] by contrast, ignores 'regression to the mean' and stresses the process of 'assortative mating' between partners of similar IQ levels, and foresees a future in which, as the environment becomes more favourable to the development of intelligence, social mobility increases, and technological advance sets a higher premium on intelligence, social classes will become ever more caste-like, stratifying society into a hereditary meritocracy. Finally, Jensen, observing that some racial groups, especially American whites and blacks, differ markedly in their distribution of IQ scores (the mean IQ differing from 10 to 15 points), concludes that, since no known environmental factors can explain such differences, their explanation must be largely genetic. In his latest book, he affirms the hypothesis that 'something between one-half and three-fourths of the average IQ difference between American Negroes and Whites is attributable to genetic factors, and the remainder to environmental factors and their interaction with the genetic differences'.[63] He attaches much importance to this conclusion, since he believes that IQ is a major determinant of success in our society.

These claims obviously cannot be adequately considered here, but a few remarks are worth making. First the estimate of 80 per cent genetic determination of IQ is controversial. Others suggest a substantially lower figure. According to Jencks it is something like 45 per cent: Jencks and his colleagues estimate that 'genotype explains about 45 per cent of the variance in IQ scores, that environment explains about 35 per cent, and that the correlation between genotype and environment explains the remaining 20 per cent.'[64] Moreover the evidence with respect to genetic determination is far less univocal than these writers imply: 'different methods of estimating the heritability of test scores yield drastically different results' and 'studies of different populations yield somewhat different results'.[65] Again, children's test scores are not immune to considerable improvement by effecting changes in their environment. Eysenck suggests that 'Clearly [sic] the whole course of development of a child's intellectual capabilities is largely laid down genetically',[66] yet this is strikingly contradicted by a number of twin and adoption studies.[67] Secondly psychologists notoriously differ about what IQ tests measure: some, such as Jensen, Herrnstein and Eysenck, believe it measures some basic property of the intellect; others believe that intelligence is multidimensional, that it cannot be measured by a single number, and (according to many authorities) that that number in any case measures educationally and culturally specific aptitudes with limited wider applicability. Thirdly, and related to this last point, it has been established (at least for the US) that (1) social class is not, *pace* Eysenck, 'determined strongly' by IQ; (2) educational attainment depends less on IQ than on family background; and (3) IQ is not a major determinant of economic and social success.[68] Fourthly, the difference in average IQ test performance between blacks and whites is consistent with all three of the following hypotheses: that it is explained by genes, by environment, and by both.[69] Moreover it appears indisputable that present data and techniques cannot resolve this issue. It certainly has not been established that one can extrapolate from genetic determinants of differences within a population to explain mean differences between populations. And it is worth observing that, in any case, genetic differences within races are far greater than those between them, accounting for 60–70 per cent of all human genetic variation. In general, it appears entirely reasonable to conclude with Jencks that it is 'wrong to argue that genetic inequality dictates a hierarchical society'.[70] This is so even if Jensen should turn out to be nearer the truth than Jencks, and heredity does substantially constrain the maximum achievable by different individuals in the best of all possible environments. For, as we have argued, the principle of equal respect requires, in Tawney's words, that society's organization be planned so that 'whether their powers are great or small, all its members may be equally enabled to make the best of such powers as they possess'. Since this requires the equalization of rewards and privileges, biological differences would correlate with social positions but not with unequal rewards and privileges attaching to those positions.

Sociological arguments for the inevitability of inequality are of two broad types. One is that inequalities are functionally necessary for any society, the other that they are inherent in the very nature of social life. A much-discussed example of the former is the so-called functionalist theory of stratification; an interesting instance of the latter is furnished by Ralf Dahrendorf.

Davis and Moore's 'functionalist theory of stratification' seeks to demonstrate 'the universal necessity which calls forth stratification in any social system'.[71] It advances the following propositions:

1. Certain positions in any society are functionally more important than others.

2. Adequate performance in these positions requires appropriate talents and training.

3. Some such talents are scarce in any population.

4. It is necessary (a) to induce those with the requisite talents to

undergo the sacrifice of acquiring the appropriate training; (b) to attract them to the functionally important positions; and (c) to motivate them to perform in these positions adequately.

5. To achieve these objectives, differential incentives must be attached to the posts in question – and these may be classified into those things which contribute to (i) 'sustenance and comfort'; (ii) 'humor and diversion'; and (iii) 'self-respect and ego expansion'.[72]

6. These differential incentives (unequal rewards) constitute social inequality, which, in securing that the most talented individuals occupy and adequately perform in the functionally important positions, fulfils a necessary function in any society: 'Social inequality is thus an unconsciously evolved device by which societies insure that the most important positions are conscientiously filled by the most qualified persons.'[73]

Controversy over this theory has raged for well over two decades,[74] and it is fair to say that the balance of the argument has largely lain with the theory's critics. There is the evident difficulty of identifying the 'functionally important' positions, as distinct from those which a given society values as important (bankers or miners? elementary or university teachers?) and the dubious assumption that training for these positions is sacrificial (especially since there would, presumably, be no material loss in an egalitarian society). Also, it ignores the point that a stratified society itself restricts the availability of talent and the further point that an advanced industrial society is in principle able substantially to increase the availability of talent and training. A further weakness of the theory is its assumption that unequal rewards (defined in a most culture-specific way) are the only possible means of mobilizing qualified individuals into adequately performing important jobs. It leaves out of account the intrinsic benefits of different positions, in relation to the expectations, aptitudes and aspirations of different individuals (potential surgeons being anyway attracted by practising surgery and potential carpenters by carpentry); and it fails in general to consider functional alternatives to a system of unequal rewards – such as intrinsic job satisfaction, the desire for knowledge, skills and authority, an ethos of social or public service and a diminution of acquisitiveness and status-seeking, the use of negotiation, persuasion or direct planning, changes in the organization of work and decision-making, and so on. Finally, to the extent to which the thesis does remain valid, at least for contemporary industrial societies – that is, in so far as unequal rewards are needed so that certain jobs are adequately filled – this in no way implies a society-wide system of structured social inequality, linking wealth, income, status and power (indeed, it would probably imply the reverse); nor is it plausible to suggest that the range and scope of actual inequalities, such as those surveyed in the previous section of this essay, can be explained in this beneficently functional manner. It is, incidentally, noteworthy that liberal reformers in East European countries have used arguments analogous to Davis and Moore's to justify the widening of income differentials (as did Stalin in the 1930s). But the Davis–Moore theory does not specify any particular range of inequality as functionally necessary – or rather, it all too easily serves to justify any such range which its proponents may seek to defend or establish.

Dahrendorf's theory seeks to demonstrate that 'inequalities among men follow from the very concept of societies as moral communities . . . the idea of a society in which all distinctions of rank between men are abolished transcends what is sociologically possible and has its place in the sphere of poetic imagination alone'.[75] The thesis is essentially this: that '(1) every society is a moral community, and therefore recognises norms which regulate the conduct of its members; and (2) there have to be sanctions connected with these norms which guarantee their obligatory character by acting as rewards for conformism and penalties for deviance',[76] from which Dahrendorf concludes that 'the sanctioning of human behaviour in terms of social norms necessarily creates a system of inequality of rank and that social stratification is therefore an immediate result of the control of social behaviour by positive and negative sanctions'.[77] But the conclusion does not follow from the premises. It does not follow from the mere existence of social norms and the fact that their enforcement discriminates against those who do not or cannot (because of their social position) conform to them that a society-wide system of inequality and 'rank order of social status' are 'bound to emerge'.[78] Dahrendorf slides unaccountably from the undoubted truth that within groups norms are enforced which discriminate against certain persons and positions (he cites the example of gossiping neighbours making the professional woman an outsider) to the unsupported claim that, within society as a whole, a system of inequality between groups and positions is inevitable. To support that claim he would need to show the necessity of society-wide norms whose enforcement necessarily discriminates between persons and social positions, and this he fails to do. Nothing he says rules out the empirical possibility of a society containing a plurality of norms, each conferring and withholding status and prestige (so that gossiping neighbours look

93

down on professional women, and vice versa), without themselves being ranked within a single system of inequality or stratification.

Finally, I turn to the argument that inequality is eradicable only at an unacceptable cost. This argument has been voiced in many forms, by those both friendly and hostile to socialism. A forceful contemporary formulation is that of Frank Parkin, who argues that

> A political system which guarantees constitutional rights for groups to organise in defence of their interests is almost bound to favour the privileged at the expense of the disprivileged. The former will always have greater organizing capacities and facilities than the latter, such that the competition for rewards between different classes is never an equal contest. This is not merely because the dominant class can more easily be mobilized in defence of its interests, but also because it has access to the all-important means of social control, both coercive and normative. Given this fundamental class inequality in the social and economic order, a pluralist or democratic political structure works to the advantage of the dominant class.[79]

What this argument perhaps suggests, Parkin writes, is that

> socialist egalitarianism is not readily compatible with a pluralist political order of the classic western type. Egalitarianism seems to require a political system in which the state is able continually to hold in check those social and occupational groups which, by virtue of their skills or education or personal attributes, might otherwise attempt to stake claims to a disproportionate share of society's rewards. The most effective way of holding such groups in check is by denying them the right to organise politically or in other ways to undermine social equality.[80]

But historical experience of this approach has been pretty uniform: gross abuses of constitutional rights, terrorism and coercion, and, even when these latter are relaxed, the continuance of party control over all areas of social life, including literature and the arts. As Parkin observes,

> The fact that the humanistic ideals central to the socialist tradition have found little, if any, expression in the European socialist states highlights an unresolved dilemma; namely, whether it is possible to establish the political conditions for egalitarianism while also guaranteeing civil rights to all citizens within a system of 'socialist legality'.[81]

Conclusions

Fortunately, this is not the place to enter into the whole question of the 'socialist transition'. I merely wish to conclude this essay with three brief observations. The first is that the massive inequalities of power and privilege outlined in the second part are, for many socialists, intolerable mainly because they violate something like the principle of equal respect delineated in the first part – a principle which derives from liberal premises, but which takes them seriously. The second is that the arguments for the unrealizability of equality considered in the third part all fail to show that these inequalities are ineradicable, whether on psychological or sociological grounds. And the third is that the argument that the costs of implementing equality are too high is the most crucial facing any socialist today. And it is perhaps the inclination to see the accumulated weight of historical evidence for the apparent need to pay such costs – from the rise of Stalin to the fall of Allende – as a challenge rather than as a source of despair that is, in the end, the distinguishing mark of an egalitarian socialist.

SOCIALISM, REVOLUTION AND VIOLENCE

Gajo Petrović

Introductory

Most of us seem to like socialism. None of us seem to like violence. Unfortunately, it seems that socialism cannot be achieved without revolution, and that it is impossible to have a revolution without violence. In other words, it seems as if we must choose between socialism with violence and a non-violent life without socialism. This is certainly not an easy choice.

Before we try to make up our minds, we should first try to see whether the choice is real or merely apparent. Would it somehow help if we try to analyse the three concepts involved?

It might seem an inadequate, elementary approach to begin a discussion of what may be important and urgent questions of social life with a theoretical clarification of concepts, or with an analysis of the meanings of the words involved. However, how are we to decide about the relationship between socialism, revolution, and violence, if we do not know what those three are?

It would be insincere to pretend that we all know and agree on what socialism, revolution and violence are, and that the only difficulty is to express that agreement in the form of definitions. As a matter of fact the number of different concepts of socialism, revolution and violence which circulate nowadays is enormous, and behind these different concepts there are big differences in thinking about basic problems of the contemporary world. To discuss socialism, revolution and violence without trying to clarify the concepts involved could only help to increase confusions and misunderstandings. Thus let us try to see first what we mean by socialism, revolution and violence.

I. Socialism

There are many different concepts of socialism today, so many and so different that the term tends to lose all definiteness and meaning. Which of these different concepts should we choose? To which of them should we give preference? Shall we make an arbitrary choice or shall we decide on more or less rational grounds? What ground or criterion should we use?

Two basic courses of action seem open, if we want to make a well-founded choice. One is to derive the concept of socialism from the existing socialist reality, by an analysis of the states or societies which call themselves socialist, another is to derive it from the history of socialist thought, from all or some socialist thinkers of previous ages.

It might seem at first that it would be better to start from the existing socialist realities, not merely from thoughts. However, this would be a dubious way. The concept or idea of socialism has not been developed as a tool for understanding the existing socialist countries, it has been deployed by a number of thinkers long before these states came into existence. The so-called socialist states emerged and developed not as a result of a spontaneous development of capitalism, but rather as a conscious attempt at creating a new type of society predicted and advocated by great thinkers of the past. This is why it would be wrong to take the existing 'socialist' countries as a criterion for judging the concept of socialism. On the contrary, the concept of socialism as it has been elaborated in the history of socialist thought may be regarded as a criterion for deciding whether a society which claims to be socialist is really so.

The concepts of socialism of the many thinkers in the history of socialist thought are far from identical. Which should be regarded as the most relevant? I hope that I am not eccentric in maintaining that Karl Marx was the most profound of all socialist thinkers up to now. This is not to say that he discovered the whole truth or that everything contained in his writings was true. I believe that some socialist thinkers, including some of the direct opponents of Marx, have seen at least some problems better than he. And I think that not every word in Marx is true. There have been two opposed tendencies in Marx's thinking, one representing his new thinking of freedom and revolution, and another reflecting the positivist spirit of his age (a line of thought which has been continued in Stalinism). However, I do not think that both tendencies were equally strong. The real Marx is not somewhere

97

in the middle between these two tendencies, his basic line of thought was that of revolutionary humanism, not economic determinism.

However, Karl Marx was not only the most profound, but also the most influential of all socialist thinkers. Nearly all attempts at creating a socialist society have been inspired, or at least claimed to have been inspired, entirely or chiefly by Marx's concept of socialism, which can thus be regarded as the chief criterion for judging the socialist character of the allegedly socialist countries.

There is no generally accepted view of Marx's concept of socialism among Marxists. It has been understood and interpreted in many different ways. Its most widespread interpretation is still the Stalinist one. According to this interpretation, as canonized by Stalin and accepted also by a number of non-Stalinist Marxists and 'Marxologists', socialism is a 'lower phase of communism' which is supposed to develop after the 'period of the dictatorship of the proletariat' and before the 'higher phase of communism'.

The distinctive traits of socialism as the lower phase of communism, according to this view, are: (1) social ownership of the means of production (a trait which it shares with the higher phase of communism); and (2) the principle of distribution according to work (the trait which distinguishes it from the higher phase of communism, or true communism, where distribution should be carried out according to needs).

On a number of occasions[1] I have criticized this Stalinist scheme and argued that although it has its roots in Marx (in his *Critique of the Gotha Programme*), it is nevertheless a negation of the essence of Marx's views on socialism. A brief summary of these arguments will suffice for our purposes here.

First of all, I think it is a negation of Marx's thought to separate the dictatorship of the proletariat into a special period between capitalism and communism (or socialism). If the dictatorship of the proletariat is regarded as a special transitional period which is neither capitalism, nor socialism, and which can be basically different from both developed capitalism and developed socialism, then it can be also conceived as a period of unlimited terror and violence. However, for Marx the dictatorship of the proletariat would really be a dictatorship of the proletariat only if it represented the first phase of socialism and communism, and began immediately to create a humanist society.

Just as it is dangerous to single out the dictatorship of the proletariat as a special period different from both capitalism and socialism, it is unjustified to differentiate between the 'lower' and 'higher' phases of communism. The usual distinction between the two, that of the difference in distribution (in socialism according to work performed, and in communism according to needs), suffers from hopeless defects. One of these is that it takes distribution as the sole criterion for distinguishing phases of communism and ignores all other aspects of economic life, especially production. But this scheme would remain defective even if we took the whole economic structure as a criterion. In socialism as viewed by Marx, the division of society into 'spheres' and the supremacy of the economy are overcome. Therefore, for distinguishing phases of socialism we should use a more complex principle which takes man as a whole.

According to one of Marx's formulations, communism is the emergence of humanism, but, in contradistinction to atheism, which is 'the emergence of theoretical humanism', communism is 'the emergence of practical humanism'. As such, it cannot essentially differ from humanism nor can it contradict it; it is already humanism but it is a humanism mediated by the abolishment of private property. Only through this mediation can *positive* humanism emerge, humanism which begins positively from itself. In other words, if we insist on a 'transitional period', then *communism* is a period of transition from *capitalism* (and class society in general) to *humanism*. However, we may speak about a period of transition only if we keep in mind that communism is only communism in so far as it is humanism.

What, more specifically, does communism as the emergence of humanism mean? According to Marx, communism is the reintegration or the return of man to himself, the abolition of man's self-alienation. This de-alienation means 'the return of man from religion, family, state, etc., to his human, that is social existence'. Accordingly, communism is not only a new socio-economic formation, it is the abolition of the primacy of the economic sphere and the appropriation of human life in its fullness.

Some will concede that the prevailing form of distribution cannot be the sole criterion for distinguishing the phases of humanist society, but will add that even so the question of the principle or principles of distribution in humanist society is neither meaningless, nor unimportant. Even if distribution is not everything, the question remains whether distribution in a truly human society should be carried out according to work, according to needs, or according to a third principle.

Marx thought that the principle of distribution according to work is a principle of bourgeois right which applies *equal* standards to *different* people and thus despite formal equality results in inequality and injustice. At the same time he maintained that the communist society, in its first stage of development, will not be able to do away with the injustice which is inherent in distribution according to work. Only in the higher stage of communism will the conditions be created for transcending the narrow horizon of bourgeois law and for distribution according to needs.

These thoughts of Marx, with which I basically agree, have acquired in the interpretation of some 'Marxists' a simplified, caricatured form. Thus it has been maintained that in the first phase of communism *all* distribution shoud be according to work. This principle should be applied in the 'first phase' unconditionally, strictly, without any exception.

Contrary to this, I believe that the principle of distribution according to work can be relatively 'progressive', 'Socialist', and 'humanist' only when it is applied to those who have the necessary preconditions for work (primarily, ability and opportunity for work). But I believe that it turns into its opposite and becomes antisocialist and inhuman when it is applied to old people, sick people, invalids, pregnant women, children and others who cannot work, or to those who have biophysical and psychological abilitities for work but no opportunity for it. Even in the beginning stages of socialism, even in the most difficult situations, the principle of distribution according to work is socialist and humanist only if combined with a specific form of the principle of distribution according to needs, i.e. with the principle that the minimal life needs of *every* human being must be satisfied.

This is not to say that we must reject the view according to which socialism should develop from distribution according to work, to distribution according to needs. This means only that we must beware of oversimplifications, absolutizations, and abstract confrontations of the two principles. We must take care that no other principle be given more importance than the *basic principle of socialism* which follows from its essence as a truly human society, *the principle that a society is to that extent socialist in which it provides the possibilities for a free creative development of every individual.*

I know that the concept I have sketched of socialism is not generally accepted and will probably never be. But I believe it is the concept of socialism which most adequately expresses the basic insight of Karl Marx, and also the concept of socialism which might be of the greatest interest for the contemporary man. I also know that the acceptance of the above concept of socialism cannot help us to solve more easily the problem from which we started. It could make it even more difficult.

For one whose concept of socialism is Stalinist, the objection that violence has been used to create or to support socialism cannot be of a decisive importance. He might grant that violence is undesirable, and at the same time insist that the existence or non-existence of violence cannot change the nature of socialism. Socialism, according to his view, is the social ownership of the means of production combined with the distribution according to work, and where these two characteristics are found, we have socialism.

On the other hand, if we assume that capitalism is by definition in-human, and socialism by definition human, then we are not allowed to have any violence in socialism. According to this view the use of violence is a negation of socialism. However, how can we break a violent social order without using any violence? And if we start using violence on a broad scale for breaking capitalism and for 'constructing' socialism, shall we be able to stop it at some point?

In other words, by accepting the suggested concept of socialism our initial difficulty is only increased, not diminished or eliminated. We still have to deal with the question: Is a revolution possible which could create a non-violent society, not merely replace one violent form of society with another? The answer certainly depends on what we mean by revolution.

II. Revolution

In contemporary social science, journalism and philosophy we find many different concepts of revolution. We cannot discuss them all here; it will be quite enough if we succeed in clarifying the concept of revolution found in Karl Marx. He was not only the deepest socialist thinker but also the profoundest thinker about revolution. And the very fact that we started with Marx's concept of socialism, forces us to continue with his concept of revolution. Whether Marx's concept of socialism can be realized is a question to which the Marxian theory of revolution must first give an answer.

Marx's concept of revolution, it seems to me, is best understood when compared with some simpler concepts with which it is sometimes confused. This is why I want to start with the ordinary concept of revolution such as it is found in everyday life and then gradually move to the authentic view of Marx.

The simplest of the current concepts of revolution is the concept of revolution as a violent overthrow or replacement of persons or groups in power. This pre-scientific concept is not entirely unjustified. It is not difficult to see that in social life struggles for power and shifts in power occur. That some shifts of power take place in a peaceful way and some rather violently – this is also a difference which is easily noticed on a pre-scientific level. The concept of revolution as a violent overthrow or change in power is the most widespread in everyday opinion.

A further step consists in realizing that behind the political groups and individuals fighting for power there are more deeply rooted groups such as social classes and that struggles for power which are continuously going on in a class society have most frequently a class character. With this insight begins (and not far from it ends) what we call vulgar Marxism, that kind of Marxism which is certainly most widespread but also most remote from Marx.

Despite all critical reservations towards the vulgar Marxist, we must do justice to him. The vulgar Marxist insists that revolution is not every transfer of power, but only one in which power passes from one class to another. By this insistence he certainly does not want to say that this is the only possible meaning of the word 'revolution', but that we should distinguish between the two essentially different transitions of power: one in which power passes from one group to another inside the same basic class, and one in which power passes from one class to another.

The vulgar Marxist knows also that different social classes are not only factually different (and opposed), but that they can be divided into progressive and regressive. This is why he insists that the shift of power from the regressive class to the progressive class should be called 'revolution' and strictly differentiated from the shift of power from a progressive class to a regressive one (which should be called 'counter-revolution').

Vulgar Marxism has learned very well from Marx that social changes should be regarded from the standpoint of the class struggle and that a revolution is not a *putsch*. However, it has also too often forgotten to investigate from a class standpoint the process following the 'revolution' conceived as the capture of power. The revolutionary capture of power has been strictly distinguished from so-called post-revolutionary development. Revolution as a short act and post-revolutionary development as a long-term process have been regarded as two mutually independent things, and it has been considered that the character of revolution does not depend on the nature of the post-revolutionary development which follows after it.

The difficulties in such a view are obvious. How can we decide whether a shift of power means the transition of power into the hands of the progressive class, not just to another faction of the old ruling class, if we leave aside the way in which new rulers use their power? Only if the new rulers use their power for a radical change in society, for constructing a new social order which corresponds to the interests of the progressive class, may we rightly speak of revolution.

Marx and Engels, and later also Lenin, insisted that revolution is a radical change of the social order, and that the capture of power is at best a moment of revolution. In the most vulgar forms of Stalinism, revolution has been reduced to the conquest of power, and the practical activity of Stalin could be perhaps regarded as an attempt to kill revolution soon after the conquest of power. However, in his theoretical writings he knew that the conquest of power represents only one moment or phase in the development of revolution. Interpreting Lenin, he insisted that the bourgeois and the proletarian revolution differ essentially in the phase in which and the task with which the shift of power occurs. Thus when we criticize the identification of revolution with the capture of power, we are still not very far away from Stalin. Here we merely defend the 'better' Stalin from a 'worse' one.

If we want to part ways with Stalinism we must see the difference of principle between the socialist and all other revolutions, a difference which is so profound that only the socialist revolution can be a revolution in the fullest sense. Of course Stalinism will not protest against stressing the qualitative difference between the socialist and all other revolutions. The quarrel begins when we maintain that only the socialist revolution can be revolution in its fullest sense.

This thesis might seem not only logically dubious, but also historically untrue and even reactionary. Great revolutions of the past have shaken and transformed the world of their time, leaving lasting traces for posterity. To diminish their importance in comparison with a revolution which has hardly begun – is this not to negate in a nihilistic way the great deeds of mankind in the past (and thus to prevent them in the future)?

With this question we have come to the point at which it becomes obvious that the essence of revolution cannot be successfully discussed without touching on the question of the fundamental potentialities of thinking and Being.

Our view according to which not all revolutions are equally revolutionary and only the future socialist revolution can be revolution in the full sense is certainly a failure, if there is a constant, unchangeable essence of revolution and if it can be grasped by a firm concept which sums up what is common to all revolutions, remaining equally neutral to all specific forms of them. In other words, our concept of revolution is untenable if we live in a closed, finished world in which nothing new could arise, in a world which consists of hierarchically ordered static essences.

The situation is quite different if we live in an open world which is not completely determined by the past. If the future can bring to life something new, essentially different from the past, then past revolutions cannot be models for future ones.

It could be objected that a future revolution should not be taken as a standard for the present either. Because how can we think in advance the future, something which is not yet (and perhaps will never be)? The objection seems convincing, but we must think what it implies and requires from us.

If the thinking of the future is inadmissible, we must restrict our thinking to the present and the past. Seemingly, in this way something is required only from our thinking, not from our Being. However, if we are not allowed to think the future, are we unrestricted in our Being? Are we allowed to transcend the limits of the existing in our Being and bring to life something new? If not, then we have limited not only thinking to the past, but also our Being. If so, then we are condemned to create the new without thinking, and our thinking and our Being fall apart. Perhaps this is not so catastrophic? Would it not be possible to think the old, to respect the existing as the holy limit of our thinking, and nevertheless in our practical activity, in Being, to produce something new, even to progress to higher forms of life? If so, then the new would be entirely irrational, mystical.

With the view that only the socialist revolution is revolution in the full sense, our concept of revolution is still not finished; it is still halfway. We still do not know what revolution in general is, or the socialist revolution in particular. Can socialist revolution be reduced to the abolition of exploitation?

If we understand revolution as a radical change of society, the question naturally arises of what we think under such a change and to what extent it presupposes, includes or requires a change in man. Rather often revolution is conceived as a change of social structure which does not affect the nature of man. It is assumed that society can be fundamentally changed and man may remain basically the same. Others dream about a new man, but believe that creation of the new society and creation of the new man are two different things in an external causal relationship; by revolution a new society is created, and in the new society a new man can be educated. Thus the new man emerges as a passive product of the new society and, in the last analysis, of revolution. However, who makes revolution? If the old man can make it, how can it lead to the new man? The product shoud not differ too much from the producer.

Revolution as we see it is possible only as an activity through which man simultaneously changes the society in which he lives and himself. This insight is clearly expressed in Marx's third thesis on Feuerbach. The vulgar Marxist idea that we should first create the new social structure (which would easily produce a new man) is as much a failure as the Christian belief that we should first achieve a change in man's heart (because the changed man will easily organize a better society).

If the change of 'society' and the change of 'man' are inseparably linked (because in both cases it is a story about man), is it justified to separate these two sides of the same process into two entirely different and independent processes? Is it not more adequate to try to consider the whole process a (differentiated) unity? It is certainly not of great importance whether we are going to call the whole process 'revolution'. What is important is to think the possibility of overcoming man's self-alienation, that alienation which in the contemporary world hits equally the individual man and human society, and can be abolished only by creating a truly human society and truly human human beings.

However, what does the socialist revolution as the overcoming of human self-alienation more precisely mean? Where is its place in Being? Most frequently revolution is conceived of as a form of transition. On one level it is a transition of power from one group or class to another, on another, the transition from a lower form of society (or man) to a higher one. In both of these views revolution is nothing in itself, it has no content, value or importance independent of the goal at which it aims. It is simply a transition to a higher form of Being, a means which is justified by its end. In this way, it seems like a non-Being, emptiness, a hole in Being, a split which divides two real and really different states of Being.

In opposition to such a view I think that revolution can lead to a higher form of life only if it is itself an epoch of intense creativity, in which man uncovers, creates and fulfils his new possibilities. Far from being merely a jump *to* a higher form of Being, revolution already *is* a higher form of Being, a creative activity which distinguishes man as man. The end of revolution, including the so-called successful end, would mean the interruption of creativity, at best, stabilization at an already achieved level.

When, if at all, should the creativity of a socialist revolution stop? Obviously when every self-alienation is abolished, when man becomes fully human, and society also completely human. However, when should such a moment actually arise? Hopefully never. To realize all human possibilities would mean to close man, to interrupt his develop-ment, to negate his creative essence. If man is to continue to be, develop-ing to the full extent his potentialities, then the socialist revolution is thinkable only as a never-ending process. Only in living revolutionarily can man fulfil his essence.

Man, as I see him, is different from any other being because he is a being of praxis. This does not mean that he is determined by his political, commercial, or some other 'practical' activity in the colloquial sense. In the spirit of Marx praxis is the structure of man's activity in so far as it is free and creative. As a being of praxis man is a free and creative being, and as such he is a being of revolution. Revolution is not a special phenomenon in history, but the most concentrated form of human collective creativity, a form in which the creative nature of man most clearly comes to the fore.

As is well known, revolutions have been relatively rare in human history, and very short in comparison with the non-revolutionary periods. How can this be reconciled with the thesis that revolution ex-presses the essence of man? According to Karl Marx, history up to now was only prehistory in which man was alienated from his essence. This is not to say that he possesses a given, firm essence. It means that he does not realize his historically developed creative potentialities. Man, on the contrary, is not self-alienated when he at the same time realizes and enlarges his creative possibilities, and in social life acts as a being of revolution. In the self-alienated history-prehistory up to now, man only at times and very incompletely succeeded in fulfilling himself as a being of revolution, but this does not contradict the thesis of revolution as the essence of history.

All revolutions up to now included a greater or lesser degree of violence and bloodshed. If we celebrate revolution as a possible lasting form of human life, do we not want to turn man to the road of violence and cruelty? This is far from the intention. The essence of revolution is not bloodshed and cruelty, but the creative activity by which the new man and the new society are born and developed. Even in the past bloodshed and cruelty were the subordinate moments of revolutions, and on the whole there was more humanism in revolutions than in the epochs of 'peaceful' evolutionary development which have often been marked by terror and violence.

However, past revolutions, although attempts at realizing a better humanity, still belonged to the alienated prehistory of mankind; they were heroic attempts to break through the ring of alienation. The socialist revolution as a radical negation of the whole inhuman class history of mankind should bring us something new in principle, a development of human creative power which radically eliminates violence and cruelty, an association in which, in Marx's words, 'the free development of each is the condition for the free development of all'.

III. Violence

In our attempt to clarify the concepts of socialism and revolution we have already expressed a view about the relationship between socialism, revolution and violence. Socialism has been interpreted as a truly human society in which the self-alienation of man is overcome, and man can live on the level of his creative potentialities; revolution has been conceived as a collective creative activity through which socialism as a truly human society is being realized. Both have been opposed to violence as an inhuman mode of being, which has to be eliminated by revolution.

But are we right in regarding violence as something opposed to socialism and humanism? Are not power and violence among the distinctive traits of man? And regardless of whether we regard violence as something human or inhuman, is it not indispensable for overthrowing a violent social order such as capitalism?

Before trying to answer these questions we must first say what we mean by violence. Pretty often violence is identified with power, a confusion which may have serious consequences. In order to avoid such a confusion in a paper published in *Praxis* under the title 'Macht, Gewalt, und Humanität' I tried to analyse the concepts of power and violence in their relationship to humanity.

Starting from certain differences found in Nietzsche I tried to distinguish between the three forms of power. According to this analysis the first form of power is mere power or force (*die Kraft*), neutral in relation to what is human, power which is not specifically human, but common to man, animal, machine and nature. This is the power to stay and to remain, the power to move and to clash. A second form of power is power as more strength (*mehr Kraft, mehr Macht*), power as predominance. This is the power to rule and to govern, the power to command, to repress and to exploit, the power to usurp and to rob. And finally, as a third form, there is a concept of power as ability, capability, or potentiality; the ability to experience and to live, to love and to wonder, to discover and to bring to life the new, to create and give presents.

If we now ask about the relationship of power to humanity, we cannot disregard the existence of different forms of power. Thus there can be no general answer to the question. Power as mere force is something prehuman, something not-yet-human. Power as rule and domination is a form of non-authentic, self-alienated human Being. Power as creativity and present-giving is a really human form of Being. Power as domination and power as creation, enriching humanity, are in irreconcilable opposition. However, both of them presuppose power as mere power or force. Creativity cannot be powerless!

If power as creativity is a negation of power as domination should not we in the name of humanity try to overcome power as domination by means of power as creation? Or would it be an 'exaggeration'? Perhaps it is not power as domination that is inhuman in itself, but only that misuse of predominance which we call 'violence'? Perhaps the demand to overcome power as domination should rather be to overcome violent domination, power as *violence*?

Some people think that, as the eighteenth century was called 'the age of enlightenment', ours could be called 'the age of violence'. However one-sided or exaggerated this characterization might be, it is hard to dispute that in the contemporary world, at every step, we meet both physical and mental violence in most different forms.

Many contemporary thinkers who dream of a non-violent socialist society consider that the violence which is a characteristic of contemporary society can only be overcome by counter-violence. The argument is very simple: love and other non-violent 'means 'are powerless when confronted with violence. Violence can be removed only by a stronger counter-violence.

Opposed to such a view we find another according to which violence cannot be overcome by counter-violence. To preach a violent reaction to violence means to support a new form of the violent society, to advocate changes within the limits of the old violent society. The new society can be created only by reacting with love and truth to violence and obscurantism.

Recognizing that considerable difficulties are contained both in the view that violence can only be overcome by counter-violence and that every use of violence is inadmissible, some progressive thinkers have tried to find a way out by distinguishing two different forms of violence, such as revolutionary and counter-revolutionary violence, or progressive and reactionary violence, or repressive and liberating violence, or aggressive and defensive violence and so on.

It seems, however, that this distinction does not solve the problem and that those who defend the viewpoint of revolutionary violence also come into difficulties. Revolutionary violence is also a form of violence and it is very difficult to see how, if at all, we can stop and eliminate violence after it has been accepted and used. Perhaps we should think a little more about the concept of violence.

In his Reflections on Violence Sorel insisted that we should draw a distinction between 'bourgeois force' and 'Proletarian violence'. I do not want to quote his definition of the two concepts here, because I do not want to follow his proposals. I mentioned his distinction simply because I find it terminologically interesting in a reverse sense, because I propose a distinction between (sometimes proletarian) force and (sometimes bourgeois and never proletarian) violence.

Violence, as I see it, is a form of power as domination and oppression. In the same way as every power is not oppression, not every use of power is violence. It is certainly no violence, in this sense, if somebody who is attacked in the dark defends himself with all his strength, and it is also not violence if a country defends itself with arms from military aggression. Violence is only an application or use of power which tends to destroy what is human in man, to limit his freedom, to prevent his creativity, to deform his personality. It can be directed at the physical destruction of man by inflicting upon him bodily injuries or by imposing upon him physical strains, but it can also restrict itself 'merely' to mental destruction by pressure, intimidation or delusion. Thus I suggest that we speak of violence only where power is used for the destruction of humanity, for suffocation of man's abilities, for preventing man's creative activity.

It is obvious that violence in this sense is essentially connected with power as superpower or predomination. Only where there is predominance is violence possible, and it can be exercised only by one who is stronger in relation to one who is weaker. A hare cannot exercise violence over the hunter.

Growing out of power as predomination, violence cannot be essentially different from it. Power as predominance contains in germ violence and 'naturally' develops to violence which is merely its manifested and developed essence.

The question about the relationship between violence and socialism can thus be answered by saying that violence is something essentially inhuman, and cannot serve as a means for achieving a human goal such as socialism. This does not mean that we are not allowed to oppose violence by force, because the toleration of violence is not humanism, but an inhuman reconciliation with inhumanity. If we want to achieve socialism, a human form of life, this requires the negation of power in the sense of violence, and the victory over it by power in the sense of human creative activity.

ON THE DEVELOPMENT OF MARXISM TOWARDS PRECISION

Fritz J. Raddatz

Defining the traditions of Marxism has usually been understood until now as the question: what has been modified, what has been correctly or even incorrectly handed down through tradition since Marx's original insights? Marx's own precepts are true; if something has gone awry, then it is to be blamed on disciplines or disloyal followers. They have many names, some are called revisionists and others Stalinists, as the case may be.

I am not sure that the question is formulated correctly. Christianity is good – but the popes, bishops and priests are fallible? Feudalism was nice – but Marie Antoinette was an intriguing fool? Capitalism creates the best of all possible worlds – but Krupp or Onassis are annoying abuses? However, what if it is a product of *the situation itself*? This assertion seems a necessary banality for past social precepts and forms. Should it not therefore be allowed in relation to that which calls itself 'omnipotent, because true'?

Ernst Bloch formulated the problem in a most alarming but precise manner: we must decide not so much whether Marxism has evolved towards imprecision, but rather whether it has evolved towards precision (*Kennt-Lichkeit*). What does he mean? To put it another way what can we recognize as contradictory in the concepts which Marx himself established?

The early writings, terminating with the key word 'alienation', which Marx later disavowed, demonstrate a clear orientation towards the humanistic. 'To be radical means to grasp things by their roots. The root of humanity is man.' This sentence of reflective beauty originated in 1843.

The influence of Marx's early writings was not felt until late, perhaps too late in the socialist countries, where they are still largely ignored.

Neither Rosa Luxemburg nor Lenin knew them. Many of them were published in 1931-2, less than three years before the first Stalin trials. I do not mention this date incidentally; it is a fixed historical point for these theoretical considerations: the role of the individual in history. Does the Marxist image of man contain the possibility – a possibility which actually does not exist – that man can dehumanize himself? It was no accident that Arthur Koestler's novel *Darkness at Noon*, mistakenly stamped as the strategic plan of the cold war but in fact a historical dialogue written with the intensity of Diderot, triggered Merleau-Ponty's furious study on *Humanism and Terror*, which appeared several years later. Koestler's book identifies in the figure of Rubashov not only the inner structure of Bukharin with the external physiognomy of Zinoviev, it also presents accused individuals who surrender themselves having seen the necessity of injustice. His novel examines whether at certain historical turning points the individual is superfluous, a *quantité négligeable*. Merleau-Ponty takes up his study, with its indicative title, at exactly this point, proposing for the first time that there is no divergence between ends and means. A possible utopian goal which justifies all means in order to reach it – both are concepts which Marxism does not recognize. Rather, revolutionary action is the continuation of a process which is already latent in history. This historical process, at the same time an objective force, has only one agent, the proletariat. The perspective of revolutionary action arises when the lines of proletarian development are extended into the future. However, that is not the goal, a concept which Lenin explicitly denounces: 'No man can assure the advanced phase of communism.' Rather, it is the logic of history, a value-free process.

> Because the proletariat is both an objective factor in the political economy, and a scheme of consciousness (Bewusstseinssystem), or rather a style of community life, a fact and a value, and because the logic of history unites in the proletariat the energy of labour and the true experience of human life, use becomes identical with value, not because value is measured according to use, as in the case of a Commissar, or because use is measured according to value, as in the case of the Yogi, but rather because proletarian use is the value which is active in history.[1]

Marx mentions that the proletariat has no ideals to realize. The denial of goal and utopia, of forecasting ,and of morality sounds so convincing that it can be considered as *the* Marxist discovery, that which Engels meant in his eulogy to his lifelong companion and comrade when he said: 'He discovered the law of history.' Yet, at exactly this radical point begins the divergence between the philosophical system and man himself.

Marx characterizes the time of his early writings as his Feuerbach period. The Feuerbach Theses mark the end of this period. The definition of the Sixth Thesis: 'But the human essence is no abstraction inherent in each individual. In reality it is the sum of social relations' is a clear answer to Marx's own *Manuskripte* of 1844 in which he wrote: 'The individual is the social being.' In his excellent book *Marxismus und Theorie der Persönlichkeit*, Lucien Sève describes the step which Marx took here by following closely the formulations of Marx himself:

> The social being is understood here as something quite other than the individual. It is the 'sum of productive energy, capital and forms of social intercourse with which every individual and every generation must come to terms as something given'. This is the basis of what philosophers have called the 'substance' and 'essence of man'. In other words, the concept of man must be radically inverted.[2]

This inversion can be substantiated by numerous textual citations, be they from *Deutsche Ideologie*, *Grundrisse* or *Das Kapital*. Whether there actually exists such a clear break between the theoretical concept of the *Ökonomischphilosophische Manuskripte* of 1844 and later writings of 1845-6, as Sève's thesis indicates, is open to question. Themes and motifs, even metaphors and images of the early writings emerge repeatedly at later stages. For example, the discussion of the power of money based on a motif from Shakespeare's 'Timon of Athens' can be found in the *Manuskripte*, in *Deutsche Ideologie*, ten years later in the original text of *Zur Kritik* and again ten years later in *Das Kapital*. One cannot doubt that historical materialism, as Marx developed it, is directly related to scientific anthropology.

Here lies the problem. In a sort of constantly interrupted continuum man is conceived of as both creator of, and creation of history. The determined denunciation of the traditional concept of freedom (in *Deutsche Ideologie*) which 'is no more than the right to enjoy undisturbed the fruits of contingency within certain conditions', contrasts with indecisive and misunderstood judgements in the form of a 'just-as-much' balance; '. . . that conditions form human beings just as much as human beings the conditions'. The postulate of practice of the Feuerbach

Theses is certainly clear; but it remains unclear whether its application is not a kind of historical mechanism, in other words, *not an application by persons*. Perhaps the statement of the aged Friedrich Engels is not only a simple slip of the tongue: 'Thus past history has elapsed in the form of a natural process . . .'?[3]

To this day the most burning question in the dialogue both inside and outside Marxist circles has been whether individuality is not at bottom secondary to the objective social infrastructure. That then would be Bloch's 'precision' towards which Marxism has moved – not the simple *aperçu* of a play on words. In a long interview concerning this thesis Bloch introduced detailed deliberations in which he characterizes the dominating form of Marxism as a sort of critique of pure reason for which there has not yet been written a critique of practical reason – an exposed but not yet developed picture of man. If this is true, if we understand the existing socialist forms of society as a frightful demonstration of the fact that the process of socialization of the productive forces does not bring into play what should actually be understood under 'social wealth', then a situation has been abolished in which hardship and misery exist, but a situation has not been created in which there are no oppressed or humiliated.

In her eclectic essay (which is more descriptive than analytical) the Italian communist Rossana Rossanda formulates the problem as follows: 'The socialist revolution cannot be conceived simply as a transfer of property from which a more equal distribution of profit results, whilst all other relationships remain alienated and objectified.'[4] It is especially typical of the French Marxists, such as Merleau-Ponty, Paul Nizan, Louis Althusser or Roger Garaudy – who have always distrusted the orthodox catechism – that they return again and again to this question, for, abstract as it might appear, it is of direct practical application. If Marx ultimately needs no subject for the historical process, then there is no true dialectic between the individual and history but rather a scientific rationalism. In this case 'one can and must speak openly of a theoretical antihumanism on Marx's part'.[5] Althusser, who goes so far as to claim this theoretical antihumanism as 'the precondition of Marxist philosophy',[6] does not reproach Marx (as Sève implies) for having neglected the theory of man as the common agent of all social relationships. Just the opposite is the case: the main objection of Althusser, Etienne Balibar, and others concerns Marx's concept of the total dependence of the individual on the structure of the productive process or the mode of production.

He indicated in the terminology itself the theoretical fact that we are dealing not with concrete human beings in the analysis of 'relationship', but rather with human beings as carriers of certain functions in the structure: carriers of productive labour (in formulating the theoretical concept which defines the analysis of the labour process, Marx speaks not of 'human beings' or 'subjects', but of 'expedient activity'), representatives of capital.

To characterize these individuals Marx systematically employs the expression carrier (*Träger*). In theory, human beings appear only as carriers of relationships immanent in the structure, and the forms of their individuality appear only as certain consequences of the structure.[7]

If taken literally, this agent, or representative, function is a process of de-individualization. Individuals are reduced to miniature reproductions of the whole social structure. The counter-model, where human beings form the centres from which perception of the connection between forms of the praxis in the structure as a whole would be possible, that is, where the practice is conceived as the centre of ideological subjects (with varying forms of consciousness), this model is excluded from Marx's analysis. Social relationships would then be no longer the expression of the structure of forms of praxis, of which individuals are only consequences, but rather the product of the multiplicity of such centres. It is certainly no accident that Althusser speaks here of 'practical intersubjectivity', a term employed already much earlier by Herbert Marcuse, one of the first critics of Marx's *Manuskripte* (1932). The Stalin critique in this context is only an apparent contradiction; indeed the personalization, or better, the reduction to 'personal degeneration', invalidates any dialectical connection between the individual and the historical process. It introduces a mechanistic concept of political action: the improvement of certain power mechanisms or 'organs' could then eliminate the deeply rooted imbalance of politics and morality.

We are speaking here of a process of cognition, that is, the step-by-step perception of social relationships, which the French word 'conaissance' expresses. Such concepts are not contained in Marx's formulations. 'Society does not consist of individuals, but rather represents the sum of those relationships and affinities which these individuals have with one another.'[8] This is a small but decisive distinction. One is forced to ask whether comments which seem so illuminating at first glance –

such as the following from *Deutsche Ideologie*: that division of labour does not derive from differences between individuals, but rather that differences between individuals derive from division of labour – whether such materialism does not ignore many categories of communication. The result is perhaps just that state of 'non-being' which Marx himself meant when he wrote 'Ein ungegenständliches Wesen ist ein Unwesen.'[9]

The uncertainty of Marx's concept of man cannot be misunderstood as a dated leap in development or as a difference between the 'pre-Marxist' Marx and the 'Marxist' Marx. Erich Fromm refers precisely to this in his study on Freud and Marx:

> Marx argues against two points of view here: the ahistorical, which postulates the nature of man as a substance existing since the beginning of history, as well as the relativistic, which endows the nature of man with none of its own properties but considers it the reflection of social conditions. However, he never formulated conclusively his own theory of the nature of man in order to transcend both the ahistorical and the relativistic points of view ... For this reason the interpretations of his theory are so variant and contradictory.[10]

If, however, Marxist anthropology comprehends only one side of the personality – its origin as social product – and not the complete structure with its individual life and characteristic activity, then we can identify some meaningful implications for political practice and ideological tradition.

From the break between Marxists and Anarchists after the Congress in The Hague in 1872 and Bakunin's exclusion, to Lenin's 'advice' to Gorki to emigrate, his displeasure with Mayakovski or his concept of a party of cadres, to Daniel Cohn-Bendit's denunciation by Georges Marchais, we can follow this disastrous but consistent line in the European labour movement. In short, those are the way stations of practical politics. The present level of discussion in countries such as Italy and France indicates the dependence of these political facts on ideological disagreements; their differing development can be understood in the framework of our deliberations. The subjective element in many variants plays a role for philosophers such as Georges Sorel or Petr A. Kropotkin, for Alexander A. Bogdanov, and later for Benedetto Croce, Antonio Labriola, Antonio Gramsci, Anton Pannekoek, Karl Korsch and Georg Lukács. The Italian development is particularly stringent, not only because fascism established itself earlier there, but also because the intellectual concept of non-dogmatic Marxism has had acute political consequences. The contemporary independent position of the Italian Communist Party has one source – expressed in the protest against the invasion of Czechoslovakia or the strangulation of philosophers such as Robert Havemann. The mixture of materialistic premises, anarchosyndicalist ideas and élitist idealism is to be found in the writings of Benedetto Croce and his Roman teacher Antonio Labriola, an early socialist law professor and philosopher. One of Labriola's first essays on socialism consists of a series of letters addressed to Georges Sorel, whose principal work, *Réflexions sur la violence* (*Reflections on Violence*), was published with Croce's help in Italian *before* the first French edition. Sorel must be considered one of the fathers of the Syndicalist Movement. He was secretary of the Fédération des Bourses du Travail, founded in 1892, and was an initiator of the Confédération Générale du Travail in 1895. The programmes of both groups supported the general strike as an especially effective instrument in the revolutionary struggle. At the same time Sorel was striving for a 'cultural revolution' as a commentator on and popularizer of Marx – at times together with Labriola and Croce.

Sorel's collaboration on numerous journals of a materialist or Marxist character not only brought him into contact with leading theoreticians such as Friedrich Engels, Karl Kautsky, Eduard Bernstein, August Bebel or Jean Jaurès (who all contributed to *Ere Nouvelle* for example). but also acquainted him more fully with Marxism as such. Sorel expanded the fourth edition of his *Réflexions sur la violence* in 1919 with an essay entitled 'Pour Lenine'.

Labriola, in his time one of the most knowledgeable interpreters of Marx, turned sharply against Bernstein and at the same time broke with Croce and Sorel. The latter, however, had written in 1897 the introduction for the French translation of Labriola's principal work *Essais sur la conception matérialiste de l'histoire*. In 1898 a nineteen-year-old prisoner in a jail in Odessa read this edition and became a convinced Marxist through its argumentation. He was called Trotsky.

Georgi V. Plekhanov continued the critical dialogue with Labriola. The Italian translator of Marx, Giovanni Gentile, a prominent student of Labriola and one of the main collaborators of the journal *Critica*, seized at this time upon the phrase 'the philosophy of practice', a phrase which was to become one of the main features of Gramsci's life work.

Gramsci is a clear descendant of this idealistic and revisionist presentation of Marxism. Indeed, in all of his important essays, even those of the later years, Gramsci refers to Labriola and Croce. The resistance to orthodoxy and catechization (a concept which must be understood essentially as misgivings about Stalin) is apparent from the earliest phases of Gramsci's development through to his final writings. Undoubtedly he has left a decisive mark on the evolution of Italian communism in refusing to consider theory only as a complement or appendage to practice, but rather as the marketplace of practice.

Gramsci's form of Marxism can be characterized as both intellectual and individualistic. Here, as in almost all the discussions of the Second International, a phenomenon of pseudo-simultaneity becomes apparent: various contradictory concepts are simultaneously criticized and developed further. Thus, for example, we can recognize that Gramsci appropriated the same critical concepts as Korsch. Like Korsch, and from time to time even Lukács, Gramsci believed that Marxism, as a part of the superstructure, can become ideology in the sense of false consciousness. It remains a 'philosophy of practice' if it is not subject to its own reflective process of critical revision.

Gramsci's political concept is comparable to that of the Jacobin Revolution. Bogdanov's assertion that a cultural revolution must precede the social revolution – he even had a plan for a 'Proletarian Encyclopedia' – was shared by Gramsci. It is his ideal of a new, integral mass culture that possessed the enlightened elements of eighteenth-century France and the German Reformation, as well as the classicism of Greece and the Italian Renaissance. It is a culture that synthesizes Robespierre and Kant. (It is hardly an accident that as early as 1908 Lenin reacted extremely negatively to Bogdanov's plans in a letter to Gorki.)

In addition to the ideological dialogue, the debates on literature and art make this tradition even clearer. The rather lightly-propagated tenet that theory becomes material power when the masses take it up should make one sceptical, even of its verbal form. It signals an undialectic relation – between above and below. The agitated masses are passive. The theory is external to them.

Georg Lukács' sociology of art illustrates clearly the confusing contradictions in this concept. The new world spirit is called the spirit of the time; *Weltgeist* becomes *Zeitgeist*. This observable process of depersonalization constitutes two patterns of thought which only apparently contradict one another. There is a kind of historical psychology, but no individual psychology; the author is also a 'translator' of something existing objectively – a something for which there are diverse but no divergent translations, different versions but only one original text. The author is the interpreter of the objective musical score. Transposed into the realm of aesthetic theory, this means art is to be understood as a substitute for harmony, literature as the projection of a veiled but existing totality. Art becomes calocagathy: the identity of the good, the true and the beautiful. Transposed into the realm of formal aesthetics, this means Aristotelian aesthetics, cognition by means of identification. Not Brecht but Thomas Mann, not Joyce but Shaw. Yet identification in the sense of a guide for life is only possible with models and derived figures.

At this point the circle is complete. Lukács' theoretical concept of the artist's totality favours closed forms because they can make visible the latent possibilities within the insufficient reality, that is to say, they can transcend. The ambivalent, open and imponderable is filtered out. Derived figures instead of characters, reality (at least) instead of truth, sexuality instead of eroticism, to be driven to death instead of death. This is the root of what Brecht considered an unacceptable concept of realism, a concept which was none. Even Engels doubted his own (and Marx's) method of research in his famous letter to Franz Mehring:

Otherwise there is only one aspect which is lacking, but an aspect which has not been systematically enough stressed in discussions between Marx and me. Namely, we have all placed, and had to place, the emphasis on the economic derivation of political, legal and other ideological ideas and the actions arising from these ideas. As a consequence, we have neglected the formal aspect in favour of the content: the way in which these ideas come to pass. This has provided the enemy with a welcome opportunity for misunderstanding and distortion. Paul Barth serves as an excellent example.

Ideology is a process which is consciously executed by the so-called philosopher, but with a false consciousness. His real motivations are not apparent to him, otherwise it would not be an ideological process. Therefore, he imagines false or ostensible motivations. Because it is a reflective process, he deduces its content and form from pure reflection – be it his own or that of his predecessor. He works with purely conceptual material, which he uncritically accepts as the product of his reflection, not examining further whether there might be a source independent of the reflection. This is self-evident to him because he regards all action as the product of reflection, and thus substantiated in the reflection.[11]

To be sure we can laugh today at the Marxism which, as Adam Schaff once put it, derives the source of Mickiewicz's Totenfeier directly from the rise and fall of grain prices in Lithuania. However, we do know that the irrational component of the human psyche is practically excluded from Marxist research, a component whose origin can be rationally explained.

Theory, which is taken up by the masses and which then becomes powerful, resembles the image of a natural catastrophe. Here lies the hubris which lead to Lukács' concept of the *élite*, his theory of partisans and his leftist rigorism. Again the root is the concept of man. A minor example: if the singularity, the uniqueness of the individual is not accepted, then one cannot comprehend the totality of the psycho-physical structure, the complex of attitudes, predispositions, preferences, passions, fears. Two aspects are missing in the artistic image of man as propagated by socialist art: Eros and Thanatos. No accident that Ernst Bloch repeatedly refers to Kant's notorious definition of marriage as 'the relationship between two persons of different sex for the vital and mutual possession of their respective sex characteristics'. After all, the impetus of Bloch's life's work is to redefine the subject–object relationship. Bloch regards Hegel's comment that 'terror is Kant converted into action' not an historical diagnosis but as a concept to be used in research. Kant's is not the only name that can be inserted. As if that same terror does not also lie in this formulation of marriage in terms of a commodity, for example; the beginning of seeing what is individual but not what is human? Bloch's concept of materialism is a process. Matter is not being, but ability – 'matter on the move' – is.

Thus, materialism is the impetus of responsible human action. Bloch's concept of 'action' is the human consequence of matter in motion. The 'honest motion' is threefold: condition for action, for labour; prerequisite for consciousness; possibility for what is human, thus for what is political. That is dialectical materialism.

If Bloch postulates the concept of the contradiction not only as a form of reflection but also as an objective movement of matter, then it is more a summons to dispute. Contradiction marks individuality. Human beings are not only representatives of logically deduced socio-economic structures. Brecht's comment 'there are people who have no right to be right' can also be reversed: 'there must be people who have a right not to be right'.

Yet it is the general stigma of past socialist art that just this human contradiction is excluded. The female characters of the only important female communist prose author, Anna Seghers, are defeminized organisms. Death exists as a function, not as the end of a non-repeatable whole, therefore it can hardly be tragic. Brecht's only play that does not deal with the moral débacle of the old world but with the moral categories of communism is a play about death – Die Massnahme. For forty years it has been suppressed.

All this has implications, easily understood in the non-existence of the Fine Arts, a bit more complicated in the analysis of literature. The drama of East Germany, for example, sways between two extremes which qualify each other: on the one hand, the complicated is transposed into the comical, social conflicts are not utilized as a source of tension but emasculated. Banality as folk wisdom – 'to laugh is healthy'. Comedy as the emergency exit for a society. On the other hand, there exists a 'high' literature which searches for truth in unreality, in resignation. The insight of Heiner Müller's Macbeth is historically pessimistic in the same way as that of 'Philoktet'. In the latter the sum of all experience is expressed as 'your fish is coming, net'. In the former, 'the only exit from this world is to the knacker. The career is with knives to the knife'. That is the passé défini of Peter Huchel's verse, the precision of the hopeless:

Solitude becomes history.	Die Öde wird Geschichte.
Termites write it	Termiten schreiben sie
With their tongues	Mit ihren Zungen
In the sand.	In den Sand.[12]

This 'historical materialism' is close to that of Polansky. The new application of myth in so-called Socialist Classicism indicates a new concept of destiny – guiltless destiny. This process of cancelling guilt easily becomes a process of apology: when the realm of myth is conceived as that where speech, discourse, reflection and action are separate from each other, then we are faced practically with a scared denial of reality. Myth and world, present and past, real and unreal have become identical. For our comments on the theatre this implies that the distinction between world and its 'designation' – that is, art – becomes invalid. Not only are the general context and historical causality assumed as known quantities, so that accident and surprise are banished, but also the audience is persuaded to accept the inevitable.

What does this mean, though, for the sphere beyond dramaturgy? It means that guilt no longer exists, for within a generally known and accepted context guilt can hardly be judged. The moral trespass of an individual no longer has a place – what remains is a sort of 'objective guilt', similar to an unavoidable fate, whether it strikes Oedipus or Kepper Paul Bauch. They are not 'responsible'. However, if no one is 'responsible', not even Stalin, not Beria, not Gomulka, then we are presented in the 'high' literature of East Germany with the same effect as in the social comedies: truth is filtered out.

It is against this rigid inevitability that Robert Havemann directed his polemics. After all, this is a degradation of historical materialism to Kismet, of dialectics to inevitability. Here also a clear effect of exculpation: if this fatalism defines the role of personality in history, then there is simply no personality in history and, therefore, also no possibility of personal responsibility in action. Stalin was just an operational failure. Hitler too.

The process of cancelling guilt is not moral but essentially political. De-individualization means de-politicization, to the point that was touched upon in the comments on Koestler's and Merleau-Ponty's interpretations. That was humanity as the totality of social relationships – this generic concept stops before the possibility of choice or torment, that possibility which we all have, perhaps, as a burden: on the one hand, to pursue a Marxism which inevitably must turn against the historical reality of the USSR or the various communist parties; on the other hand, to opt for the 'socialist camp' without inquiring whether that is 'strait-jacket and legerdemain' socialism (R. Rossanda). To refuse this possibility its fruition, that is, *not* to make a choice, means to ask about tradition in a different way. We must not ask whether it is false *how* tradition was handed down, but whether *what* is handed down can be false. It is to ask whether mental hospitals for Soviet intellectuals or concentration camps for Cuban homosexuals are really only 'operational failures' or whether they are mistakes in the construction of the building. In Angola or the Greek Islands we already know.

Is it only the amputated leg that hurts? Are only the remaining nerve endings still sensitive? Is the phenomenon of alienation in socialism simple a residue of amputated capitalism or is it a phenomenon of socialism itself? Marx turned Hegel's world on its feet; has the head now been amputated?

— 9 —

SOCIALISM AND THE WORKING CLASS

Tom Bottomore

I. The Problem

The historical connection between socialism and the working class – however complex and diverse its forms – is quite obvious. Working class movements produced socialist ideas, and when more systematic socialist theories (in particular, Marxism) were elaborated, they found their most responsive public among workers. At the very least one can speak of an 'elective affinity'.

The questions that have been raised more recently about this connection or affinity seem to me to involve the following aspects:

1. The changing economic and social situation of the working class in advanced industrial societies.

2. The factors influencing the political consciousness of the working class.

3. The capacity of a working class movement to create a socialist society.

I propose to examine these three aspects separately before venturing upon any more general comments.

II. The Economic and Social Situation of the Working Class

All observers seem to agree that economic developments – the rapid progress of technology and sustained economic growth – in the Western industrial countries since the war, have brought about significant changes in the environment of the working class. There is no such agreement, however, about the effects which these changed circumstances have had upon the social role or outlook of the working class.

During the 1950s some sociologists began to write about a 'new working class', meaning by this expression that a part, a substantial part, of the working class was being assimilated into the middle class or as the phrase went, was undergoing a process of *embourgeoisement*. According to this view, rising levels of living, universal welfare services, better educational opportunities, changes in the occupational structure, new residential patterns, increased chances of social mobility, were together tending to break down the barriers between the middle class and a section of the working class, and to diffuse very widely a middle class way of life. To some extent this process was seen in Europe as a movement towards the American type of society, conceived as being already predominantly middle class, or to put the same point in other terms, as being relatively 'classless'. Such a view was formulated very plainly by S. M. Lipset, in an essay published in the early 1960s, when he said that '. . . instead of European class and political relationships holding up a model of the United States' future, the social organization of the United States has presented the image of the European future'.[1]

The picture thus presented of the emerging society was that of a large middle class occupying the foreground, a more vaguely portrayed small upper class or set of *élite* groups, and an 'underclass', also regarded as being fairly small (and diminishing in numbers), made up of specific groups in the population (the old, some ethnic groups, workers in declining industries) who were living in relative poverty. This picture is no longer generally accepted as accurate, though it may still be necessary, I think, to consider whether it was not simply drawn prematurely. In considering the objections to it I shall leave aside such matters as that the 'underclass' of those in poverty turned out to be much larger than the more optimistic commentators suggested, and also the problems concerning the social and political significance of the upper class or *élites*, and shall concentrate on the position of the working class.

What most critics of the *embourgeoisement* thesis have noted is that the working class is still a much more distinctive group, more sharply separated from the middle class, than has been claimed. Although there are 'affluent workers' the general level of income of manual industrial workers is still well below the income level of white collar and professional workers.[2] Moreover, there are a number of other differences in the work situation which separate the working class from the middle class: less security of employment, more restricted opportunities for promotion, a stricter external control over the conditions of work. Outside the work situation there are other elements of distinction which have been explored particularly by Lockwood and Goldthorpe in *The Affluent Worker*.[3] Do the economic and social changes, which have certainly occurred however much they may have been exaggerated, bring about a change in the social relationships and social outlook of industrial workers? The conclusion at which Lockwood and Goldthorpe arrive is that: 'Broadly speaking, our findings show that in the case of the workers we studied there remain important areas of common social experience which are still fairly distinctively working class; that specifically middle class social norms are not widely followed nor middle class life-styles consciously emulated; and that assimilation into middle class society is neither in progress nor, in the main, a desired objective'.[4] And after quoting Marx's characterization of alienated labour in the *Economic and Philosophical Manuscripts* they go on to suggest that 'the alienated worker (in the above sense) is, at all events, far more readily recognisable in our research data than the worker "on the move towards new middle class values and middle class existence".'[5]

Other studies, at various times, have come to similar conclusions; for example the work by Popitz and others,[6] which found that there is still a very strong working class consciousness in which society is seen as sharply divided between 'them' and 'us', the importance of physical work as the principal creator of value is emphasized, and there is a profound sense of belonging to the community of workers. More recent studies in Germany by Kern, Schumann and others[7] and in France by Andrieux and Lignon,[8] arrive at much the same results.

Another version of the *embourgeoisement* thesis is to be found in Marcuse's *One-Dimensional Man*, though here it is not so much a question of the absorption of the working class into the middle class as of its integration into a national society as a whole, and its pacification as an agent of revolt. According to this view, 'changes in the character of work and the instruments of production change the attitude and the consciousness of the labourer, which become manifest in the widely discussed "social and cultural integration" of the labouring class with capitalist society ... Assimilation in needs and aspirations, in the standard of living, in leisure activities, in politics, derives from an integration *in the plant* itself. ... The new technological work-world thus enforces a weakening of the negative position of the working class: the latter no longer appears to be the living contradiction to the established society.'[9] Evidently, Marcuse's argument and conclusions are open to some of the same objections as have been brought against other versions of the *embourgeoisement* thesis; in particular, that there is little evidence of the change in consciousness which is the main support of the argument (and a good deal of evidence to the contrary).

Marcuse, however, also gives prominence to another aspect of the situation – the changes in technology and especially the progress of automation – which was not emphasized so much in earlier studies, but which has assumed considerable importance in a different kind of discussion of the future of the working class. This aspect has been presented with particular force by Daniel Bell in some recent writings.[10] Bell's main argument is that there is now apparent a decisive shift in the nature of work in American society; male blue-collar workers, although their *numbers* have continued to increase, and will increase up to 1980, will form a smaller *proportion* of the labour force by the latter date. On the other side, the professional and technical occupational category is now 'the central one in the society'. Bell's general conclusion is that while labour issues may become more 'salient and even rancorous' they are unlikely to become ideological or 'class' issues: 'In the economy, a labor issue remains. But not in the sociology and culture of the society, and less so in the polity.' A similar view is taken by another contributor in the same issue of *Dissent*, David M. Gordon, who also points to the tendency to a decline in the proportion of male blue-collar workers, and emphasizes the extent to which there are now quite distinct categories of workers who cannot easily be brought together in a coalition, or engage in what Marxists would think of as a 'class' action.[11] From a different perspective Alain Touraine has given a somewhat similar account of the changing role of industrial workers, and I shall look at this more closely in the following section.

This kind of argument, about the declining economic and social importance of the traditional working class, has also attracted criticism. It is suggested that the rate of development of automation (and hence the decline of manual work) has been greatly exaggerated; that even if the worker comes to be employed at a control panel rather than an assembly line this may not significantly change his work situation or his class allegiance; that the balance between white-collar and blue-collar work is misunderstood if it is not recognized that a high proportion of white-collar workers are women (one of the most significant occupational changes in the industrial countries is certainly the rapid increase in the numbers of married women at work) and that many of these women, the wives of manual workers, cannot be regarded in any sense as having moved from the working class into the middle class.

Nevertheless, even taking into account such criticisms, this change in the nature of work is a phenomenon of real importance. At the least, one has to distinguish between the situation which prevailed roughly from the mid-nineteenth century up to the end of the 1930s, with an expanding industrial working class, and in some countries a large peasantry or farmworker class; and the likely situation towards the end of this century, when the industrial working class will have declined as a proportion of the working population, and perhaps in absolute numbers, while the numbers of technical and professional workers will have increased still more. In such conditions it seems probable that the working class, even if it *were* radical and committed to socialism, would have considerably less weight and influence in determining the direction in which society moves.

III. Political Consciousness

In any thorough consideration of this aspect it would obviously be necessary to take account of the divergences between countries, resulting from different historical experiences and political traditions. The differences between the American working class and the European working class are evidently great, but there are also differences within Europe between those countries in which the working class is wholly or mainly committed to reformist political parties, and those in which a substantial part of the working class supports parties which claim, at least, to be revolutionary, and in which there is a stronger revolutionary tradition. In what follows I shall consider only some general features of working class political consciousness, but the variations which I have just mentioned should be borne in mind.

The issue can be approached in two different ways. First, one can examine the historical development of political consciousness in the working class, as it is expressed in the doctrines of working class movements and parties. Second, one can look at the emergence, and prevalence, of political doctrines and preoccupations which do not arise from the working class movement but may affect it in various ways.

As to the first: the *embourgeoisement* thesis which I considered above proceeds from an analysis of the economic and social situation of the working class to an assertion of its declining radicalism; and Marcuse's version of the thesis seems to arrive at the conclusion that this radicalism has been totally extinguished. However, there is little evidence to support such views. What needs to be recognized is that no substantial part of the working class in the Western capitalist countries has been radical or revolutionary for a long time (roughly since the period from 1913 to 1919); and no working class party has ever been able to establish itself at the head of a broad revolutionary movement. Thus the situation in the 1950s and 1960s was not that the working class had become politically less radical, but simply that it was as little radical during that period as it had been for the preceding thirty or forty years. Its lack of radicalism appears in all the studies with which I am familiar;[12] and it reappears even in more recent studies,[13] in spite of the revival of radical doctrines among intellectuals in the 1960s.

The question to be posed, therefore, is not whether radicalism is declining, but whether working class radicalism is likely to increase in the future; that is, whether the historical process envisaged by Marx of the formation of a 'class for itself', committed to a radical transformation of society, is likely, in the end, to be accomplished. Leaving aside the kind of answer given by very orthodox Marxists, which involves a large element of dogmatic assertion, there seem to me two more interesting answers, sketched by Serge Mallet and Alain Touraine.

Mallet's argument[14] is broadly that the 'new working class' (comprising the technically qualified and professional workers employed in the most advanced sectors of production), while it is not revolutionary in the sense of being ready to make a revolution at all costs, especially because it has no desire to see the existing apparatus of production destroyed, *is* revolutionary in the sense that it is led by its situation in the labour process to aim at a fundamental change in social relations. The main evidence brought forward to support this thesis is that workers in some of the most advanced sectors of production have gone beyond wage demands to a more general confrontation over the organization of production in the enterprise and the management of the economy as a whole.[15]

Touraine argues in a similar way, except that he envisages a new structure of classes altogether.[16] In his view, the social conflict between capital and labour is losing its central importance in the capitalist societies of the late twentieth century, but new types of domination (which have also appeared, in more authoritarian forms, in the societies of Eastern Europe) are giving rise to new social conflicts, between those who control the institutions of economic and political decision-making and those who have been reduced to a condition of 'dependent participation'. Touraine illustrates this change from the events of May 1968 in France, which revealed that 'sensibility to the new themes of social conflict was not most pronounced in the most highly organized sectors of the working class. The railroad workers, dockers and miners were not the ones who most clearly grasped its most radical objectives. The most radical and creative movements appeared in the economically advanced groups, the research agencies, the technicians with skills but no authority, and, of course, in the university community.'[17]

Such a view could, of course, be interpreted along the lines of Marcuse's argument to mean that the working class has now ceased altogether to be a radical element in society. How it is interpreted will depend in part upon conceptual choices – whether the new radical groups are regarded as forming a 'new working class' or a 'new class' – but also upon judgements (influenced also by these conceptual differences) about the degree of continuity between the traditional labour movement and the new social movements. Touraine suggests that there is a large element of continuity, in doctrine and organization; so that the new social groups could be regarded as carrying on a class struggle which is similar in some fundamental respects to that which occurred between bourgeoisie and proletariat. However, there may also be important differences in the formulation of aims and aspirations, in forms of organization, and in modes of political conflict.

But there is a more fundamental question about the development of radicalism in and through the new social movements of the 1960s. The events of May 1968 in France, and the movements of protest and opposition in other industrial countries, may be seen either as some kind of historical accident or aberration, interrupting the smooth upward course of these societies, or as harbingers of a new revolutionary movement, based largely upon the working class, or particular sections of it, but also involving other social groups, which will eventually express, in a persuasive and effective manner, the opposition to present social inequalities and to a culture dominated by money, speculation and acquisitiveness. It is still too early to forecast with any confidence the future development of political attitudes in the working class, or in other groups which were involved in recent social movements. In some countries there has been a distinct leftward movement in the trade unions, though a study such as that by Michael Schumann and his colleagues[18] indicates that it has not gone very far, at least in Germany. The renewed interest in workers' control or self-management reveals a change in outlook, but it is still confined to a very small section of the working class. Nevertheless, the events of the past decade do suggest that it may be more realistic to pay attention to the revival of radicalism, and its prospective development, rather than to the decline of radicalism which was the favourite theme of the 1950s.

In taking this view, however, it would still be essential to consider the extent to which there developed, during the 1960s, political doctrines and concerns which were not radical at all, or were radical in a fashion which marked them off very distinctly from the mainstream of working class and socialist politics. I described, in an earlier essay,[19] four styles of political thought and action which seem to me to have little connection with the working class movement: the politics of new *élites* committed to, and justifying themselves by, the extension of rationality and efficiency in the system of production; those radical movements, especially among students, which attacked bureaucracy and technocracy and broadened out into a general cultural criticism, expressed sometimes in the notion of a 'counter-culture'; the politics of ethnic or nationalist movements in many parts of the world; and the politics of various supra-national movements, as exemplified by the creation and development of the European Common Market. It is clear that these different styles of politics are still active, that they have affected, and will continue to affect, the working class movement, and that a profound uncertainty about what are the central political and social problems of the world in the late twentieth century still persists.

IV. The Working Class and Socialist Society

If the working class *were* radical, and if it were successful in becoming the ruling power in society, would it establish socialism? In other words, is there a necessary connection between the working class movement and socialism? One rather crude version of Marxism, which nevertheless has had a great influence, asserts this connection very strongly: the victory of the working class will abolish classes, just as the victory of the third estate abolished estates – and a classless society simply *is* socialism. Another twist was given to this doctrine when a political party, claiming to be *the* representative, or vanguard, of the working class, also claimed that *its* victory, *its* seizure of power, was equivalent to the abolition of classes and the inauguration of socialism. In a sense Marx himself gave some plausibility to such an interpretation of his ideas when he disclaimed any desire to produce 'Comtist recipes for the cookshops of the future'; which might be taken to mean that there was no need to think about, or prepare, the institutions of a socialist society, and that somehow everything would fall into place after the revolution.

The criticism of such conceptions has grown as experience has accumulated of the difficulites and deficiencies of those societies in

Eastern Europe which call themselves socialist. Within Marxist thought itself this criticism found expression especially in the writings of those thinkers who formed the Frankfurt School; and it is well summarized in a recent work by Albrecht Wellmer:

> Since history itself has thoroughly discredited all hopes of an economically grounded 'mechanism' of emancipation, it is not only necessary for a theoretical analysis to take into account entirely new constellations of 'bases' and 'superstructures'; in fact, the criticism and alteration of the 'superstructure' have a new and decisive importance for the movements of liberation. In order to reformulate Marx's suppositions about the prerequisites for a successful revolution in the capitalist countries, it would be necessary to include socialist democracy, socialist justice, socialist ethics, and a 'socialist consciousness' among the components of a socialist society to be 'incubated' within the womb of a capitalist order. In short, elements that would have to be included are institutions, forms of life, political *praxis*, that could become the nucleus of a new, emancipated organization of social life . . .[20]

This sets out the issues admirably. In so far as the working class movement is the principal bearer of the socialist idea we should expect to see a development, in working class organizations and through working class political action, of new institutions and new forms of social life. To some extent this has happened, but it has certainly not gone far enough for anyone to see clearly the outlines of a new society taking shape within the old one. What conclusions should we then draw? In the first place, I would say that we have to recognize that the period of gestation of a socialist society is likely to be very much longer than was envisaged by the early socialists, including Marx. A long, complex and difficult process of development is a necessary precondition of socialism: it must include, especially, the attainment of a sufficiently high level of production of goods and services (so that there are no acute scarcities which would require authoritarian allocation and coercive control of those who are deprived); the achievement of a much higher level of general education for the whole population, and its institutionalization as a normal feature of society (which has not yet happened anywhere); the historical experience, over several generations, of the practice of political democracy, which requires the existence of many autonomous, strongly established associations able to express the aspirations and defend the interests of diverse social groups, and to contest or oppose the authority of society's rulers for the time being. These preconditions are only now beginning to appear in some of the advanced industrial countries.

Secondly, if there is, as Wellmer argues, no economically grounded 'mechanism' of emancipation, and if criticism of the 'superstructure' has a new and decisive importance, then the activities of intellectuals, of social and cultural critics, are likely to become more prominent in the movement towards socialism; and this does seem to have been a feature of the recent radical movements. This is not to cast the intellectuals in a Lukácsian role, as party theorists who are able to express the 'correct class consciousness of the proletariat' by virtue of some privileged insight into the ultimate meaning of history, but only to claim that intellectuals, through their reflection and criticism, can sketch possible new forms of social life, diffuse new outlooks, extend the range of education, and awaken or deepen the capacity for independent critical judgement in ever larger numbers of people, and that through this activity they contribute directly to the realization of socialism.

Thirdly, however, I would say that not only is there no economically grounded 'mechanism' of emancipation, but there is no such 'mechanism' at all. We have to give up entirely that element in Marxism, and in some other socialist theories, which conceives the transition from capitalism to socialism as a historical necessity. Socialism is only a *possible* future. All the experiences of the twentieth century show how many and varied are the obstacles which the movement towards socialism has to overcome, and which it has so far failed to overcome – the concentration of political power in a party or a bureaucracy (which develops all the more easily where there is public ownership of large scale enterprises), the obsession with economic growth which has corrupted socialist thought itself, the rapid growth of population and of urban congestion, the vast inequalities between nations and the extent of the rivalry and conflict which arise from national sentiment and interests.

It may be that the word 'socialism' has become so corrupted by its association with authoritarian regimes, with centralized planning, with the obsessive pursuit of technological innovation and economic growth, as to be unsuitable any longer to describe the objectives of movements of liberation in the late twentieth century. But until a new term is found we must make do with it, only taking care to interpret it always in such a way that it does adequately express the idea of liberation; that is to say, the creation of a social order in which there is the maximum feasible equality of access, for all human beings, to economic resources, to knowledge, and to political power, and the minimum possible domination exercised by any individual or social group over any others. The striving for such a state of society, it is plain, is not only the concern of the working class, but of many other groups and organizations in present-day society; and the development of such groups – of radical students and young professional people, ethnic groups, community associations, and many others – in relation to the traditional labour movement will have, I think, a profound influence on the outcome of our ongoing social struggles.

SOCIALISM AND THE NATION

Peter C. Ludz

In the past one hundred and twenty years of European history 'socialism' and 'nation' have been indicators of completely different socio-political outlooks. At some points, however, similarities between the two concepts can be traced. 'Socialism' and 'nation', while differing in their meaning, represent existing social and political entities. Furthermore, both encompass ideas about how social and political affairs should be organized. These ideas, of course, may spring from two different general orientations: the justification of the existing world or the creation of a new world.

Terminological Clarifications

In whatever way one chooses to organize one's remarks on socialism and the nation, a brief outline of how these terms will be employed seems helpful. Such an approach may be recommended because in contemporary discussions both words are used in a variety of ways. A preliminary terminological clarification may further be advisable since in everyday usage the distinctions between both terms and their respective related concepts have become blurred ('people' with nation, for example, or 'democracy' with socialism).

However, we do not aim at abstract definitions here. Rather we want to clarify the two terms with regard to those historico-political realities which form the basis of our deliberations.

(*a*) SOCIALISM. 'Socialism' here stands for the socio-political doctrines in Western Europe which go back to Marx and Engels and were fully developed under the auspices of the Second International. In German history we are referring to the social democrats and, as far as the theory of democratic socialism is concerned, their forefather, Eduard Bernstein. Bernstein defined socialism as 'the movement towards a co-operative societal order'. This definition includes the notions of participation and equality both of which are as much constituent parts of co-operatively oriented forms of socialism as is the idea that, step by step and in a common effort, society must be democratized via reforms.

Bernstein regarded socialism as the theory of workers' emancipation. But he did not intend to limit socialism to the workers; rather, in accordance here with Ferdinand Lassalle, he wanted socialism to be open to all citizens. Thus, the ancestry Bernstein acknowledged for his definition of socialism included not only Marx and Engels but also – and *expressis verbis* – Robert Owen and Charles Fourier, Henri Saint-Simon and Pierre Leroux, Louis Blanc and Etienne Cabet.

Probably Bernstein's most important theoretical achievement was the linking of socialism to parliamentary democracy. For him, existing democracies provided the means to fight for the ultimate goal of socialism; at the same time democracy as such represented the form in which the socialist idea might materialize. Consequently, Bernstein refused to recognize the class struggle as the motor of all historico-political development. He also renounced dialectics, which were for him an empty formula which could be used universally for the interpretation of history, politics, and society.

In his view, the roads that lead to the societal order of democratic socialism are in principle open and not predetermined. Socialism rooted in democracy stabilizes the value of freedom by opposing all suppression of the individual. Thus, Bernstein's concept of socialism extends to such programmatic slogans as 'more justice', 'more security' for the individual and 'more solidarity'.

Relating Bernstein's theory to the German Social Democratic Party's Godesberger Programme, we should like to emphasize a considerable similarity between the two, at least as far as the 'fundamentals of socialism' are concerned. We can only state, but not discuss, this here. As for the emphasis on individual freedom and the assertions of a close relationship between socialism and democracy, there may also incidentally be some interesting parallels between Bernstein's suppositions and contemporary propositions, as advanced by Yugoslav (Svetozar Stojanović) and Czech (Ivan Sviták) thinkers, which we are also unable to outline here. Czech and Yugoslav views which differ from those of Bernstein are probably those on democracy; the Czechs and Yugoslavs we have in mind tend to conceive of direct and immediate rather than indirect and representative democracies.[1]

(*b*) NATION. As for 'nation', the terminological confusion is much greater than in the case of 'socialism', at least in the German-speaking countries. In the English and French languages 'nation' is commonly used to identify people that are bound together by political and governmental organization, while in German 'nation' is also a synonym for people (Volk), irrespective of political organization. The German word *Nation* means, on the one hand, people organized in a political or state constituency; on the other hand, it serves as a shelter for those concepts which – while transcending specific state and societal orders – call for common cultural and ethnic bonds among people. In this latter usage *Nation* borrows from the word *Volk* – a term which describes cultural appearances (e.g. *Volkstum*) rather than political ones.

In what follows we want to keep to a meaning of nation that is linked to the tradition of socialism as described above. Analytically we may distinguish between three aspects characteristic of 'nation' within (democratic) socialism: firstly, at different locations and not only in the *Communist Manifesto*, Marx and Engels had claimed that the nations (or national questions) will merge in an international community (or internationality); and that the national revolution is followed by the social(ist) revolution. On the other hand, and secondly, the founders of Marxism displayed a rather traditional concept of the nation. For example, when discussing problems of the Poland, Alsace-Lorraine or Schleswig-Holstein of their time, their arguments were quite patriotic or nationality-bound. Thirdly, in Marx and Engels and similarly in Lassalle as well as Bernstein, we find a further aspect of the nation. Nation is understood in terms of what Friedrich Meinecke later called the *Kulturnation* (cultural nation); national culture is regarded as a functioning part of world culture and of the cultural development of mankind.

Socialism and the Nation: Some Historical Remarks

(*a*) THE LACK OF A THEORY OF NATION AMONG GERMAN SOCIAL DEMOCRATS DURING THE SECOND INTERNATIONAL. The foregoing discussion points to the fact that neither Marx and Engels nor Bernstein, Lassalle, August Bebel or Wilhelm Liebknecht had developed a theory of the nation. These fathers of socialism displayed an attitude towards the nation which resulted from a mixture of ideas. Their adherence to the bourgeois revolutions of 1848, i.e. the ideas claiming the rights of independent existence, self-determination and self-defence for, at least, every great cultural nation, is evident, and they acknowledged this themselves. Lassalle gave the most penetrating description of socialism in relation to democracy and the nation. For him the 'free, independent nationalities' represented the roots of democracy. The workers who were fighting for democracy were simultaneously struggling for national unity, at least in Germany.

On the other hand, the fathers of socialism in Germany were governed by the idea that there is no *Vaterland* (fatherland) for workers. In his contributions to the *Neue Rheinische Zeitung* (1850) Marx had already seen the national revolution merely as a preliminary step in the direction of the proletarian revolution, but this idea was never fully integrated into his historical philosophy. Finally, Marx and Engels, as well as later socialist leaders, believed that each war between nation-states would lead to an increase in the workers' international solidarity and that the working class would thus profit from such wars.

Between 1848 and 1870 and for the entire period of the Second International, no consistent attention was given to the contradiction between socialism, nationality, and internationality. As for the German-French War of 1870–1, the Lassallean as well as the Eisenach social democrats declared that they would be willing to help to defend German territory against 'Napoleonic' and all other arbitrary acts. Later on, even when the so-called *Sozialistengesetz* (Bismarck's law of 1878 against the 'public danger caused by the social democrats') was in effect, social democrats in the German Reichstag (among them Auer, Bebel and Liebknecht) stated that social democrats were prepared to serve their fatherland in the same way as all other citizens. And in the summer of 1913, shortly before he died, Bebel reportedly said in a meeting of the Reichstag Budgetary Commission on the occasion of consultations on defence expenditures that nobody living in Germany would like to see his fatherland defenceless and abandoned to foreign powers.

Bernstein's programmatic statements that socialism is the legitimate heir of liberalism served to counterbalance the conceptual exclusion of the nation from social-democratic theories of the state, democracy, and society. The same function may be ascribed to the notions that – through the efforts of the Social Democratic Party, especially in educational affairs – the proletarians have grown up and become 'citizens'.

In Marx, there was strong emphasis on the fact that workers were not integrated into a national body; that they lived their lives apart from what was called the nation; and that for the bourgeoisie appeals to a concept of 'the nation' were instrumental in their class struggle.

Bernstein quoted the relevant Marxian phrases in his *Voraussetzungen des Sozialismus und die Aufgaben der Sozialdemokratie*;[2] but he gave them a completely different interpretation. Marx's doctrine, in Bernstein's eyes, was referring to the workers of the 1840s who had no civil rights or were excluded from public life. For Bernstein the later workers who had equal rights in federal and community elections had become 'co-owners' of the 'property' called the nation. To recapitulate, for Bernstein as well as for many other German socialist leaders, the workers were integrated into the nation-states from at least the late decades of the nineteenth century onwards.

With his interpretations Bernstein revitalized some of the ideas of J. G. Fichte, especially those from the 'Speeches to the German Nation', and of Lassalle. According to Bernstein, Fichte started from the individual's freedom and made nation the ultimate culmination of humanity. Thus, nation denotes that in a common effort all citizens do fight for freedom, realized within the context of a national community. Two arguments which Bernstein derived from Fichte should be mentioned here: firstly, that education is the decisive instrument in the nation-building process; secondly, that there is no contradiction between patriotism, love for one's homeland, and cosmopolitanism.

(*b*) BELIEF IN THE NATION AND INTERNATIONALISM. Not only Bernstein but also Georg von Vollmar and Bebel opposed any opinion that claimed incompatibility of belief in the nation with the workers' class interest or class consciousness. For them nationalism and internationalism were not contradictory beliefs. In 1899 Bernstein emphasized that the German social democrats should look after their class and national interests simultaneously and thus demonstrate their internationalism. Vollmar said at the Stuttgart Congress of the Socialist International (1907): 'Es ist nicht wahr, dass international gleich antinational ist. Es ist nicht wahr, dass wir kein Vaterland haben.' ('It is not true that international is the same as anti-national. It is not true that we have no fatherland.') Such statements must be related to the discussions within the Second International on international anti-militaristic actions and on the use of international general strikes as a weapon in the political fight. At the Stuttgart Congress and later up to World War I, these endless debates did not produce any binding declarations on international actions. In these discussions it was the German social democrats who wanted the other groups to agree on a platform that would concede the right of self-defence to a nation if attacked by an enemy. Formulations in this vein by Bebel can be found in the protocol of the Erfurt Party Congress of 1891.

What the social democratic leaders called internationalism was, in its essence, a philosophically conceived idealistic cosmopolitism. In actual politics their loyal attitude towards the nation, towards the Prussian-German nation-state, became effective – although in retrospect we can hardly assume that at that time the workers and their leaders were integrated into the state. However, many statements by party officials supported the nation-state as clearly as the one by Bebel on the occasion of the Essen SPD Congress in 1907:

> Wenn wir wirklich einmal das Vaterland verteidigen müssen, so verteidigen wir es, weil es unser Vaterland ist, als den Boden, auf dem wir leben, dessen Sprache wir sprechen, dessen Sitten wir besitzen, weil wir dieses Vaterland zu einem Land machen wollen, wie es nirgends in der Welt in ähnlicher Vollkommenheit und Schönheit besteht.

> (If one day we actually have to defend our country, then we will do so because it is our fatherland: on whose soil we live, whose language we speak, whose morals are ours – all because we want to make of this fatherland a country whose perfection and beauty is unsurpassed in all the world.)[3]

(c) LENINISM AND THE NATION. In the literature on the problems of socialism and the nation we very often find authors (lately Leszek Kolakowski) hinting at the fact that, of the socialist leaders of the Second International, it was those who either lived in a multinational state or belonged to repressed minority groups who stressed the nation question or the problem of nationality. Thus, the national question was of considerable concern to Austrians, Russians and Poles. Contrary to other socialist ideologues who rather neglected these concerns, Lenin took them into his strategic concept of the class struggle. Nevertheless, like Marx, he believed that the socialist revolution would solve all problems of nation as well.[4]

Rather early, in his work on the 'Characteristics of Economic Romanticism' (1897), Lenin had subordinated the national question to that of class antagonism. Later, in his 'Critical Remarks on the National Question' (written in 1913), he opposed the concept of a uniting 'national culture'. In his view there were two elements within national culture: the 'bourgeois' and the 'democratic' or 'socialist'. While the bourgeois commitment to 'national culture' was simply the outcome

of 'bourgeois fraud', the living conditions of the exploited masses produced a socialist and democratic ideology or national culture proper.
Thus it is not surprising that in his pamphlet 'On the Nationalities'
Right of Self-Determination' (which he wrote in 1914 and in which he
discussed, in particular, ideas of Rosa Luxemburg and Karl Kautsky),
Lenin argued for the convergence of all nationalities which existed
within the Russian state under the guidance of the Russian proletariat.
In referring to the London Agreement of 1896, he advocated the right
of self-determination for the nations (Nationalities) inside and outside
Russia; but he made it clear that self-determination could only provide
the basis for the 'amalgamation of the workers from all nations'.

The political relevance of Lenin's conceptions concerning socialism
and the nation was not fully visible until the end of his life, when in June
1920 he wrote the 'Original Draft of the Theses on the National and
Colonial Question'. These 'Theses', which Lenin had sent to Stalin,
were prepared for the Second Congress of the Communist International. Here Lenin utilized the national and colonial question for his
defence strategy, for his fight against the 'world bourgeoisie'. He defi-
nitely subordinated the nation question to the interests of Soviet power
and propagated the RSFSR (the Russian Social Democratic Party) as
the model for a federation of the workers from all nations. At the same
time he ridiculed freedom and equality in bourgeois democracies.
Furthermore, he divided the world into 'oppressed, dependent and
non-equal' nations, on the one hand, and 'exploiting' nations endowed
with colonial power, on the other.

With his class concept of the nation Lenin went in a direction quite
opposite to the one Stalin had taken in 1913. Stalin's early views of the
nation were not determined by a class theory; rather, he described
nations as composed of a variety of elements: an historically developed
community of men; a commonly shared language, territory, economy,
and culture as well as a specific psychological character as expressed in
the culture. The apparent lack of a class concept of the nation in Stalin
has been critically emphasized in recent Soviet discussions (since the
22nd Communist Party of the Soviet Union Congress in 1961) on the
national question.

Socialism in the German Democratic Republic (GDR) and the Concept of Nation

From 1966 on, having successfully prevented the planned exchange of
speakers with the West German Social Democratic Party (SPD), the

East German Socialist Unity Party (SED) has developed a programmatic political concept of the nation which serves both offensive and defensive purposes. Roughly speaking, it is a Leninist class concept of the nation which the SED uses to counterbalance its lack of legitimacy in the GDR (defensive function) and to direct the class struggle in the Federal Republic (FRG) (offensive function).

At the core of the SED's concept of nation (which can be traced back to the late 1940s), we find the German Democratic Republic workers' 'historical right of self-determination'. This means that the nation concept is reduced to an orthodox class scheme: The GDR is ruled by the working class and its party, the SED, while the FRG is dominated by the monopolbourgeoisie under the guidance of the trust barons, the rightist social democratic leaders and their helpers. Thus, according to the SED, there exists no national unity in Germany, no German nation any more. This has been the official GDR doctrine at least since Erich Honecker's speech at the 8th SED Congress in June 1971. The German nation is split into a socialist nation (GDR) and a bourgeois, i.e. a historically surpassed, nation (FRG). Furthermore, in their efforts to complete the socialist revolution, the workers in the GDR are compelled to settle the national question in their state by an alliance with all other working people, classes, and social strata in the GDR.

According to Honecker and other SED leaders (Kurt Hager, Albert Norden), the basis for class antagonism, in which hostile parties with irreconcilable national ideals are principally involved, has been eliminated in the GDR. Although the SED still admits the existence of class (or social) conflicts in the country, its representatives are also convinced that there is a common creed in the socialist nation which deactivates all conflict. The GDR is believed to be continuously developing those characteristics of a socialist nation which Lenin and Stalin laid down: a stable community of men, speaking the same language and living in the same territory; a specific economic system; a socialist culture which is rooted in the humanist traditions of German history.

After a long historical process of rapprochement between all socialist nations, especially the Soviet Union and other countries of East and South-east Europe, the GDR is supposed to merge into a 'unified fraternal league of free people' (einheitlicher Brüderbund freier Voelker). By thus internationalizing the nation concept, Honecker goes beyond the late Walter Ulbricht, who advocated instead the doctrine of a 'socialist state of the German nation'.

(*a*) SOME POLITICAL CONSEQUENCES. This concept of nation has a considerable impact on inter-German politics because, among other things, it claims that the working class together with its party, the SED, will establish a new and united Germany in a 'socialist way'. According to this doctrine the GDR represents the political homeland for all German workers and working people, even those living in the FRG. The 'progressive forces' in the FRG receive their right to self-determination from the 'party of the working class' in the GDR. Or, put otherwise, from this doctrine it follows that in Germany, irrespective of the FRG–GDR state border, there exists a class border-line.

From this point of view the class struggle has different aspects for the GDR leaders: firstly, it is a struggle of socialism (GDR) against capitalism or imperialism (FRG); secondly, it is a struggle of progressive versus reactionary forces within the FRG; thirdly, it is a struggle of the West German workers assisted by the East German workers and their party against the West German bourgeoisie and its supporters; fourthly, it may be seen as a 'conflict' of the East German workers and their party with bourgeois residua in the GDR – a social conflict which the SED has often fought by setting up the image of a West German class enemy.

Of course, a doctrine – even if eloquently presented – should not be confused with the realities of international politics. However, the SED doctrine on the nation may be indicative of an increasing significance which the German question may gain in international politics in the seventies. In the coming years it could well happen that – on the question of nation – the SED would try to carry out its Leninist strategy politically.

The SPD and the Nation

Contrary to the SED leaders, the SPD authorities in recent years have argued that despite the two German political and social systems, there exists one German nation. As often stated by Willy Brandt, the two German states have their place within the framework of one German nation, now as before. Brandt advanced three main arguments for the existence of one German nation: the persistent feeling of belonging together among people living in both systems (family bonds); the commonly shared political and cultural history, which especially includes the experiences of the 1933–45 period; the comparable duties of both Germanies, in so far as a European peace order is concerned.

For the SPD leaders too, the question of nation is bound to socialism. But they adhere to a democratic socialism which lives on the European socialist and humanist tradition. Democratic socialism renounces the orthodox concept of the class struggle as well as that of the dictatorship of the proletariat; it also opposes the ideology of Marxism–Leninism in its totalitarian version. These fundamentals are agreed upon by all SPD leaders, however they may differ in their individual political standpoints. Now as before, democratic socialism for them can only be conceived as built on the principles of individual freedom, justice and solidarity and must be based on a pluralism of world views and on toleration. Democratic socialism also includes the desire to democratize further the social system; it thus aims at further materializations of the principles of equality and co–determination (participation). Democratic socialism is oriented towards social reforms and not revolutions. In the FRG, as acknowledged by the SPD, the institutional framework for such desires is the democratic and social *Rechtsstaat*. Thus, the SPD's socialism is not supporting anti–state emotions; it rather wants to develop the democratic and social components of the FRG Constitution. It aims at a reasonable balance between general public interests and particular group or individual interests.

We may conclude from these remarks that the SPDs concept of nation is part of a broader social outlook. However, it is not an outcome of Leninist class theory, but rather is embedded in the – albeit vague – theory of the democratic and social *Rechtsstaat*. The legitimacy of the state as it exists in the FRG remains undisputed. And more: in the view of the SPD representatives the further strengthening of this state's legitimacy should be achieved not only by further controllable acts of legitimization, but also by materially developing the democratic and social dimensions of the state. Several prominent social democrats in the FRG assume that in the long run these latter tendencies will lead to the decay of nationalism in Europe and promote the emergence of a European political consciousness.

Concluding Remarks

Reviewing the ground covered above, we find that the concept of the nation within socialism has never been so defined as to exclude internationalism completely. This holds for what we have here termed 'democratic' socialism; but it is also true for the totalitarian version of socialism. Generally speaking, this state of affairs has contributed to the concept's elasticity and multiple application; it is also responsible for never–ending socialist discussions on the concept of the nation.

Despite a certain terminological confusion there seem to be two versions of the nation concept which can be distinguished in principle: the class concept of the nation (i.e. the concept that strongly emphasizes internationalism) and the state concept.

Historically speaking, the class concept of the nation is related more to the Leninist version of socialism, while the state concept is more embodied in democratic socialism.

At present we find specific manifestations of both concepts playing their roles on the stage of the divided Germany. While the SED employs a class concept of the nation, the SPD resorts to a state concept. However, as far as nationalism-internationalism antithesis is concerned, both display a certain flexibility.

The SED, although loudly propagating the class concept of the nation, is undoubtedly also holding on to a state concept. And on the part of the social democrats we can observe a state concept of the nation which is kept open for transformation into an inter-state concept. In contrast to SED internationalism, however, the SPD inter-state concept does not derive its internationalism from class theory.

SOCIALISM AND NATIONALISM

Vladimir V. Kusin

We have been invited to comment on relationships between several different factual and conceptual notions (technology, planning, market, nation, ownership, equality, etc.) and the 'socialist idea'. Which socialist idea? Whose socialist idea? Saint-Simon's? Marx's? Bernstein's? Jaurès's? Lenin's? Stalin's? Dubček's? Brezhnev's? The New Left's? Eric Heffer's? Dick Taverne's? The exercise appears to me singularly futile. As long as someone does not define the term of reference more precisely, we cannot measure anything against it, although, of course, one can spend a lifetime comparing socialisms.

The elusion goes even further since the other concept suggested to me, nationalism, also means different things to different people. Which interpretation are we to consider? The awareness, 'essentially secular and essentially democratic',[1] that gradually superimposed itself on tribalism and replaced loyalty to the Church and the ruler by loyalty to the nation? The defensive reaction to German, Ottoman, Russian or Soviet conquest of Central and Eastern Europe? The combination of 'myths about the past and the dreams about the future'?[2] The 'revolutionary dogma' or 'artificially fostered group feeling' that 'has to be inculcated by education and propaganda into each member of each generation'?[3] The forcible removal of men, women and children from their homes in order to create homogeneous national units,[4] Venizelos, Hitler, Stalin or Potsdam fashion? Or, to end a list that is much longer, Mr Ceauşescu's insistence on freedom of foreign political gesture for the sake of something he himself may not be quite certain about?

In other words, the wealth of comparable permutations militates against generalised meditation. What good would transpire, for example, if we juxtaposed an unmatchable pair? Moreover, there will always be enough special cases to invalidate an abstract analysis. It reminds me of the Czech grammar. As soon as you succeed in teaching a complex rule to a brave student, you have to start reciting a long list of exceptions.

Nevertheless, one learns not to avoid discussions on a general plane, even if only because so many student promoters of permanent revolution and the appended internationalism challenge our right to deal with the world *in concreto*. I must, however, make one reservation arising from reasons of competence. My argument will be based on Central and East European experience. Its validity for any other part of the world or a different constellation of power will not be claimed.

Professor Kolakowski's outline suggests incompatibility between Soviet-type socialism and national sovereignty as well as an inherent conflict between communism and national awareness. It may, but need not, follow that a happy coexistence of national sovereignty and democratic socialism is possible. Broadly speaking – and always mindful of the stubborn peculiarity of specific cases at specific moments of time – I would agree with both propositions.

The theory emerging from East European reformism (Polish, Hungarian, Czech and Yugoslav) can be convincingly argued to be better equipped than the Soviet system to solve all of the problems which the countries in question face in the 1970s. In practice there is one crucial exception: reformed East European socialism cannot as yet ensure its own sheer survival, something which Soviet communism has done successfully. Democratic socialism in Eastern Europe has thus the great handicap of having been frozen on the drawing board while Soviet communism has long emerged from the research and development workshop. None the less, pilot schemes have been put to practical tests, and not all have met with a sad end.

Emancipation from Soviet influence (to a differing degree, from more elbow room in external affairs or economy to full-scale independence of political decision-making) evidently concurs with the mainstream of reformist striving. A democratically socialist programme of action in Eastern Europe must entail a national element because Soviet authority has demonstrably exceeded the accepted dimensions of an international alliance. More 'nationalism' and less 'internationalism' is a part of the reform, be it open or unsaid. Implementation of this desideratum represents one of the trickiest tasks the reformers face. Rather than knowing how to go about it, they know what they must not do.

Where applicable, i.e. in multinational states or countries with strong minorities, such a programme would also feature a prescription to alleviate and hopefully to remove causes of national strife within the country's borders. No entirely novel policy to guarantee national peace has been devised, and success would once again depend on how benign a content the central (federal) government granted to such time-honoured frameworks as self-government, industrialization, distribution of the national income and indigenous education.

The Yugoslav warning looms high, more recently complemented by the danger that centripetal suppression of nationalism can fairly easily turn into all-round counter-reformation. Whether Yugoslav-type federation would have worked better in conditions of political pluralism is difficult to say. Open competition of, say, a nationalist party (or parties) with a federalist party would certainly provide an outlet for national passions, possibly less damaging than pent-up feelings in an artificial political monolith. In a one-party state all conflicts, including national strife, must find reflection within that party. One should also not forget that, the Soviet Union aside, Yugoslavia is unique in Eastern Europe in that it comprises more than two full-nation elements. Czechoslovakia has two (in addition to minorities), two countries embrace substantial minorities (Romania and Hungary) and four have none or almost none within their present borders (East Germany, Poland, Bulgaria and Albania).

If we probe deeper, hoping that the exercise will show us what every political system in the area, including all kinds of socialism, has, or would have, to cope with, we discover in fact three types of outward-oriented nationalism. There is anti-Sovietism, as mentioned above, undoubtedly the most potent of them all. Then there still exist national feelings which hark back to past subjugations by no longer existing empires and colonial powers (German/Austrian, Turkish and Phanariot Greek, and Italian; in some areas the anti-Soviet feelings of today are amplified by anti-Russian echoes of the past). And finally there is national friction in the intricate network of former relationships between national units which now belong to different states (especially Slovak–Hungarian, Hungarian–Romanian, Albanian–Yugoslav, Bulgarian–Serbian and Polish–Czech). Smaller national entanglements are too numerous even to mention.

Four communities pursue national aspirations *vis-à-vis*, and sometimes against, each other within a joint state ('internal' nationalism): the Serbs and the Croats in Yugoslavia (with the added complication of involvement by other nationalities), and the Czechs and Slovaks in Czechoslovakia.

Finally there is the special case of East Germany where ideological *Abgrenzung* has and will have to vie with the pull of national gravitation.

Not all these national quarrels naturally propel themselves with the same intensity. Some have remained acute throughout the era of communism, others stay potent but are blanketed by a heavy load of other worries, yet others wax and wane, and some have reached the threshold of disappearance. Nevertheless, even if the governments of the area and their patrons in Moscow had no problems with the economy, the younger generation, the political dissidents and the cultural intellectuals, they could hardly complain of lack of preoccupation. (Note that I am not bringing in the Ukrainians or the Baltic nations, East European as they undeniably are. Suffice it to point to A. Marchenko's *Testimony*: members of these national communities are well represented in the various Soviet institutions of incarceration.)

Why should this be so, twenty-five years after the introduction of communist power? Has the recipe for the 'solution of the national question' and its replacement by internationalism failed so miserably?

The answer must be yes and no. The idea that economic advancement coupled with an internationalist ideology originally devised for Germany, England and France and adapted beyond recognition on Russian experience can bring about a state of brotherly bliss has proved largely abortive. It simply cannot work in the form of a supra-national hierarchy which derives its power relations from the national communism of the strongest member. That Soviet communism is national communism there can be no doubt. Let me quote E. H. Carr at this point: 'Once the workers' state was effectively established, "socialism in one country" was the logical corollary. The subsequent history of Russia and the tragicomedy of the Communist International are an eloquent tribute to the solidarity of the alliance between nationalism and socialism.'[5]

In fact the wheel of history has once again turned screechingly on its prophets, Herder, Schleiermacher, Kollár and the other romantic eulogizers of the exclusiveness and messianism of the Slavs as the chosen people. Communism, having found the internationalism of its doctrine impracticable, lifted Russia on to the pedestal of supreme nationalism. The nineteenth-century romantic dream came to be fulfilled in a hideously distorted manner.

Not that all of the nineteenth-century Slav nationalists were overwhelmed by Russian-led Panslavism. František Palacký, himself called the Father of the Nation, sensed the power-political undertone with an almost uncanny prophetic clarity. Rejecting a fusion of Czech aspirations with German nationalism, he wrote to the Frankfurt Parliament in April 1848:

> You know, gentlemen, which power holds the entire Eastern expanses of our part of the world; you know that this power, already grown to vastness, waxes every decade stronger and more powerful of itself and in itself, more so than can happen in the countries of the West; that, its own core beyond almost any attacker's reach, it has long become dangerous to its members . . . [It] threatens at an ever faster pace to beget and establish universal monarchy, an unfathomably and unspeakably evil thing, a disaster without measure and limit, which I, a Slav in body and soul, for the sake of the good in man, would not regret less if this monarchy were Slavic.[6]

Whatever its vicissitudes and disguises, nineteenth-century East European (non-Russian) nationalism was essentially secular and essentially democratic. 'Fundamentally . . . the idea of nationality contains within itself that of the sovereignty of the people.'[7] Or, as Arnold Toynbee put it, 'The spirit of nationality is a sour ferment of the new wine of democracy in the old bottles of tribalism.'[8]

This inherent, traditional-oriented conflict between superior national communism and subordinate communist nationalisms, let alone democratic nationalisms, cannot be resolved within the limits of the existing ideological gospel and the present political configuration. It even gets further entangled in the wake of critical situations. Witness Czechoslovakia and the Brezhnev Doctrine, Yugoslavia and its post-1948 history, and Romania in relation to the Sino–Soviet rift.

Internationalism of the first phase of communism, before the seizure of power in Russia, works in theory, but not in practice. It had to be abandoned in Russia (and is being abandoned by China) and it would have to be discarded by our New Left friends should they, God forbid, find themselves in power. It looks paradoxical, but socialism was international in the nineteenth century; it is national in the twentieth.

Communism understands 'the national question' as a tactical problem. With offensive simplicity it pushes national feelings around as if they had not evolved over centuries of passionate and bitter experience. National awareness is a long-term historical category, communist power politics a short-term one.

Take, for example, the fifty years of the Czechoslovak Communist

Party. It accepted independence of the Czechoslovak state in the first few years of its existence (under Šmeral), then it declared the country imperialist and professed national alienation for a decade only to change its attitude – unpopular and untenable – into a 'Defence of the Republic' under the impact of the Seventh Congress of the Communist International. It switched back to internationalism when World War II was labelled imperialist by Moscow, resumed the national cloak after Hitler's attack on Russia, put itself fully at the service of socialist internationalism, by then understood as supreme loyalty to Moscow, from 1948 – 67 ('With the Soviet Union for ever – and never otherwise!'), embraced some of the country's democratic national tradition under Dubček, and finally endorsed the Brezhnev Doctrine having been invaded by Russia. (Nancy Whittier Heer, writing about Soviet historiography, speaks about the 'attraction-repulsion' syndrome in the communist approach to the national past, arising from and coupled with the reflection of current policies in historical writing.)[9] This kind of zig-zag politicking may appear natural to someone who sees the 'national question' subserving a superior strategic aim, but it will seem positively revolting to the man in the street, let alone an intellectual steeped in his nation's cause. This kind of intellectual is not a rare bird in Eastern Europe and, incidentally, not quite so comic as the West often sees him.[10]

Equally oblivious of the reality of fact and human sentiment is the worn cliché about respect for the 'national peculiarities' within a wider 'internationalist' striving for power. While there certainly were periods in the life of young nations in which they had to dissociate themselves from others in order to attain the standing of a separate entity when they themselves stressed their own house-styles, the real point at issue now cannot be interpreted as measuring institutions, processes and operational modes against an artificially created, unitary socialism. Whatever we may think about the liabilities and assets of a world organized on the basis of national units, no once-for-all improvement can transpire from the infliction of drastic supra-nationalism.

Communism expects national exigencies to disappear and national aspirations to be automatically fulfilled with the 'building of socialism' and the accompanying removal of material grievances. We must give credit where it is due. Practically all national problems in history have had some material background, such as that arising from inequality, poverty or avarice. Advancement of economic well-being cannot but reduce the vehemence of a nationalist stance. There will always be those for whom a hearty meal, let alone a car and a weekend hut, dissolve a less tangible dedication. Education also bears on the younger generations who emerge to commanding posts in public life less marked with passion than their fathers. On the other hand, better economic conditions and a higher standard of education breed the propensity to political preoccupation. Barbara Ward observed: 'Communism does not act as a dissolvent [of nationalism.] On the contrary, by modernizing the economy, increasing literacy, and creating a sense of popular participation, it can even become an agent of national self-consciousness. At first, confronting these paradoxes, the true believer rejects the evidence in favour of the dream. Later, he accommodates himself to it.'[11] Thus the old nationalisms are being pushed out. They were trained on national constitution, seizure or retention of territory, purity of language, homogeneity of religion, native education. New ones take their place, much more orientated towards political participation.

To recapitulate:

1. The internationalism of communist theory has given way to nationalism in practice. There is no such thing as internationalist communism any longer.

2. In Eastern Europe non-communist nationalisms have been changing; their content reveals an increasing inclination towards political participation, and they have largely become anti-Russian.

3. The reform movements in Eastern Europe incorporate an attempt to blend nationalism with enlightened communism. In doing so, they find some common ground with traditional national consciousness.

4. Russian national communism is in conflict with both.

What about democratic socialism? Socialism of any colouring has no chance of 'solving the nationality question' as long as it does not recognize that the international socialist community must not be organized on the lines of 'democratic centralism'. As the 'leading role of the party' forms the insurmountable obstacle to full internal reform, so does primacy of one socialist country in a supra-national bloc. Freedom of choice between political parties, possibly coupled with a mechanism of direct democracy on socio-economic lines, must be matched by a similar arrangement in international relations. Nations must be permitted to vote communists into power and out, just as they must be free to join or leave an international commonwealth. The projection of 'self-management' on to the international scale may represent the democratic socialist alternative to proletarian/communist internationalism.

The difficulty is not only that there appears to be no socialist theory to express all this, but above all that no one knows how to bring the coveted state of affairs about. Experience broadly hints at circumspect gradualism as the only possible road. Eastern Europe would be greatly helped if a similar development occurred in the West.

Some people abhor nationalism as a matter of principle, and they have much to base their attitude on. Without engaging in a detailed discussion, I believe that nationalism is manageable by a non-imperialist democracy in conditions of advanced economy. So would be its democratic socialist variant.

─── 12 ───

LEISURE AS THE MEANS OF PRODUCTION

Michael Harrington

Socialism, if it is to be found anywhere, is located on the far side of automation. Leisure time is its characteristic means of production.

In his *Marxism in Modern France*, George Lichtheim wrote that the bourgeoisie was 'already the bearer of a new form of economic organization', but that the working class is not.[1] Indeed, Lichtheim goes on to argue that the original socialist critique was not directed so much against capitalism as against industrialism. Eventually, he concludes, Marx understood that 'the curse of mechanical labour (and the bureaucratization which goes with it) can at best be diminished, but not removed.'[2] This analysis is, like almost everything Lichtheim says, brilliant and suggestive, but I am not persuaded by it. Or at least, I remain ambivalent about the question which he poses.

In what follows, I will suggest that there is a 'new form of economic organization' associated with socialism and that it is automation. This insight, I will try to show, is not new but can be found in Marx's writings. It points to the notion that leisure time is the unique socialist mode of production. That idea has been denied, or obscured, for functional reasons in the communist world where, from Lenin to the present, there has been a 'productionist' emphasis which is basically hostile to conceptions of the value of leisure. But in view of current trends visible in the advanced technological nations that original socialist dream is at least possible and perhaps, just as Marx thought, even a necessity.

It could be that the technology of the future will allow man no other choice except to be free.

I

In Chapter XIII of Volume I of *Das Kapital*, Marx makes a brilliant historical and theoretical analysis of the development of technology under capitalism. He describes in detail how the worker is degraded to an appendage of the machine (thus deepening themes first stated in the Paris Manuscripts of 1843–4) and asserts that

> 'The factory code, in which capital privately and arbitrarily formulates its autocracy over the worker without that separation of powers so beloved by the bourgeoisie or that even more beloved system of representation ... is only the capitalist caricature of that social regulation of the labour process which became necessary with co-operation on a large scale and the use of common means of labour, namely machines. In place of the lash of the slave master there is the punishment book of the overseer.'[3]

This discussion of technology in *Capital* is clearly foreshadowed, and worked out in much greater detail, in the *Grundrisse*. In that treatment of the subject, Marx makes explicit his analysis of automation and the way in which it contradicts the very structure of capitalist production. I recall it here at some length not simply because it has enormous historical interest but because it is a relevant point of departure for the consideration of the problems of socialism and technology in the late twentieth, and even the twenty-first, century.

The 'last metamorphosis' of the means of labour, Marx writes in the *Grundrisse*,[4] 'is the machine, or more precisely *an automatic system of machinery* ...' 'The differentia specifica of the machine is not at all, as is the case with the means of labour, to facilitate the activity of the worker upon the object; but this activity is now so designed as to facilitate the labour of the machine, its action upon the raw materials ... The activity of the workers is reduced to a mere abstraction of activity, on all sides determined and regulated by the movement of the machinery ...' (p. 584). 'Through production in great quantities,' Marx continues, 'which is part of the machine process, all relationship of the product to the immediate needs of the producers, and thereby to immediate use-values, vanishes ...' (p. 585). 'The accumulation of knowledge and of skill, the general productive powers of the social brain, are absorbed in capital and counterposed to the worker ...' (p. 586).

So far this is a familiar analysis. But then Marx broadens it to include automation and argues that there is a 'contradiction between the basis of bourgeois production (the value measure) and the development of that production itself. Machines, etc.' Through the application of science to production, 'Labour no longer appears as incorporated in production, but rather man related himself to the production process as observer and regulator (*Wächter und Regulator*)' (p. 592). 'As soon as labour in its immediate form has ceased to be the great source of wealth,' Marx argues, 'then labour time can no longer be its measure and exchange value cannot be the measure of use value.' The new measure of wealth is 'the free development of individuality, not the reduction of necessary labour time in order to increase surplus labour, but the reduction of the necessary labour of society to a minimum which is adequate for the artistic, scientific, etc., development of the individual through free time and the means which are provided.'(p. 593).

'Actual wealth,' Marx continues, 'is the developed productive power of all individuals. Labour time is no longer the measure of wealth, but disposable time. *Labour time as the measure of wealth* assumes that wealth itself is based upon poverty . . .' (p. 596). This conclusion is similar to, but arrived at in a different fashion from, a famous passage in Volume III of *Capital.*

> The kingdom of freedom first begins there where work which is determined by necessity and some outside purpose ceases; it lies, therefore, beyond the sphere of material production as such. . . . Freedom in this sphere can only emerge through socialized man, the associated producers, who regulate their interaction with nature rationally, bring it under their community control [*gemeinschaftliche Kontrolle*] instead of being ruled by it as by a blind power; and whose work is accomplished with the least expenditure of effort and under conditions worthy of and adequate to their human nature. But this still remains the kingdom of necessity. Beyond this there lies that development of human powers which is its own excuse for being [*die sich als Selbstzweck gilt*], the true kingdom of freedom which can, however, only bloom on the basis of the kingdom of necessity. The shortening of the working day is its fundamental precondition.[5]

There are many things which can be said of these remarkable passages. I will confine myself to a few comments which relate to the theme of socialism and technology and help explicate my basic thesis about leisure time as the distinctively socialist means of production.

First, Marx's anticipation of automation is remarkable. By extrapolating mid-nineteenth-century trends, Marx anticipated the assembly line (which dates from Henry Ford's Highland Park, Michigan plant of 1914) and even automated production. His description of the worker in a continuous flow technology as a 'watcher and regulator' corresponds to recent American experience in the chemical industry.[6]

Moreover, Marx was right that the society would have to encourage consumption if it was not to be ruined by its prodigious – and science-based – productivity.

Even the remarks about the breakdown of the labour time measure in a period of automated technology have been borne out. Daniel Bell, a sophisticated but resolute critic of Marx, wrote in 'Work and Its Discontents':

> Most important, perhaps, there may be an end, too, to the measurement of work. Modern industry began not with the factory but with the measurement of work. When the worth of the product was defined in production units, the worth of the worker was similarly gauged. . . . But under automation, with continuous flow, a worker's worth can no longer be evaluated in production units. Hence output-incentive plans, with their involved measurement techniques, may vanish. In their place, as Adam Abruzzi foretells, may arise a new work morality. Worth will be defined not in terms of a 'one best way', not by the slide rule and stop watch. . . . but on the basis of planning and organizing. . . . Here the team, not the individual worker will assume a new importance. . . .[7]

But perhaps most important for the view of socialism and technology which I will develop in this paper, these passages from Marx make it clear that he saw free time as the essential liberation and that, in the analysis of the *Grundrisse*, he believed that automated production would make such an emancipation not simply possible, but also necessary. That is what Marx said and, more to the point, I think that Marx was, is, and perhaps will be right.

II

Why, if the classic socialist tradition is so clear on this point, has it been obscured? For it is certainly true that many who consider themselves in the Marxian tradition not only disagree with Marx on this rather crucial point but seem to be ignorant of his attitude. One profound reason, in this area as in so many others, has to do with the Russian Revolution.

The revolution took place under conditions which Marx would have regarded as impossible for the construction of socialism.[8] Instead of a victorious working class socializing the abundance of an advanced economy, a Bolshevik minority was confronted with the problems of hunger, and then of underdevelopment generally, in the most backward of European capitalist societies. As a result, Lenin's interpretation of Marx – and later Stalin's totalitarian reading of the socialist tradition – stressed the productionist aspect of Marxism. And given the enormous authority which the revolution exercised over socialists around the world, particularly in its heroic period, an entire generation was educated in this Leninist, and then Stalinist, transformation of Marx's meaning.

Lenin wrote in 1918:

> The task that the Soviet Government must set the people in all of its scope is – learn to work. The Taylor system, the last word of capitalism in this respect, like all capitalist progress, is a combination of the refined brutality of bourgeois exploitation and a number of the greatest scientific achievements in the field of analysing mechanical motions during work, the elimination of superfluous and awkward motions, the elaboration of correct methods of work, the introduction of the best system of accounting and control, etc. The Soviet Republic must at all costs adopt all that is valuable in the achievements of science and technology in this field. . . . We must organize in Russia the study and teaching of the Taylor system and systematically try it out and adapt it to our own ends.[9]

This statement is, of course, but one expression of a basic contradiction of the Russian Revolution: that a government speaking in the name of socialism undertook to introduce that labour discipline which capitalism had imposed upon the working class with all the resulting alienation and misery that Marx had described. It proved impossible to resolve this contradiction and Soviet society turned into a new form of class rule. But in the process, Marxist–Leninist authority had been provided for the proposition that socialist technology would be even more rational, planned and dehumanizing than capitalist technology.

In more recent years, this trend in communist thought has been facilitated by the cybernetic revolution. Thus the East German philosopher Georg Klaus, sees automation as the way to end alienation. He rightly points out that the new production systems can end routine and boring labour. But he fails to take account of the degree to which the bureaucracy supervising this process can itself become an alien force counterposed to the lives of the majority of people. He does not, as Marx did, understand the potential for the reification of human and social life in even the best of scientifically planned orders. Thus Klaus modernizes the Leninist tradition and its attempt to incorporate Taylorism into Marxism.[10]

There are some democratic implications in this cybernetic interpretation of Marxism – the notion of 'feedback' and self-regulation implies that there should be some autonomy in the basic institutions of the society – but they are usually contained within a technocratic, and undemocratic, model. As Peter Ludz remarks of Klaus' protest against arbitrary decision-making in East Germany, 'the typical limitations and the hesitant, qualified character of this protest, characteristic of the development of institutionalized revisionism, can be seen in the fact that rational decisions are criticized only when they appear to counter the criterion of increased performance.'[11] In other words, the productionist emphasis is still paramount and the notion of 'scientific management', created by Taylor for the efficient regulation of capitalist society, is still alive and well within the communist world.

Ironically, the emergence of the computer caused Oskar Lange, the classic theorist of the function of the market under socialism, to adopt a much more centralized model of planning towards the end of his life. 'The market process with its cumbersome *atonements* appears old-fashioned. Indeed, it may be considered as a computing device of the pre-electronic age.'[12] Here again the gain in efficiency is paramount (as indeed it must be in a less developed economy like Lange's Poland); the Marxian dream of a technology so abundant that, in some respects at least, it burst through the confines of cost accountancy is totally absent.

So the limitations of history – and above all the impossibility of socializing poverty or underdevelopment so as to create a society of fraternity and classlessness – resulted, not simply in totalitarian regimes, but in a particular reading (or more precisely, misreading) or the Marxian tradition. In the process, its central theme of the liberating potential of technology was forgotten, or else subordinated to the drive for more and more production.

But what of that Marxist dream itself? It is not enough to demonstrate that it has been ignored or underplayed by this or that political movement. One must also examine its relevance to the last quarter of the twentieth century – and to the twenty-first century.

III

The United States, Gertrude Stein once remarked, is the oldest nation on the face of the earth, for it has lived in the future longer than anyone else. In what follows, I will take the trends of American technology as indicators, not of the inevitable path of development in the rest of the globe, but as the most important single case in point of the potential of science in the productive process. In doing so, I will, of course, make some unavoidable distortions. It is, for example, difficult to imagine a uniform level of world technology and therefore no one instance can serve as a model. Still, I think the American experience does reveal important tendencies which, in one way or another, must be faced by socialists. And with the rise of the multinational corporation, and the attendant export of technology within the advanced (capitalist and communist) nations, I think my approach has considerable relevance.

In the 35 years prior to World War II, output per man hour in the private economy in the United States rose at a rate of 2 per cent a year. Between 1947 and 1965, productivity increased by about 3·2 per cent a year. As the National Commission on Technology, Automation and Economic Progress reported to President Lyndon Johnson in 1966, 'Growth at 2 per cent a year doubles in 36 years; growth at 2·5 per cent doubles in 28 years; growth at 3 per cent doubles in 24 years. . . . not much more than half a working lifetime. . . .'[13] Part of this increase in productivity was utilized to increase leisure time in America. Participation in the labour force has been declining modestly for youth between 16 and 24 years of age (and almost 40 per cent of the young entered a college in the fall of 1972); the average weekly hours worked in non-agricultural establishments dropped from 39·8 hours in 1950 to 37·0 hours in 1972.[14]

Thus mechanization, automation and cybernation have not yet had a dramatic impact on the rations of work and leisure time. They have, however, profoundly affected the class structure of American society. The most recent government data indicate that manufacturing jobs decreased from 27 per cent of the total in 1960 to 24·4 per cent in 1970. As an article in an AFL–CIO journal described the trend,

> Jobs for the skilled craftsman, the blue-collar worker whose skill, income and educational level made him 'the middle American', are disappearing. They are being replaced by jobs for the accountant, the computer programmer and the salesman at one level and for the filling station attendant, janitor or airline porter at the other. Thus the census data reveals that the United States is on the road towards becoming a nation of 'researchers and soda jerks' . . .'[15]

There are some surprising aspects to this change. Assembly line labour is now confined to less than 2 per cent of the American work force. However, the new white-collar work is, for the most part, not independent and creative. The office has become more routinized and factory-like; and the new jobs – medical technicians, teachers aides, computer key punch operator – do not have 'professional' characteristics.[16] As a result, there has been an enormous amount of discussion in the United States in recent times of the problem of alienation.

This debate over alienation, it must be emphasized, has not been restricted to intellectuals. Perhaps one of the best statements of the problem came from Malcolm Denise, a Vice-President of Ford, in 1969:

> Many employees, particularly the young ones, are increasingly reluctant to put up with factory conditions, despite the significant improvements we've made in the physical environment of our plants. Because they are unfamiliar with the harsh economic facts of earlier years, they have little regard for the consequences if they take a day or two off. The general increase in real wage levels in our economy has afforded more alternatives for satisfying economic needs. There is also, again especially among the younger employees, a growing reluctance to accept a strict authoritarian shop discipline. This is not just a shop phenomenon, rather it is a manifestation in our shops of a trend we see all about us among today's youth.[17]

Denise is right, I think, to link the discontent on the assembly line to the general phenomenon of the youth culture. The development of technology, the achievement of a relative affluence (and it must be remembered that the majority of the American people, including almost the entire working class, is *not* affluent), the breakdown in the Puritan ethic, are subverting that attitude towards work which was once essential to capitalism. The Ford Vice-President and Marx describe the same phenomenon, the former as a worried production engineer, the latter as a humanist prophet: that the society of the future as one glimpses its origins in the present will be incompatible with the time-studies division of labour – with Taylorism – and will be characterized by a demand for leisure time.

However, it is not at all simple to deal with this trend in concrete situations today. More and more of American management is becoming concerned with alienation on the job since that affects production. Some trade unionists, the leadership of the Auto Workers among them, are trying to formulate new demands with regard to democracy on the job: an end to the arbitrary authority of the foreman, the possibility of elected foremen, etc. But many unionists are suspicious of proposals for 'job enrichment', regarding them as a management device to extract more work at the same pay and thereby prepare the way for the reduction of the plant labour force. Those fears are not idle. In most of the experiments which have been carried out, increasing job satisfaction was a means of decreasing the number of employed.[18]

Perhaps the classic example of the kind of conflict these changes can generate is found on the automobile assembly line. From the very beginning, the workers have been trying to figure out a way to perform their task in less time than the company allocates for it. Once that is discovered a man can 'bank' a minute, or even a few minutes, and be able to smoke a cigarette, to snatch some seconds from the discipline of the line. But management is aware of these practices and looks over the worker's shoulder to steal the secrets of his private productivity from him. Once those are learned, they can then be made obligatory for everyone and that margin of minutes is taken away from the creative employee. Therefore there is a profound tradition of concealing productivity improvements and of being hostile to them when they are introduced by management.

Thus, it is not easy to deal with this situation within a profit-maximizing framework. That is why the most fervid demands to be made by the American auto workers in their current contract negotiations both concern time. The younger workers are demanding an end to compulsory overtime; the older workers are rallying to the slogan, 'Thirty and Out' (retirement after thirty years at no matter what age). There is, in short, a tendency to see the greatest gains not in the humanization of industrial work but through decreasing the amount of working time required of people.

These trends, among other things, convince me that the basic Marxist attitude is compelling. Freedom will not be discovered within technology, but by means of it and outside it, i.e. through the diminution of the working day and a vast, qualitative increase in leisure time. Put in terms of an ideal – which should help us better to define the approximations of it – socialism seeks the abolition of compulsory labour. Its distinctive means of production is leisure.

IV

Positing such an ideal is simple enough. Acting on it is extremely difficult. Let me just take up one or two of the complexities that must be faced.

In a series of projections made by the futurist Herman Kahn, the outline of a 'Leisure-Oriented "Postindustrial" Society' is described:

> 7·5 hour working day
> 4 working days per week
> 39 working weeks per year
> 10 legal holidays
> 3-day weekends
> 13 weeks per year vacation
> (or 147 working days and 218 days off/year)

This would mean that a man would spend

> 40 per cent of his days on vocation
> 40 per cent of his days on an avocation
> 20 per cent relaxing.[19]

Kahn's estimates, it should be remembered, do not assume a radical–socialist – change in the planning processes of society. These figures are therefore suggested as one possible development based on an extrapolation of present tendencies in American *capitalism*.

Several comments are relevant to this last point. If there is such a vast expansion of leisure within a culture still permeated by commercial priorities, it could have very sad consequences. There is already a class struggle of sorts in the United States over scarce free time resources, for example some municipalities are passing legislation making it impossible for outsiders (who are more likely to be less affluent and possibly members of a minority group) to gain access to beaches. And the shoddiness of commercialized entertainment is already apparent. Therefore a paradox emerges: that there must be the most careful planning if free time is going to be spontaneous.

Herbert Marcuse has remarked on this problem, though I think he treats it too pessimistically. After quoting Marx from the *Grundrisse* on how leisure will transform man 'into a different subject', Marcuse comments, 'Today, advanced industrial society is creating free time, but the possessor of the free time is not a 'different subject'; in the capitalist and communist systems, the subject of free time is subordinated to the same norms and powers that rule the realm of necessity. The mature Marxian conception . . . appears idealistic and optimistic.'[20]

What Marcuse says is certainly true – but I am not at all sure that it proves his point. Late capitalist society is being forced by the exigencies of its own technological genius – and by the dignity of its workers – to invest some money in leisure. But it does so within a context which distributes and corrupts that leisure, in part at least, according to the commercial priorities of the economy. Communist society is – and I am sure Lenin would not appreciate the irony more than fifty years after the October Revolution – still at a Taylorite stage of development and even produces philosophies which put productionism at the very heart of the value system. This demostrates something which would not have surprised Marx: that the results of technological revolution within a class society are inevitably perverted to some degree. But does it prove that the vision of a society located on the far side of technology – a socialist society – is not relevant? I think not.

It would be comforting to conclude that the inexorable development of modern technology makes the transcending of it an historic certainty. Such a faith is possible only for those who have not noticed the twentieth century. Still, one can soberly and reasonably say that there are tendencies visible at this very moment in advanced capitalist technology which make the seemingly utopian Marxian vision of a society of free time practical. Socialists should understand that the freedom they seek does not lie within that technology but just beyond it and then – be it in the work of elaborating a union contract or in debating the proportions of work and leisure in society as a whole – should struggle for the hopeful possibility.

THE IMPLICATIONS OF MODERN TECHNOLOGY FOR SOCIALISM:
Comments on Michael Harrington's Paper

Wlodzimierz Brus

My comments on Professor Harrington's paper 'Leisure as Means of Production' are presented on the assumption that his paper is an attempt to examine the implications of modern technology for socialism.

Michael Harrington's answer consists – as I understand it – of four basic elements:

1. 'Freedom will not be discovered within technology, but ... outside it.'

2. 'Socialism seeks the abolition of compulsory labour. Its distinctive means of production is leisure.' The actual development of technology both confirms Marx's prediction in this respect and creates the necessary conditions for achieving the socialist ideal of the 'true kingdom of freedom'.

3. This kingdom of freedom arrives, however, not as a simple result of technological development. 'If there is such a vast expansion of leisure within a culture still permeated by commercial priorities (as in present-day primarily capitalist American society) ... it could have very sad consequences.' So, the historic role of socialism is to transform these material potentialities of the 'kingdom of freedom' into reality by means of changing the structure of goals, the principles of distribution, etc.

These three points constitute the main body of the argument. (Point 4, which will be dealt with below, concerns the assessment of the East European reality in the light of these general conclusions.) If we should consider Professor Harrington's conclusions as his answer to the question 'Is there anything wrong with the socialist idea?', this would be an astonishingly unequivocal and optimistic answer: No, nothing is wrong with it. It is a perfectly correct idea, because socialism is – as predicted by Marx – the result of the development of modern technology, and only socialism is able to use these results properly, to the advantage of mankind, by creating the 'kingdom of freedom outside technology'.

Point 4, concerning the USSR and other countries which derive their system from the Russian Revolution, is most clearly expressed in the following statement: 'The liberating potential of technology was [here] forgotten, or else subordinated to the drive for more and more production.' Professor Harrington formulates this point not so much as an accusation of actual policy carried out in Eastern Europe ('it must be [so] in a less developed economy'), but as proof of the incompatibility of socialism with conditions of underdevelopment. As he stressed again in the conference discussion: 'Abundance is the prerequisite of socialism'.

I do not think it necessary to dwell on this question, but some remarks seem to be appropriate. My conclusion from the discussion is that nobody here would challenge the proposition that one cannot look on leisure as the first priority benefit before many other needs are satisfied. Numerous proofs could be given from Eastern European experience, that the 'revealed' preferences of the working population are still very strongly concentrated on 'things' (individual means of transportation included) and basic services (housing). Many accusations might be made against the autocratic leadership of East European countries for their desire to impose attitudes on the population, but this is hardly the case with the question 'more leisure versus more goods'. I would not say also that the 'Marxian dream' (as Michael Harrington puts it) was ever forgotten in the ideological sphere. We were constantly reminded of this ultimate goal of the 'higher stage of communism', with the inevitable conclusion that in order to obtain this we had first to achieve an unheard-of level of efficiency. What is more, practical steps were even taken along the road to increased leisure-time: if I am not mistaken, there were periods in the 1920s when the Soviet working week was among the shortest in the world. It would be easy to show why this state of affairs could not be maintained. Also, more recent attempts to cut the actual labour time seem not to be very much of a success, because the hours gained by many workers are used simply to work for additional earnings, either as overtime or in all kinds of 'moonlighting'.

But this is all a digression, in fact. It is interesting in the context of the general line of our conference that, again, the main conclusions which could be drawn from Professor Harrington's remarks about Eastern Europe contribute to a favourable answer to the question 'Is there anything wrong with the socialist idea?' Because nothing in the practice of Eastern Europe is relevant for socialism as such: by definition, these countries have nothing in common with socialism – they do not satisfy the condition of abundance. If we accept such an approach (and I do not hide my position of not accepting it – for me, socialism can and has to be defined in terms of objective features of its institutions), socialism as a socio-economic system cannot be subjected to any kind of efficiency test: again by the very definition used or implied in Professor Harrington's paper we are even not entitled to ask what is the real impact of socialism on the development and application of modern technology; the function of socialism is to collect the fruits of previous development.

As usual in such cases, I may be guilty of exaggeration. I do not think, however, that I am guilty of gross distortion; by and large these are the conclusions which could be drawn from the paper. And if so, it seems to me that they run contrary to what would be commonly expected from a discussion of the implications of modern technology for socialism, particularly if – as in our previous discussions – we accept the Marxist socialist idea as the point of reference.

A careful reading even of some of the passages quoted in the paper would lead one to conclude that – in relation to technological development – socialism begins for Marx much earlier than for Harrington. 'Freedom in this sphere,' Marx, as quoted, says, 'can only emerge through socialized man, the associated producers, who regulate their interaction with nature rationally, bring it under their community control instead of being ruled by it as a blind power; and whose work is accomplished with the least expenditure of effort and under conditions worthy of and adequate to their human nature. But this still remains the kingdom of necessity.' There is no doubt about Marx's view: relations of production have changed from capitalist to socialist, but it is still not Michael Harrington's 'kingdom of freedom'. Socialism is understood by Marx as a condition, or better, a factor, of the creation of the 'kingdom of freedom'.

We see this, even more clearly stated and in more simple language, in the very well-known passage from 'The Critique of the Gotha Programme', quoted in his paper by Professor Mayer: 'In a higher phase of communist society, after ... the productive forces have also increased with all-round development of the individual and all the springs of co-operative wealth flow more abundantly – only then can the narrow horizon of the bourgeois right be fully left behind . . .'

Thus Marx expected socialism *to create* (and not simply to utilize) the conditions of abundancy, by fully opening the sources of development of the productive forces, first of all by spurring technical progress. His critique of capitalism and his case for socialism were based not only – and I would say not mainly – on ethical grounds, but on grounds of economic efficiency. He tried to identify all the obstacles and limits created by capitalism to the development of productive forces at a later stage: the 'capitalist limits' to the application of machinery; the impact of the increase in the 'organic composition' of capital and of the operation of the 'law of the falling tendency of the profit-rate', derived from the former; the fragmentation of the economy and the resulting impossibility of planning on the macroscale; the monopolistic phenomena, treated by later Marxists as decisive in blocking the development of productive forces (Lenin's 'imperialism as the parasitic stage of Capitalism'), and so on.

On the other hand, socialism was presented as the system which would create the most favourable conditions for the development of modern technology and all other aspects of the development of productive forces. The dynamic factors attributed to socialism were to be (using rather modern terminology): the internalization of externalities (on the basis of social ownership of means production), thus eliminating all obstacles to development stemming from the conflict between private capitalist interest and the interests of society; planning on the macroscale and with a long time-horizon; new social incentives for increased productivity in the broadest sense, due to the growing sense of identification of the working people with the aims and forms of economic activity, and so on.

This is all too well known to require further elaboration. It is socialism which – in the view of Karl Marx and all his followers – creates and strengthens the mutually interrelated and cumulative process of diminishing 'expenditure of effort' and conditions of work increasingly 'worthy of and adequate to human nature'. If this is true, however, quite different dimensions appear in answering the question 'Is there anything wrong with the socialist idea?' in connection with technical change. Let us look at point 2 of the 'Proposals' to call our conference:

In the traditional Marxist sense socialism was supposed to draw its historical strength from and demonstrate its superiority by abolishing the fetters which the capitalist mode of production imposed on technical and productive progress. It is obvious that social problems are by no means solved either by economic growth or by technical progress in itself either in the East or the West (the very concept of progress in this sense being more and more doubtful, considering the price paid for it by mankind). It may also be argued that societies based on capitalist modes of production have not lost the ability to stimulate technical development; rather the opposite seems to be true.

These are, in my opinion, the relevant questions for obtaining a clear view of the implications of modern technology for socialism. It would be impossible to attempt to do so in a brief comment, but what I think is important for our discussion of this topic is to be aware that, first, we cannot avoid the necessity of examining the actual record against the high expectations of technical progress under socialism and the black prospects of technical progress for capitalism; and second, the examination of the problem cannot be limited to even the most accurate presentation of facts. The latter have to be properly correlated with underlying factors, if we are to arrive at a meaningful answer.

It seems to me that *on the capitalist side of the picture* we have, first of all, to examine to what extent technological development of recent decades is due to the injection of 'non-capitalist' (some may say even 'socialist') elements of economic organization on the macroscale, and to what extent further development in this field depends on broadening the sphere of operation of these 'alien' elements.

On the socialist side of the picture, the first problem to examine is the interrelation between the 'state of immaturity' at the starting point and the poor technological performance in absolute terms, or – in other words – how do we assess the achievements of the East in relative terms? To what extent are the deficiencies due to the wrong economic organization *not* predetermined by the nationalization of the means of production? And finally the reverse, and to my opinion the crucial, interconnection: what consequences for change in the political system in Eastern Europe should be expected from the need to cope with modern technological development? Putting it in most orthodox Marxian terms: will the development of the productive forces create a need for change in the relations of production in the direction of the transformation of merely public into social ownership in the Marxian sense, i.e. effectively brought 'under community control'?

All this is not meant to deny the validity of the idea expounded in Professor Harrington's paper, only I think that we cannot limit ourselves to this idea when examining the implications of modern technology for socialism.

SOCIALISM AND OWNERSHIP

Ljubo Sirc

Definition of Socialism

The theme of this paper is ambiguous because it is only possible to discuss the relationship between socialism *and* ownership in so far as socialism is not identified with a type of ownership. Thus in the recent textbook *Les économies socialistes – Sovietiques et européennes* (Paris 1970) the French economist, Marie Lavigne, defines 'socialist' as 'based on property' and adds that state ownership makes a country socialist only if the 'state structure' is also reformed. The author does not go any more deeply into the problem of this 'reform', but since this approach is usually adopted by communists, one can safely assume that it means that the Communist Party must be in power. Others might claim that for socialism 'workers' must be in control. Be this as it may, state ownership is, without any doubt, considered a necessary, if not sufficient, condition for socialism.

If such a definition is accepted, any discussion of public ownership necessarily means a discussion of socialism itself. On the other hand, it is difficult to see what the word socialism means if Madame Lavigne's or another similar position is not adopted. The term is often loosely used to mean a system in which everybody has a good life. If that is what it does mean, then we are all socialists and the discussion shifts to the question of the means by which we are to achieve such a happy state, including, of course, the problem of whether 'socialist' ownership is the means conducive to it.

Private Ownership of the Means of Production

Many who are socialists in the sense that they want to introduce public ownership believe that private ownership of the means of production is the root cause of all evil. They expect that the abolition of private ownership would do away with exploitation, with inequality, with any limits to production and even with crime and prostitution. And the state would also be abolished. More than that, they expect that the human being would be entirely changed. To a large extent, these expectations go back to Marx himself and most certainly to his popularizer Engels.

To my mind, the experience of the last fifty years has undeniably shown that evil does not stem only from greed but can also be a consequence of the lust for power, sexual drive, irrationality, sheer madness and possibly other human properties. Greed itself is not necessarily a result of private ownership of the means of production.

Since equality and 'socialist man' are the subject of separate papers at the Reading Conference, much must not be said about these two questions here. Let us mention, nevertheless, that Engels interpreted the real content of the proletarian claim for equality as a demand for the abolition of classes, that is public ownership of the means of production. He added: 'Any claim for equality going further than that becomes necessarily an absurdity.' As to the perfect man, the very concept reminds one of millenarianism promising perfection on this earth with complete disregard for the complexities of real life.

Exploitation and Ownership

The belief that private ownership of the means of production is the source, or a source, of evil seems to be based largely on the theory of exploitation. The worker is exploited, because some people live, and live well, without working in the same way as he does. For a while, it appeared that workers were in fact entitled to the full product of their labour, but this understanding was attacked by Marx in his *Critique of the Gotha Programme*. There he explained that workers cannot be given the 'entire return of labour' because of the need for simple reproduction, expanded reproduction, cover for risk and collective consumption. Thus workers' wages, after the socialization of the means of production, could be increased only by an amount corresponding to what the capitalists spent on themselves. In so far as a capitalist reinvests, what he has appropriated cannot be given to the workers as it would have to be invested even if there were no capitalists. The only question is: does the capitalist invest efficiently or not?

Looking at the matter in this way, we discover that the part of formally-defined exploitation that matters – because it could possibly add to workers earnings – amounts to very little. It was not always so, as in the past taxation policies were different, but at any rate it has turned out that taxation policies can replace the change in the form of ownership, as far as redistribution of income is concerned. It also has to be taken into account that the share of property belonging to institutional investors is ever larger. These institutional investors provide pensions for the aged and indemnities in the case of accident, etc. This is certainly very different from the luxury consumption of an idler.

On the other hand, there is no reason to believe that exploitation can emanate only from the private ownership of the means of production. The concept of exploitation is based on the labour theory of value. The worker is paid the value of his labour power, while his product has the value of his labour, and the difference is surplus value which is equal to exploitation, if we forget collective needs and expanded reproduction.

The question of the value of labour power has, it would appear, become ever more blurred, since real wages have been rising over decades. If originally the value of labour power was defined as equal to the goods necessary for the survival of the worker (and his family?), this definition can no longer hold true unless we are prepared to claim that, in many instances, a car or television set is also a precondition for survival. Marx avoided this problem by saying that the value of labour power is determined by social circumstances. This may be so, but it can certainly not be claimed that nowadays wages are subsistence wages, while the claim that they are determined by social customs tells us very little.

Marx distinguished between simple and complex labour and claimed that the differentials between the wages of different kinds of workers are fixed so to speak behind their backs. Whatever this means, it is certain that there is no way physically or objectively to measure the labour content or the labour power content of anything.

As there is no objective way of fixing commodity and factor prices, they can be determined either by the market or quite arbitrarily. We can speak about a social convention, if we respect wage differentials as established by tradition, but otherwise wage differentials can only be determined by those in power. Even if the government is democratic, this can still mean the imposition of the subjective judgement of the majority on the minority which can feel exploited.

On the other hand, various groups can also use their monopoly power or simple violence to force their own wage demands on society, i.e. on all other groups. Nominally, monopoly or violence can be directed against profits, but, in fact, they are directed against other groups of workers and are an attempt to exploit them. They are without doubt an attempt at exploiting others if claims go far beyond what could be obtained out of profits and force prices up. But even if they only erode profits, they are still an attempt at exploiting other workers if the erosion is not shared with them.

What these paragraphs are intended to underline is the seemingly obvious fact that exploitation can be a consequence not only of private ownership of the means of production, but of any unjust distribution of income. And since injustice, particularly in this sphere, is a subjective value judgement, exploitation itself is something subjective. As pointed out, Marxism does not help us much, as there is no known way of measuring the value of labour power or labour. The principle 'to everybody according to his work' means nothing because work cannot be measured.

In Yugoslavia, where there is no private ownership in the manufacturing industry, workers strike against each other and feel exploited by each other. Kardelj has admitted as much in his latest brochure 'Contradictions of Social Ownership in the Contemporary Socialist Practice'.[1]

As mentioned, even perfect democracy can still lead to feelings of exploitation because the majority can impose its will on the minority. Only government based on absolute consensus could avoid such feelings, but it would probably be unable to govern and would certainly have to resort to far-reaching compromises. In fact, democracy can offer a way out only if it is understood – also in this sphere – as liberal democracy, if it is based not only on the majority rule but also on respect for the minority and individuals with their inalienable rights. It has to be democracy with moderation and tolerance.

What Rousseauean democracy cannot achieve, any kind of dictatorship can achieve even less. We are all human and, if given absolute power, we tend to abuse it also in the sense that we award more material goods to ourselves and our friends than to others. Whoever has the absolute power, can allot himself whatever he wishes whether he is the formal owner of things or not.

Power and Ownership

If private ownership of the means of production is eliminated, somebody has to perform the functions of owners. It was thought quite natural that this should be the state, in particular as the market was to be abolished as co-ordinator of economic actions and could be replaced only by a central plan.

The very fact that the government now had to administer, in the last instance, the whole economic machinery would enormously add to its power. But this was not all: because it was thought that the possessing class would oppose this new arrangement because of their selfish interests, the government was given dictatorial powers on behalf of the 'proletariat' to keep down the allegedly rebellious capitalists.

More than that: misled by the Marxist philosophy of history, the new rulers believed that they possessed 'the final truth' and that they knew what was best for the people. Since most of them must have had a very shaky idea of what 'natural science' is, they did not realize that science was a constant search for more truth and not the ultimate knowledge of everything. They thought that their policy was science-based and considered themselves some kind of demi-gods whose work was so valuable for mankind that they should be absolute masters of things and people in their country. This conviction, with Lenin's moral precept that whatever serves revolution, i.e. the new government, is justified, led not only to abuses but to incredible crimes.

However, even if one tries to assess the things not as they were and are, but as they could be, it nevertheless sounds rather dangerous to concentrate all economic power in the hands of a government, even if democratically elected and not burdened by 'the final truth' and Leninist morals.

Political philosophy has insisted for a long time that it is not sufficient that government be democratically elected, but that there must be checks and balances in the form of the division of power and statements of human rights. If the economy must be administered centrally, there should perhaps be an independent economic body, separate from the political government, to direct and administer it.

But even that may look overpowering to individuals. If a central body directs the whole economic life of a country, the personal initiative of the population is cut down to such an extent that it is bound to atrophy. One of the worst feelings in a centrally directed economy is that nobody is allowed to help himself to improve his own life even if he could do it without harming others or even by helping them also. Further, much variety is eliminated and replaced by uniformity. The personal sphere is so limited for everybody that one can speak about economic totalitarianism, even if there is no political totalitarianism.

Property can also be, so to speak, an extension of a human person, even necessary for his survival. To quote a romantic example: in the Wild West, the horse was so essential for human survival that a horse thief was punished as a murderer. Something of this is true even in modern society: the government cannot have a complete grip over a country so long as some individuals have independent means and can at least economically protect themselves and others. And only one who believes that a government can be in possession of absolute knowledge and absolute morality can want the government to dominate absolutely.

Of course, when property is mentioned in this context, the distinction must be drawn between means of production and property for consumption. But if we admit that it protects people's personal sphere if at least some of them are economically independent from the government, then there is no reason to assume that it is better for their wealth to be invested in luxury goods than in productive installations.

These days, one often encounters attacks on property in general. American protesters used to accuse the government of putting property before people and, somehow, deduced from this that violence against property was justified. I do not see why wanton destruction of either human beings or their product – property – should be justified. Violence against property can seem justified only to people who, like one of the accused in the Chicago Democratic Convention trial, also claimed that 'work was a four letter word'. Somebody who is spoiled by society to such an extent that he need not do any work, cannot have any respect for the work of others.

Efficiency and Centralism

The question is not only whether state ownership, centrally administered, excessively concentrates power, but also whether such an arrangement has advantages in terms of economic efficiency. In fact, the power in the hands of communist governments was justified by the abundance of goods which it would allegedly bring.

Marx himself wrote: 'Therefore, machinery would have an entirely different margin of leeway in a communist society than in a capitalist society.' And Engels echoed this statement in *Anti-Duehring*:

At the present development of productive forces, that increase in production which is connected with the socialization of productive force, with the abolition of frustrations and disturbances stemming from the capitalist way of production, with the wastage of production and of production means, is sufficient to reduce the working hours to a very small rate, at least from our present viewpoint, if all and everybody were to take part in working.

With the advantage of hindsight one wonders what Marx and Engels expected would happen when socialization came about. If one is uncharitable, one could say that they expected that the abolition of interest rates would lead to a tremendous expansion of investment. Of course, the consequences of this abolition were that investment funds had to be collected in some other way, that it was almost an invitation to waste investment funds and that it gave privileges to workers working with much capital over workers who had to work with little capital.

Perhaps they thought that the state would be able to invest much more than private capitalists. This it could; but, of course, only by limiting consumption, particularly the consumption of peasants who, at one stage, were starved and agriculture in consequence thrown into chaos. Of course, a large volume of investment does not necessarily mean maximizing output. The Yugoslav economist Rudolf Bićanić, said in the mid-1950s: 'Had we invested less, we would have produced more, because we would have invested better.'

Originally, socialized economies enjoyed impressive growth rates, but later both people there and observers abroad began to understand that growth rates in physical terms mean very little. And they were in physical terms because prices were frozen and were not linked to demand. Producing without aiming at satisfying demand is, of course, useless, as Marx himself knew since he continually stressed production for use.

Without any doubt, socialized economies made some achievements. But in fifty, or even thirty, years they could have achieved as much or more with half the effort if they were run in a more sensible way. We have it on the authority of the Soviet mathematician Kantorovich that the Soviet Union could produce 30–50 per cent more with the same resources if it achieved their better allocation.

Centralist Planning

It was also claimed that private ownership of the means of production had to be abolished because otherwise it was impossible to introduce 'planned conscious organization', another slogan of scientific socialism. In the end, such planned conscious organization was introduced in the socialized economies by people who had no clear idea what they were letting themselves in for.

They had no inkling of how difficult it was going to be to collect realistic information about the state of the economy and its enterprises, to process this information and hand down orders to enterprises in an intelligible form. The processing was done in the form of 'material balances', a very crude way, but there was no other available at least at that time. Information processed by this method arrived at the centre, garbled, partly because the enterprises did not want to give the correct information, partly because they were not able to produce it or were not asked the right questions. Orders issued after the processing, which could not make them coherent let alone optimal, were incomplete because they could not be anything else if they were to be issued in technical terms.

As if all this was not enough, the socialized economies also indulged in a few pernicious policies which could have been avoided had those in charge read a standard textbook on economics and not dismissed it as a capitalist fabrication. To wit, they thought that they must always use the most advanced technical methods instead of the cheapest, and that production or means of production must always have precedence over production for consumption.

Decentralization and Ownership

After several decades of experience with central planning in the Soviet Union and not quite a decade in Eastern Europe, some leading communists themselves became aware that, in spite of statistics, something was fundamentally wrong with the centralized economy. A reform movement started which, on the whole, was directed towards more use of the market mechanism as a link between demand and supply and as a method of solving problems of technical efficiency. In some instances the newly-discovered enthusiasm for the market went so far that the converted wanted to use the market for purposes for which it is unsuitable. In short, the market can satisfactorily and better than any other method transmit the wishes of the population with respect to their individual consumption where the population should have the choice, but it cannot solve the problem either of collective consumption or of the redistribution of income.

Nevertheless, the market under present conditions can very efficiently handle about forty to sixty per cent of final output and almost all inter-industry transactions. The market is an automatic mechanism and it would be strange to want to replace it with conscious actions at a time when 'automation' is widely used in engineering. 'Conscious actions' would be very effort-consuming, even if they were efficient.

But the introduction of markets transfers conscious economic activity to individual enterprises which have to take decisions on the basis of prices and within the general legal framework. This transfer raised the question of economic initiative, economic incentives and economic responsibility. It also drew attention again to the role of managers, in fact entrepreneurs, in organizing and running enterprises. This work is very demanding and requires not only considerable knowledge and experience but also special ability. That is a far cry from Lenin's statement that an enterprise could be run by anybody who mastered the four basic mathematical operations. Such pronouncements are idle talk and proof of irresponsibility when uttered by somebody who pretends to want to improve the life of millions.

The performance of decision-making in enterprises can be economically measured if prices express actual demand and supply conditions and if those responsible for them are not saddled with the wrong decisions taken by somebody else. If somebody is sent to run an enterprise, his efficiency will not show in terms of profits, i.e. the difference between revenue and costs, if he has to take over investment carried through by others at depreciated book costs. If a privately owned enterprise is taken over, the new entrepreneur will obtain it at approximately the value calculated on the basis of discounted future net revenue. If this value is lower than the depreciated book costs, those who have taken the wrong investment decisions will be 'punished' by the loss of a part of their capital. This possibility of loss is, of course, a strong deterrent against irresponsible decisions.

In a centralist planned economy such responsibility is impossible. Far-reaching decisions are taken concerning enormous funds and there is neither economic, political or criminal responsibility. Economic responsibility is impossible, since nobody has anywhere near enough wealth to recompense the losses to the population cause by wrong decisions. It is even impossible to ascertain with any precision whether there was a loss or not, since there are no markets. The only sign of mismanagement will be stocks of unsaleable goods or idle capacities and such like.

Political or criminal responsibility for central planning did not exist for central planners, or was entirely arbitrary. In fact it could not be any other way since real prices did not exist and, even if they did, there was no capital market to evaluate the future prospects of an enterprise. That is why there was talk in Yugoslavia of the need for capital markets, but nobody knew how to introduce them in a decentralized economy where the means of production are owned by society. Under these conditions, economic responsibility, which is a strong spur to efficiency, turns out to be very difficult to introduce.

And so are economic incentives. As mentioned, profits will depend not only on the decisions of the present management and workers (if there is self-management) but also on previous investment decisions. Therefore, profits appear to be largely a matter of luck, even for the managers, not to mention the workers. That is also the view of the workers themselves because, at least in Yugoslavia, workers in unsuccessful enterprises immediately demand parity of wages with workers in profitable enterprises if a part of the profits is shared out to these latter.

It is not clear whether these problems of economic initiative, incentive and responsibility can be solved without introducing some kind of closer relationship between individuals or groups and the means of production.

Alienation and Direct Democracy

Marx wrote about workers' alienation because they no longer produced the whole product but only parts of it, or only carried through a partial operation, and because they no longer themselves managed their enterprises as craftsmen used to. I do not doubt that this development has in one respect worsened the quality of life, but surely it has had some compensations. Through the division of labour which has made mechanization possible, productivity has increased many times over and the advanced countries are no longer constantly on the brink of starvation as they were at an earlier stage, and as some developing countries still are. Surely nobody would want to return to the state existing before the division of labour, although we are probably all agreed that the work has to be made more interesting and satisfactory.

The division between management and shop-floor work is a particular aspect of the division of labour. By now we should be clear that founding and managing an enterprise (entrepreneurship) is a highly specialized activity just like many technical or other activities requiring talent, specialist eductaion and experience. Management by rotation seems to be impossible. Thus 'industrial democracy' would, in fact, mean only the selection of skilled managers from among those qualified for this job and perhaps laying down some broad enterprise policy lines.

But even 'industrial democracy' narrowed to this level, runs into considerable trouble. An enterprise is not a self-sufficient unit and, therefore, not a law unto itself, but a part of a wider society which, according to all the rules of democracy, is entitled to define the purpose of the enterprise. This wider society will probably want the enterprise to produce goods efficiently, while the staff of the enterprise may have other wishes. But while the staff are primarily members of the enterprise as producers, they are certainly part of the wider society as consumers and, therefore, interested in the efficient production of all enterprises. It would be 'exploitation' of everybody else if they tried to featherbed their own jobs to a larger extent than everybody else does. This circumstance is often forgotten in modern industrial relations. And this circumstance requires that some kind of compromise be struck between society and individual enterprises, or better between people themselves as producers and consumers. This compromise also requires a careful balance between industrial democracy and efficient management.

There is one other consideration: alienation is certainly distressing, but it is no less distressing if somebody is called upon to perform tasks he does not fully comprehend. And this does happen when good workers are – for ideological reasons – pushed into performing managerial functions they are not even necessarily interested in.

Further, people who do not own the capital of an enterprise and earn relatively small wages cannot be much interested in the long-term prospects of that unit. On the one hand, their 'propensity to consume' will be very high as compared to their 'propensity to save', in particular if they do not save for themselves but for the capital of the enterprise which belongs to society. They may be dismissed or want to go elsewhere and then all their savings are lost to them for the benefit of nobody in particular.

In Yugoslavia, these arrangements were tried out. Not only did all workers want the same pay regardless of the success of their enterprises, but those in successful enterprises also distributed as much as possible and invested as little as possible. The result was that, after much talk about workers' deciding about everything in their enterprise, the decisions on distribution were taken away from them and the guidelines for these decisions are now set by special bodies in the various republics. The decisions concerning saving, no doubt the most coveted jurisdiction, have been taken away from direct democracy and are now decided by bodies which consist of representatives of the government, trade unions and associations of enterprises. Even if these organizations were not party transmissions, as they tend to be in Yugoslavia, but democratically elected, the new arrangement would surely no longer be direct democracy, but some kind of corporate arrangement. One cannot quite see what the advantages of agreements reached by these bodies are over acts voted by a democratic parliament.

Personal Work with Private Means of Production

In all socialized economies, there existed, at least on and off, small private enterprises which were allowed because it turned out to be extremely difficult for the socialist economy to supply goods and, especially, services requiring small-scale activity. They were always viewed with hostility by ideologues because they allegedly bred capitalism, and they were occasionally suppressed, but they tended to spring up again, as their socialized successors would not function. The excuse for their existence was that they were based on personal work with private means of production but, when common sense prevailed, 'personal' enterprises were allowed to employ up to five or so assistants. This was done out of dire need at times when attention was paid to how well the population was supplied with necessities.

While experience shows that the government has great trouble in running small enterprises, large enterprises, which are easy to supervise, have occasionally been run quite efficiently by governments, both East and West, depending in particular on how enthusiastic the man or men in charge were. The Italian Mattei comes to mind as a successful government entrepreneur. The Soviet Union has also been successful in the running of a few industries to which priority was given and which were run and supervised by highly-motivated party bosses. However, the Soviet successes can be measured only in technical but not in economic terms. In the West, government enterprises have to be efficient because they are covered by normal accountancy – their prices being the same as everybody else's – and exposed to competition, if not domestic at least foreign, so that their results can be compared with the results of somebody else.

In view of the findings:

1. that exploitation is by no means limited to earnings from capital but can result also from unjustified salaries and wages;
2. that it is impossible centrally to run a whole economy;
3. that a decentralized economy is difficult to run if there is no close link between the capital of an enterprise and those who run it;
4. that the state can efficiently run, at the best, a few large enterprises;
5. that distribution of income can be corrected by taxation; and

6. that small private enterprises exist (at least sometimes) in all socialist economies;

the question arises: why not allow small and even medium-size private enterprises to solve the problem which cannot be solved by socialized enterprises in a decentralized economy?

There is no reason why 'exploiting' five assistants is all right, but 'exploiting' more than that number is not. In fact, if we give entrepreneurial activity its due, entrepreneurial income can hardly be called exploitation. If the risk-taking function of investment in enterprises is taken into account, even the income of shareholders can escape being labelled exploitation, particularly if it goes to people saving against accidents and old age, or institutions acting for them.

To make private enterprises more acceptable and try at least partly to solve the problem of alienation, it would be possible to combine private entrepeneurship with worker participation. It would have to be organized in such a way that it would not adversely affect to any large extent the efficiency of management and the fulfilment of the social task of the enterprises, but would take care of the interests of its staff and, especially, supply them with all the necessary information and close contact with the management.

The reason for calling entrepreneurial or investment activity exploitation is further weakened, if it is taken into consideration that nowadays there is investment in human beings in addition to investment in means of production. Investment in human beings is often financed by society, but, in spite of that, the beneficiaries are allowed to use for themselves their increased earning power. They are the more entitled to it if they finance their education and training themselves.

In the same way, those who have the technical ability to invent are normally given the right to sell their work at a monopoly price. In view of this, it is hardly understandable why those whose special ability is in organizing production or finance should not be allowed to use the fruit of this ability because it shows in the form of external ownership instead of in the ownership of ideas. In the Soviet Union, people of great ability or education are 'income millionaires'.

This contradiction cannot be put right by simply confiscating the advantages of people with education and training or people with ideas. If this happened, these people would become slaves of society since it is impossible to separate them from their natural or acquired abilities. Something on these lines happened when the Soviet Jews were prevented from emigrating because of the Soviet Union's 'investment' in them.

Regarding private enterprise, at least one Yugoslav socialist, nay communist, has come to a similar conclusion. The Prime Minister of Slovenia, Stane Kavčič, dismissed in 1972, wrote in 1968: 'Private work will have to be included in our economy, as we must be aware that it contributes to our common accumulation. We must seriously consider how to utilize this far from small potential. The experience of socialist economy in the world has shown that it is not worthwhile nationalizing all productive processes.'[2] Oscar Lange said as much in 1938, in his *On the Economic Theory of Socialism*. He suggested the nationalization only of monopolistic firms.[3]

SOCIALISM AND OWNERSHIP

Domenico Mario Nuti

I shall focus on four major aspects of this issue, namely forms of socialist ownership and the problems of exploitation, entrepreneurship and efficiency in a socialist economy.

Forms of Socialist Ownership

Socialist ownership takes the form of state ownership, and of group ownership either in the form of cooperative ownership (Lenin, 1923) or in the form of territorial (e.g. municipal) ownership (Lange, 1958; Nuti, 1973b). State ownership is often regarded as a 'higher' form of socialization of ownership, and Marxists have opposed both the idea of municipal-socialism (the taking over of enterprises by towns) and that of co-operativism as *exclusive* forms of socialist ownership: group ownership is usually excluded from sectors of national importance. But forms of group ownership are recognized as sometimes better suited to deal with some of the problems of constructing socialism (Brus, 1972); and it is questionable whether a Chinese commune (Robinson, 1964) is a 'lower' form of socialist ownership than state ownership.

In the actual experience of socialist economies, group ownership has played a considerable part. Even today, collective forms occupy roughly three-quarters of the agricultural land in Bulgaria, Hungary and Rumania; everywhere co-operatives have an important share of services and small-scale production; while communes are the dominant form in the Chinese countryside.

Socialist ownership does not have to be total for an economy to be socialist, as long as private production is confined to agriculture and small-scale industry, and there are limits to the hiring of workers. Thus the private sector contributes something like 5 per cent of the national income in Eastern Europe, and a much greater share of output in some sectors. Here the notion of a 'private' sector is misleading, because a fundamental connotation of private property is free exchange in the markets for both final products and means of production (including labour), and this connotation is missing in the socialist economies. When the state is in a monopsony position (either *de jure*, when deliveries to the state are partially or totally compulsory, or *de facto* when the private sector provides intermediate goods for further processing by a sector which is entirely socialized), coupled with a monopoly position in the provision of most of the inputs of the private sector, and the prohibition to hire more than a small number of workers is enforced, the so-called 'private' sector is not much less 'nationalized' than the public sector.

'Nationalization' of the basic means of production, in the broad sense of the transfer of at least the 'commanding heights' of the economy from the private to the public sector (whether under state or group ownership) does not of course imply 'socialization' of those means, i.e. the establishment of 'social' as opposed to '*élitist*' control over those means. In 1918, Lenin distinguished between 'nationalization and confiscation . . . the carrying out of which requires above all determination in a politician' and 'socialization, the carrying out of which requires a different quality in the revolutionary' (Lenin, 1918). According to Lange, socialization implies both the use of the means of production in the interest of society as a whole and effective democratic participation of the producers and other workers in the administration of the means of production (Lange, 1958). Accordingly, the socialist character of ownership can be endangered by two extremes. 'One is the absence of trusteeship of the public interest. In this case, the ownership of the means of production, whatever its formal legal character, ceases to be socialist ownership and becomes pure group ownership devoid of any responsibility towards society'; Lange calls this 'anarchist-syndicalist degeneration'. The other extreme is 'bureaucratic degeneration' and 'consists in the absence of effective workers' self-government at the enterprises. In such cases, the socialist character of the ownership of means of production becomes rather fictitious, because the workers have little direct influence on the practical use made of the means of production; whatever the influence, it is channelled through a centralistic bureaucratic machine. There is a danger of a new type of "alienation" (to use a well-known term of Marx) of the producer from his product, and thus of a deformation of the socialist character of production relations' (Lange, 1958). *Socialization* is regarded by Brus as a *process* 'of which nationalization represents only a starting point and the fundamental premise'; 'Clearly it cannot be assumed a priori that this process will in all circumstances go favourably forward' (Brus, 1967, p. 15; see also Brus, 1973, Chapters 1–2).

Alleged lack of *social* control over the means of production has led critics of Eastern European economies both from the right and from the left to deny the socialist nature of these economies, and to regard them as instances of 'state capitalism', where private capitalists are simply replaced by a new ruling class, the party bureaucracy. Among others, Horvat labels the system adopted by the Soviet Union and other socialist countries as 'state capitalism' or 'state-bureaucratic socialism'. The Communist Manifesto states that 'Communism deprives no man of the power to appropriate the products of society; all it does is to deprive him of the power to subjugate the labour of others by means of such appropriation' (Marx and Engels, 1848); Horvat adds emphasis to 'by means of such appropriation' and suggests that power over the labour of others may be obtained by other means, such as position in the state hierarchy, and regards the state apparatus and bureaucracy as a new ruling class (Horvat, 1969). From a different angle, Kuron and Modzelewski point out that 'State ownership can conceal various class meanings, depending on the class character of the state', and argue that 'The central political bureaucracy is the ruling class; it has at its exclusive command the basic means of production; it buys the labour of the working class; it takes away from the working class by force and economic coercion the surplus product and uses it for purposes that are alien and hostile to the worker in order to strengthen and expand its rule over production and society' (Kuron and Modzelewski, 1968). This kind of criticism, however, loses sight of two most important aspects of the problem. First, the classification of the bureaucracy as a *class* broadens the concept of class out of existence; for the bureaucracy there is no permanence of membership nor ability to transmit membership simply by birthright, hence bureaucracy is a stratum, not a class; this seems a meaningful distinction to make. The possibility of conflicts of interest in a socialist economy is widely recognized (Mao Tse-tung, 1958; Lange, 1958), but these are not *class* conflicts (except in so far as classes of workers and co-operative peasants and private producers exist) and 'To overcome these obstacles there is not required a basic change in production relations, i.e. a social revolution, though it may lead to all kinds of friction in the superstructure during the period of transformation and adaptation of the superstructure to the new requirements of the economic base' (Lange, 1958). Second, as Lenin promptly said of his left-wing critics, 'It has not occurred to them that state capitalism would be a *step forward* as compared with the present state of affairs in our Soviet Republic . . .; in making a bugbear of 'state capitalism', they betray their failure to understand that the Soviet state differs from the bourgeois state economically' (Lenin, 1918); 'For socialism is merely the next step forward from state-capitalist mono- poly . . . State-monopoly capitalism is *material* preparation for socialism, the *threshold* of socialism, a rung on the ladder of history between which and the rung called socialism *there are no intermediate rungs*' (Lenin, 1917).

In view of the difference between 'nationalization' and 'socialization', it is best perhaps to redefine 'socialist ownership' not in terms of rela- tions between men and objects (i.e. means of production), but in terms of relations between men. I propose the following definition, that *socialist ownership relations are production relations such that no direct com- mand may be acquired, by whatever means, over labour other than one's own.* This leaves open the question of *indirect* command by individuals or groups over the labour of others; this is the question of *exploitation*.

Exploitation

Sirc states that 'The concept of exploitation is based on the labour theory of value' (see p. 172 above); he rejects the labour theory of value and with it the concept of exploitation; he suggests that only capitalists' consumption could be considered as exploitation, while pointing at other forms of exploitation which in his view are subjective (i.e. arbi- trary) notions, and continue to prevail even in a socialist system.

The approach followed by Sirc requires a brief digression into the Marxian theory of value. Sirc's statement that 'there is no way physi- cally or objectively to measure the labour content or the labour power content of anything' is rash. If labour is considered to be homogeneous, the labour content of commodities can be derived from knowledge of the direct labour input coefficients and of the other input–output co- efficients; there is nothing metaphysical about labour values, and their computation becomes a simple exercise in matrix algebra. If labour is not homogeneous, as long as differences between types of labour are due to education and training, 'complex' labour can be reduced to 'simple' labour, again by means of a simple mathematical procedure (Rowthorn, 1973). If differences between kinds of labour are physical differences, the difficulties generated by these differences are not significantly greater than those encountered in any aggregation process.

The Marxian proposition that commodities (including labour) exchange according to their labour values is not a statement of what actually happens in economic reality, but a provisional assumption made to understand the origin of profit, on the ground that if profit cannot be explained under that assumption it cannot be explained at all. Marx was well aware that, outside the case of uniform organic composition of capital, if relative prices correspond to relative values, the profit rate earned in the production of different commodities would vary; the procedure he suggested for the 'transformation' of labour values into prices of production embodying a uniform profit rate was defective, but the vexed question of the 'transformation problem' has been satisfactorily solved in modern economic literature (see Morishima, 1973; Nuti, 1973a). The notion of the value of labour power does not rest on the assumption of subsistence wages but is an aggregate notion which can be determined, at any moment of time, for a *given* level of real wage. The main results of the Marxian analysis based on labour values is the proposition that profit originates not in the process of circulation of commodities, but in the process of production, including the production conditions of labour power as a commodity; and a *measurement* of exploitation which we can regard as a more satisfactory measure than that obtained by economic observations at actual prices. The ratio between surplus value (defined as the labour time worked in excess of the labour necessary for the production of the given real wages) and necessary value (defined as the labour embodied in the real wage) indicates exactly how much per cent more work the working class has to perform, than they would have to perform to produce their real wage by means of the same technology (Nuti, 1973a).

Given the appropriate political premises, the notion of exploitation could be derived, conceivably, from a more conventional framework of economic analysis – though it is perhaps no accident that more conventional economic theory addressed itself primarily to the justification of the *status quo*, not its critique. Once it is recognized that labour is the only human contribution to economic activity, any claim to the net product of the economic system acquired other than by the exercise of labour can be recognized as exploitative, whether or not one accepts the viability of the Marxian value system. Hence Sirc's criticism of the notion of exploitation on the ground of alleged drawbacks of the Marxian value system is beside the point.

Sirc sponsors the view that exploitation consists of capitalists' consumption, not their accumulation, since 'workers' wages, after the socialization of the means of production, could be increased only by an amount corresponding to what the capitalists spend on themselves'. Now, 'exploitation' can of course be defined in many ways: as monopoly pricing (as in Pigou), or as exploitation between different generations, or races, or regions, or nations, or sexes, and not just classes. There is no conceivable social role for capitalists' consumption out of profits (unless we regard profits as the reward for entrepreneurship, see below); but it cannot be forgotten that the accumulation of profits in the form of capital investment confers upon capitalists as a class social power over others, and – as an alternative – potential power over consumption (regardless of how well capitalists *as a class* provide for capital accumulation in the economy, individual capitalists are not unknown to squander and consume their assets, while other capitalists may show above average restraint and keep accumulation up). Is there any virtue in the accumulation of profits? If capitalists 'abstain' from consuming *part* of their profits for a while for the sake of greater future consumption, workers have to 'abstain' permanently for the consumption of *all* they produce over and above their wages *and* from the additional future potential consumption that capitalists derive from it. Profit may appear as reward for the thrifty, but it all started really from 'primitive capitalist accumulation' (Marx, 1867) and continues to arise from that source. 'After the socialization of the means of production', as long as the economy keeps growing at a rate lower than the profit rate prevailing before the socialization, a situation can be envisaged where – other things remaining equal – the economy can switch to a different technology and get on to a higher consumption path (Goodwin, 1970, Chapter 4). In any case, *if* workers in a socialist economy have control over the amount of collective consumption and capital accumulation, it can be said that they acquire *collectively* whatever they do not acquire directly *individually*. If workers do not have the opportunity to exercise that kind of control, it may be argued that their condition is one of 'exploitation', but it will still not be *class* exploitation, and their condition will be capable of being redressed by a 'cultural' revolution, rather than the complete change of production and property relations needed where class exploitation prevails.

Sirc's view that wage claims by a particular group of workers in a capitalist economy are nominally directed against profits but, 'in fact ... are directed against other groups of workers and are an attempt to exploit them' presupposes the uncritical acceptance of the level of profits and rents. This is a well-known part of the ideology underlying wages policy, i.e. the direct use of the state machine against the working class (Schweitzer, 1946; Nuti, 1969). There is no economic agreement for rent as an income category (as opposed to a price category used in resource allocation). The traditional argument for profit rests on the notions of efficiency and entrepreneurship, both in the capitalist and the socialist economy. These notions deserve a closer investigation.

Efficiency

The Soviet-type system based on centralized planning mostly in physical terms and on physical indicators of the performance of enterprises ensured reconstruction and fast industrialization (and victory in war), but also had drawbacks which in the 1960s appeared to become overpowering. There was not sufficient pressure on enterprises to provide a satisfactory assortment of commodities, especially of consumption goods; the use of physical indicators to assess the performance of enterprises introduced powerful biases as to the weight, area or volume of the commodities produced, and had unfavourable effects on the efficient use of intermediate products, labour and equipment; bonuses to managers of enterprises were based on the fulfilment and overfulfilment of plans, and managers tried to be assigned the lowest possible targets, concealing productive potential and overestimating their requirements of all inputs. These are the phenomena that brought about some decentralisation and the use of value indicators and especially profit in Eastern Europe in the 1960s (Dobb, 1970). But the implications of these problems and reforms for the relative efficiency of alternative economic systems are not as simple as Sirc makes them.

Sirc's implicit model of the capitalist economy is a Walrasian general equilibrium model. Individuals maximize utility, producers (whether individuals or firms) maximise 'profits' (or, more rigorously, the present value of their production activities); they all operate in perfectly competitive markets; under certain conditions concerning the nature of technology and tastes (namely substitutability, externalities, etc.) an allocation of resources will result which is unique, stable and efficient, in the sense of Paretian efficiency, i.e. nobody can be made better off without making somebody else worse off. It is assumed (or hoped) that these conditions are satisfied in the economy; if the resulting distribution of incomes is unpalatable, the government can step in and redistribute by fiscal measures, possibly at the expense of the 'national dividend'.

The inference of the efficiency of the capitalist system drawn from this model is an easy target for criticism, once it is recognized that a general equilibrium solution (even if it exists and is unique) may be unstable, i.e. may never be reached unless economic agents happen to be confronted from the start with equilibrium prices; that there may be increasing returns to scale; that there are externalities both in production and consumption (such as pollution, benevolence, envy, etc.); and that there are oligopolies and monopolies in any actual capitalist economy. But even if none of these problems arose, one still could not draw the inference of the efficiency of the capitalist system from the general equilibrium model of resource allocation. In fact, modern versions of this model (such as Debreu, 1959) have stressed that when the model is extended to include intertemporal allocation and uncertainty about the state of the world, the notion of 'markets' must also be extended to include perfect *forward* markets for the intertemporal exchange of commodities, and perfect *contingent* markets where deliveries are conditional on the realization of particular states of the world. Now, forward markets – let alone contingent markets – are the exception, not the rule, in capitalist economies as we know them (and Sirc admits that much; see Sirc, 1969, p. 75), while even in principle the assumption of a forward market for labour is inconsistent with the assumption of a capitalist economy (because such a market would imply feudal or slave-type permanent links between labourers and assets or masters, of a kind inconceivable for wage-labourers). Therefore the general equilibrium model cannot be used to represent a capitalist economy and from that model nothing can be inferred about the efficiency of such an economy, except that intertemporal allocation in a capitalist economy is highly unlikely to be efficient. It is precisely the absence of forward and contingent markets, which is a most conspicuous feature of the capitalist economy, that turns general equilibrium analysis into a most special case, a *curiosum*, and lends generality to the Keynesian theory of investment, employment, and income determination. It is the *incompleteness* of markets that turns many traditional statements about the efficiency of a capitalist economy or of decentralized socialism into wishful thinking. It is simply not true that 'the market' can 'satisfactorily ... transmit the wishes of the population with respect to their individual consumption', since 'the market' – without forward markets – cannot possibly transmit the wishes of the population with respect to intertemporal consumption. As Keynes taught us, the interest rate is a monetary phenomenon, and does not measure intertemporal preferences of the population; there is *anarchy* in intertemporal productive transformations – a proposition which will not surprise Marx's readers. Thus Keynes, who was certainly not on Marx's side in the class war ('The *Class* war will find me on the side of the educated bourgeoisie', Keynes, 1925) argued that the volume and composition of national investment should be the object of 'some co-ordinate act of intelligent judgement' and not 'left entirely to the chances of private judgement and private profits, as they are at present' (Keynes, 1926); while Sirc believes that profits have 'the ability to allocate or steer resources to the most advantageous use' (Sirc, 1969, p. 71), and praises 'the market' as 'an automatic mechanism', he argues that 'The performance of decision-making in enterprises can be economically measured if prices express actual demand and supply conditions ...' (p. 178 above); the important point is that market prices do not express *actual* future demand and supply conditions, but the *state of expectations* about future demand and supply conditions; these expectations are in general different for different individuals, and even if they were uniform they would not be necessarily correct. Hence the need for 'some co-ordinate act of intelligent judgement', i.e. central planning of at least the main macroeconomic variables in the economy. If 'The only question is: does the capitalist invest efficiently or not' (p. 171 above), the answer is 'No, he does not.'

The same arguments hold in the case of decentralized socialism, if decentralization is pushed to the point where investment decisions are delegated to enterprises, and even a capital market is envisaged (Sirc, p. 178 above). Discussing the relative scope for centralization and decentralization of economic decisions, Brus quite rightly restricts such a scope to the *current* decisions of enterprises, while *macroeconomic* decisions are taken by central organs (and individual consumption and labour decisions are decentralized) in any model of socialism, whether centralized or decentralized (Brus, 1972). As Dobb clearly put it:

> The capitalist entrepreneur takes his decision of the basis of *expectations* as to the future trends ... and because these expectations are necessarily mere guesses, mistakes and subsequent jerks in development and fluctuations develop. On what is the industrial manager in a socialist economy to base his decision? If on similar guesses, then similar mistakes and jerks and possibly fluctuations (if not quickly corrected) will result. In order to estimate the future trend of interest-rates and the price of his product, he will have to guess, not

only what the State policy with regard to investment is going to be (of this, as Dr Lange points out, he may have a pretty fair idea), but what the current reaction of industrial-managements is going to be to the current interest-rate – how much current construction work is being undertaken in the economy at large, and its results. In other words, the future trend will itself be affected by his own decision and that of all his fellow-industrialists; and his decision will have to depend, in part, on what he guesses the response of his fellow-managers will be, including a guess as to what *they* will guess *his* decision will be. It seems inconceivable that this guessing-game can be reduced to any simple set of rules (Dobb, 1939).

These are the problems facing a decentralized socialist economy, and the weakest points of current economic reforms in Eastern Europe. And it is within the framework of the role of expectation and the missing forward markets that the problem of 'entrepreneurship' can be best analysed.

Entrepreneurship

Sirc praises the virtues of private entrepreneurship, combined with a system of punishment and reward geared to entrepreneurial performance measured by profits and losses, to the point of advocating the enlargement of the private sector to include medium-size productivity units and the abolition of current limits to the hiring of workers by private firms.

There are two separate basic elements in the function of the 'entrepreneur'. One is the ability to organize, adjust, and innovate; it consists in 'getting things done' (Schumpeter, 1943, p. 132). The other element is the ability to formulate correct expectations about the future, i.e. to guess the general trends in the economy and the actual decisions and potential responses of other entrepreneurs (see the quotation from Dobb above; also, Dobb, 1924). Writing about 'the obsolescence of the entrepreneurial function', Schumpeter (1943, Chapter XII) argued that the function of 'getting things done' 'is already losing importance and is bound to lose it at an accelerating rate in the future even if the economic process itself of which entrepreneurship was the prime mover went on unabated' (1943, p. 132). The second element has its *raison d'être* in the absence of forward markets in the economy, because such markets would dispel the kind of 'market uncertainty' with which the entrepreneur has to cope, and which represents most of the uncertainty facing him (since he can insure himself against 'risk', i.e. situations in which alternative outcomes exist with *known* probabilities). 'Profit', in the old-fashioned sense of reward for entrepreneurship, is a residual revenue over and above the payment of interest, rents and wages; it is partly the reward for organizational ability above that of the worst entrepreneur in business, partly the reward for accurate guesses, i.e. the pay-out on gambling with national resources.

In a socialist economy, central planning of the general directions of the economy should take the place of the second element of entrepreneurship, i.e. should replace those missing markets. The main aspect of entrepreneurship is the element of organization, adjustment and innovation, which is not by any means 'obsolete'. The presence of 'profits' in a socialist enterprise operating in a planned economy but enjoying some autonomy with regard to its output and price is an ambiguous signal. It may indicate two things: (i) that managers (or workers) of that enterprise have got a greater organizational ability or are harder working than those of other enterprises; or (ii) that there have been *mistakes* in the enterprise (e.g. if too low an output is produced and sold at excessively high prices in view of the small quantity) or in other enterprises (e.g. if an excessively high price rules because other enterprises operating in the same sector have underfulfilled their plan) or at the central level (e.g. if demand for the product of the firm has been underestimated). In the first case, the presence of profits may or may not be a sufficient reason for rewarding the managers and workers of the enterprise, but is not a sufficient reason for expanding the production of that enterprise. In the second case there may or may not be a good reason for expanding production in that enterprise (or sector), but there is no good reason for rewarding the member of the enterprise. The same happens with losses as well as profits: losses may be due to absenteeism and incompetence, but also to mistakes elsewhere in the economy. In practice profits (and losses) are due to a combination of different degrees of organizational ability (and hard work) and good planning, and they cease to be a reliable indicator either for directing production or for assessing performance (Nuti, 1972).

The mobilization of entrepreneurial energies in the broadest sense, as initiative, imagination and organizational ability, both at the central and the enterprise levels, is a most important issue in any socialist economy, though it is frequently neglected. Sirc's suggestions of a wider scope for private enterprise and stricter managerial responsibility do not seem entirely satisfactory for the reasons mentioned above. It seems that the problem of 'enterprise under socialism' could be better treated within a wider context of participation – not only of enterprise managers but also of workers, consumers, local and central decisional levels – in the process of economic initiative and decision-making.

Conclusion

Sirc's blueprint for the ideal socialist economy is basically a mixture of the capitalist and the socialist system; with a few state enterprises in key sectors, without monopolies, with some workers' participation, and with the state being in charge of redistribution by means of fiscal measures and catering for public goods.

The problem is, as Dobb puts it, that 'Changing an economic system is not like making a cake or a pudding where you are fairly free to mix ingredients according to taste' (Dobb, 1966). The most likely outcome is a situation where exploitation will remain, the private sector will try to frustrate social control and dominate the public sector, the struggle between capital and labour would continue, perhaps even acerbated, and no effective social planning of the economy as a whole would be possible.

Sirc's diagnosis of the problems of the socialist economy and the remedies he suggests are very strongly influenced by the experience of the socialist countries of Eastern Europe. Other socialist countries, such as China and Cuba, have been developing different patterns of socialist ownership and economic organization (Gray, 1972; Guevara, 1965). In Guevara's words:

> Pursuing the chimera of achieving socialism with the aid of the blunted weapons left to us by capitalism (the commodity as the economic cell, profitability, and individual material interests as levers, etc.), it is possible to come to a blind alley. And the arrival there comes about after covering a long distance where there are many crossroads and where it is difficult to realize just when the wrong turn was taken. Meanwhile, the adapted economic base has undermined the development of consciousness. To build communism, a new man must be created simultaneously with the material base (Guevara, 1965).

It may well be that *more* socialism, not *less*, is the answer to many of the problems of the socialist economy.

INDUSTRIAL DEMOCRACY, SELF-MANAGEMENT AND SOCIAL CONTROL OF PRODUCTION

Maria Hirszowicz

No concept seems to be more fashionable among progressivists of different orientations than that of 'industrial democracy'. The programme of industrial democracy is promoted by the labourites and the conservatives, it has become the battlecry of the militant left and the law abiding citizens; it is supported and praised on both sides of the 'iron curtain' by hawks and doves alike.

Managers hope that the participation of workers in industrial decision-making will make them more satisfied with their work and more co-operative, more inclined to identify with managerial goals and more willing to contribute voluntarily to the efficient running of enterprises. All sorts of social reformers believe that industrial democracy provides the world with an uncontroversial answer to the alienation of labour and bridges the gap between the privileged and the underdogs. Radicals advocate industrial democracy as a fulfilment of anarcho-syndicalist dreams and expect it to serve as an instrument of the proletarian revolution against the deviations of power-seeking dictators. Revisionist communists adopt the programme of industrial democracy as the only orthodox way of following the Marxist road to socialism against the attempts of the 'red bourgeoisie' to maintain state capitalism in the guise of the proletarian state.

All these trends contribute to the tremendous appeal of the idea of industrial democracy. Social scientists carry out innumerable investigations demonstrating all over again the psychological and social benefits of democratic participation. Left-wing scholars collect every scrap of information to prove that workers' pressure for self-management is becoming the dominant target of class struggle. The democratic opposition in the East European countries investigate Yugoslav experiments to corroborate their view of the economic superiority of workers' councils over all other forms of industrial management.

Yet the facts and findings about industrial democracy in the modern world seem to be pretty confusing. In most experiments carried out on group participation, its impact on individual satisfaction and group performance has been repeatedly demonstrated by (to mention only a few) White and Lippitt's studies, reports of the studies about overcoming resistance of workers to technological change, and Triest's investigation sponsored by the Tavistock Institute. And yet in most reports on participation as it is applied in industry we find the same statements about workers' apathy and lack of interest in the schemes introduced and promoted by management.

Managers are invariably enthusiastic about any idea of participation, as long as it is presented by professional psychologists and sociologists, and readily support scholarly attempts to study the problem more and more thoroughly; but in spite of that there are only very few industries where managers try seriously to implement the elaborate devices for worker participation in management. The labour movement seemed from the very beginning sympathetic to the programme of social control of industry and yet the trade unions are most reluctant in encouraging the development of workers' councils and give lukewarm support to the present shop steward movement. The concept of workers' control seems to be deeply embedded in the ideology of socialist supporters of the nationalization of industry, and yet it is in the nationalized sector that worker participation seems confined to trivialities. The communist countries, which started their revolutions with appeals for workers' (and soldiers' or peasants') councils, were in the end most determined to prevent any attempts at workers' self-management, as opposed to the centralized power of the state. In Yugoslavia, where the implementation of the programme of industrial democracy seems most advanced, there are steady complaints about the lack of influence of workers in the councils, as compared with the growing influence of engineers and white-collar employees. And the whole system does not seem to counterbalance the dictatorial power of the political *élite* in the country.

The explanations which are at hand to account for these contradictions consist either in arguing that the deficiencies in the working of industrial democracy are due to the capitalist setting within which democratic rights are exercised or, on the contrary, point to the menaces of the excessive demands in that respect resulting in the last resort in the disappearance of all democratic institutions under communist rule.

It is to the credit of the New Left that they try to discuss the concept of industrial democracy in the wider context of participative democracy: the ideas promoted once upon a time by J. J. Rousseau, J. S. Mill and later on by G. D. H. Cole seem to re-emerge from oblivion as a new device in social and political theory. And yet the utter disregard of many New Left movements for social and political realities accounts for the failure of all attempts to stimulate any mass support for their demands.

However, we get nowhere by adopting liberal dogma and arguing that democracy has an inherent social value and that participative democracy must thus be regarded as a higher and more perfect stage of human development; this assertion turns out to be false in the light of comparative and cross-cultural studies. And it is by no means 'true socialism' that consists in emphasizing the virtues of democratic participation, since for so many decades the workers' movement has been quite indifferent to the programme of industrial democracy. Where does the sudden interest in the issue come from? Can we just assert that the syndicalists were right and all others were wrong in their discussions about the future shape of socialist society? Or is there any significant change in the economic, social and political structure of the modern world that accounts for the change of emphasis about workers' control? And, if so, why has the problem of industrial democracy reemerged with new force in the late 1960s and early 1970s after being discussed only academically a few years earlier?

It does not seem that any answer can be found by treating industrial democracy as a response to one factor only, be it the technological development of large-scale industries, the growth of administrative and managerial structures, the class conflict of modern capitalism or the contradictions coming to the fore in the communist world. It is rather the combined impact of all these forces which seems to account for the renewed pressures on behalf of industrial democracy. And yet it is quite plausible that the common denominator of all these factors is linked to the emergence of what we could call 'organizational societies' (whether of capitalist or communist types) which shape a new political balance between the decision-makers and decision-takers, the ruled and the rulers, the *élites* and the masses, the planners and those who are subject to their planning, the administrators and the administered, and so on.

If the clumsy concept of Weberian bureaucracy has had a life far beyond its analytical value, if C. W. Mills' writings on *élites* and mass societies have been best-sellers for many decades and if studies on organization have turned out to be the favourite topic among sociologists and political scientists, it has happened because of the growing awareness that a new type of social order has emerged, which has to be incorporated in the modern ideological perspective whether we like it or not. No wonder that those who dismissed the new issues as conservative, anti-communist or non-Marxist have been left behind, unable to face the new dilemma posed by recent technological, economic and social developments. The problem of workers' self-management is particularly controversial in that respect: it reflects the old socialist standpoint towards the working class and its historical targets and at the same time it implies applying traditional values to highly developed bureaucratic systems. Too many problems are actually involved in the implementation of the programme of industrial democracy to be dealt with by any simplified formulas and it is only by making some basic distinctions between them that we can try to draw a line between manipulative devices, utopian dreams and political demands.

The Seamy Side of the Division of Labour and Shop Floor Participation

We should first make a distinction between the levels at which workers' control might be exercised. One usually points to the 'shop floor level', i.e. the control over units in which basic productive functions are performed, as the major scene of democratic participation by rank and file workers. The shop floor level in a factory means that of producing goods or semi-products; in a department store it means that of selling goods to the customer or typing in the office; in a school it implies just teaching and in the post office serving customers or taking care of deliveries, and so on.

It is on that level that the managers find workers' participation most beneficial for the enterprise, since it increases their interest and enthusiasm for work without necessarily encroaching upon the authority structure of the firm. There are also many spokesmen of socialism who believe that one cannot eliminate alienation and give the worker 'a sense of belonging' and enable him to 'fulfil himself' without making him participate at that level. C. A. R. Crosland, who seemed to be particularly concerned with that form of alienation which cannot be ascribed, as it was by Marx, 'to the system of property relations, nor yet to the absence of workers' management', emphasized this point by writing:

> But the predominant view among social psychologists appears to be that the problem is basically one of 'democratic participation' – not, however, the mass participation of all workers in the higher management of the enterprise, but the participation of the primary work group in deciding how its own work should be divided, organized and remunerated. On this view we must study the enterprise as a social organism, unravel the natural group relationships and endeavour to align these with the technological necessities of the work process. The emphasis is on creating structured work groups, rationally related to the production process, and endowed with increased group responsibility and internal group leadership.[1]

The impact of mass production on the alienation of work has been studied with great detail in the last few decades. In recent years many scholars support Blauner's view that the limitations of the individual and group initiative on the shop floor is but a passing stage. With the further progress of automation they expect that workers will be able to rediscover the meaning of work and to participate more and more in the processes of decision-making by being assigned to jobs which require high individual responsibility and effective team work.

Other scholars continue to argue that, so far, automation does not seem to increase the number of highly skilled jobs and to revolutionize the nature of work on the shop floor. They believe – along with, for example, Blumberg, the author of the widely read *Industrial Democracy*[2] – that it is the social organization of work rather than technological change that provides us with the solution to the dilemma.

One has to take into account new arguments related to the recent rise in living standards and the development of new consumption patterns in highly industrialized societies. In all countries where we observe any evidence of transformation of work processes (i.e. any genuine attempts at job-redesigning and extending workers' control over the operations they perform) these processes seem to have been generated not so much by new technologies as primarily by the pressure of the workers themselves, who are much more reluctant to work on the assembly line and to perform robot-like functions than they were before. There is a growing gap between the general cultural pattern of highly developed societies and the conditions of industrial work. The whole educational system, the new mass culture based on ideals of hedonism, the extension of leisure and the increased consumption of semi-luxury or pseudo-luxury goods among the workers – all this stimulates new and wider interests, engenders new habits, makes young workers prone to reject dirty and dull jobs, shapes attitudes incompatible with performing very hard and unpleasant duties. At the same time the welfare state alleviates the plight of unemployment, so that the workers can afford to be more choosy in their search for convenient jobs. In those conditions many firms institute programmes of job redesigning so as to make work more attractive and more interesting.

Can we expect that these trends will contribute in the not too distant future to a complete transformation of the nature of work in industry? One must not be too positive about it, since there are many factors that act against it. One of them is the economic pressure of the market: firms which face the necessity of competing for an exigent labour force may find it cheaper to solve their difficulties by further automation, which brings about a further decrease of workers in industry, increases unemployment and makes the workers less militant and hence better adjusted to industrial requirements. On the other hand the effect of the pressure of workers upon the employers depends largely on the scarcity of labour: as long as large numbers of immigrant workers from developing countries are available, there is always the possibility of transforming western societies into highly stratified systems, in which native workers are eligible for more interesting and responsible jobs while immigrant workers perform the most unpleasant and repetitive functions.

In communist countries, where the growing dissatisfaction of workers with hard and boring occupations is also in evidence, there is still the large residue of the rural population to take the most unattractive and unpopular jobs. And the scarcity of consumer goods in those countries makes people inclined to endure harsher conditions of work as long as they believe that their contribution may result in increased production of these goods.

There is, however, a growing dissatisfaction among industrial workers in most advanced areas of communist countries with the working conditions of mass scale production. Many Russian and Polish sociologists report that the better educated the workers the more they resent boring and repetitive jobs. Some social scientists in Russia thus raise the suggestion of adapting the educational level to the changing needs of industry by imposing limits on the number of those who receive a full education that cannot be applied in their jobs. The trend towards better and more extended education in the communist countries seems none the less too deeply entrenched and hence clashes of the kind just mentioned seem to be more and more likely. The workers with ten or more years of education want to apply their minds to the work they perform; they want to have a say and to exercise their independent judgement in work processes and, as soon as they come across unimaginative and dull jobs in big factories in Moscow, Warsaw or Novosibirsk, they become frustrated, embittered and resentful in spite of the relatively good wages and social benefits they enjoy. Attempts to extend their leisure time and to compensate for lack of stimulation on the shop floor by material rewards does not seem to be a satisfactory answer to those problems either in the West or the East.

One wonders, however, whether that is not the very approach that has necessarily to be incorporated into socialist ideology. One might argue that as long as labour remains a commodity, pleasure-orientated attitudes are bound to increase among workers utterly indifferent to the *social* meaning of the work. Can any civilization survive while relying on utterly individualistic and hedonistic motivations and values? And does the appeal of collectivism really mean that people become liberated from any external constraints by converting work into play? Or is that trend an expression of the system in which the worship of consumption, leisure and enjoyment have become the only unchallenged patterns to rely upon?

The Fads and Foibles of Industrial Democracy at the Managerial Level

So far we have discussed worker participation on the shop floor without taking into account the authority structure and pressures towards industrial democracy at the managerial level. It is at that level, however, that organizational factors seem to be at odds with any substantial development of workers' self-management.

There is no need to discuss the impact of organizational growth on the authority structure in industrial enterprises. Since Weber, hundreds and thousands of studies have been written to demonstrate the general trend towards professional management based on full-time participation in administrative processes and requiring more and more specialized training to cope with the complexity of industrial management.

A layman, even if very interested in the running of a big organizational unit, cannot assess what is going on within it unless (a) he is supplied with full information about what happens behind the scenes; (b) he has the training and experience to handle the information he receives; and (c) he has time to absorb it and convert it into relevant aggregates of digestible knowledge. As a rule, highly specialized experts and specialized organizations are necessary to cope with the control of big organizational units and as long as the workers are not able to assess what is going on at the administrative level, they are not able to implement their legitimate rights to control management.

For these reasons full participation in managerial activities is pure utopia: participation must be replaced in most cases by selective control, by disregarding pure technicalities and concentrating on general issues which are relevant for the interested parties for one or another reason.

Even in political parties, where rank and file members naturally are most interested in the running of political affairs, the professionalization of administrative functions poses a serious problem and contributes to the emergence of organizational *élites* able to manipulate easily the system of institutions regarded as safeguards of party democracy. The same happens in the relationship between the rank and file shareholders and the managerial *élites* in big corporations, and within the trade unions, where the issues of democratic control are widely discussed in that context. It is no wonder that in industrial enterprises the workers under the pressure of everyday work do not seem too enthusiastic about extended participation in management, especially as it does not bring any immediate change in the issues they are most interested in.

In addition, all participative arrangements seem to contradict both the concentration of capital spreading throughout industrial countries and building up international empires, and the structure of the trade unions linked to national bodies, whether based on trades or on industries.

One could argue, as some critics of mass scale production do, that in the long run the non-participative character of management would change by becoming less and less 'mechanistic' (to use Burns' and Stalker's term)[3] and displaying a more and more 'organic' administrative pattern. To believe in spontaneous evolutionary change means, however, to give up any reasonable hope that any substantial improvement will take place in the forseeable future. Such over-optimistic views usually do not take into account self-perpetuating forces in industrial and managerial bureaucracies. One could assume that, even when challenged by the requirement of profound change and under the pressure of improving administrative methods, the managers would resist any reform that might endanger their authority and would use all the power at their command to defend the system they are entrenched in.

This resistance comes to light not only in privately owned industries, where the authoritarian hierarchy is usually supported by vested interests of big property, but also in the state-controlled industries. The same resistance is evident in the communist countries, where the ruling *élites* may rely upon the wholehearted support of the managers in their efforts to maintain authoritarian rule. Apart from Yugoslavia, all forms of participative democracy in industry – if indeed there are any – are thus limited in communist countries to insignificant institutions of no real importance.

The whole issue is very complex, since one could hardly argue that industries could be run by majority vote and expect the workers to take an interest in controlling their managers in their everyday performance. The better qualified the managers, the more they identify with their firms, the more likely it is that they will perform their duties in an efficient and reliable way and too close a control can only be anathema to them. Some scholars argue on these grounds that the rule of participative democracy hardly applies at that level: all that can be done consists of appointing managers and holding them responsible to those whom they are supposed to serve, without any attempt to tighten control.

One could try to solve this contradiction by making a distinction between managerial activities and the power structure in an enterprise, the former involving decisions related to the tasks performed, the latter to the position of the people involved. Technical problems and personnel policy overlap, however, to such an extent that any clear-cut division of rights and duties at the managerial level is very difficult. It seems that there is no possibility of giving a group of managers the instruments of organizational power without running the risk of their abusing their position to the detriment of those who are subject to their control in the financial, technological, informational and occupational setting. Those at the top are always endowed with highly effective weapons against the rebels, deviants and reformers and it is no wonder that in all institutional systems there is always discontent with authoritarian rule and pressure on the part of the rank and file members to relax it. To defy this sort of inequality means, however, to challenge the whole system of organized hierarchies, i.e. the very organizational principles on which the enterprises are actually run.

It seems that there is no way out of that dilemma but to acknowledge the contradictory nature of the principle of effective leadership and of participative democracy at the managerial level in the same way as the above contradiction has been acknowledged in political theory, where the administrative apparatus and democratic framework have to co-exist somehow and to limit each other by constant clashes and readjustments. What really matters is the real balance of power between parties involved: in that respect evolutionary changes in the West obviously work in favour of industrial democracy.

Throughout Europe there is renewed pressure towards creating workers' councils. In France there are *comités d'entreprise* created by the law of February 1945 and developing with renewed vigour after the events of 1968. In Germany, where the first councils in the 1920s were abolished with the consolidation of the Nazi régime, they were brought back under the Industrial Constitution Act in 1952. In Italy, where after the defeat of Fascism the demand for workers' councils was increasing, new status and functions were awarded to the internal commissions of workers; since then the commissions and, after 1968, the workers' councils have become more and more active. In Belgium, factory councils created in September 1948 received much greater powers in 1967. A very similar line of development has taken place in the Scandinavian countries with even greater emphasis on co-operation. In Great Britain, the shop steward movement seemed to achieve new vigour and the militancy of the shop stewards created a new framework for worker participation in the late 1960s and early 1970s.

The significance of this development is obvious. The new institutions seem to challenge the existing authority structures by enforcing – at the level of the firm – the principle of co-government and by creating new instruments of permanent, though selective, control of managerial activities by the workers' representatives. As a result, a new pattern emerges: the big corporations and the multinationals are faced by closely-knit organizations of workers linked with factory units and dealing mainly with local problems.

The idea of co-partnership is thus running through the large-scale organizations and counteracts some of the deficiencies of super-centralization and the excessive uniformity resulting from it. In that respect the trend could be welcomed by top managers who are only too eager to combine the growth of their industrial empires with a flexibility that would be impaired by bureaucratic development. The contradiction inherent in extending workers' participation lies, however, within the area of the power game, where any shift of balance between the managers and the employees jeopardizes the targets pursued by top executives at the expense of the workers. Thus a new pattern emerges: the executives, who previously tried to counteract any attempts by the workers at interference, may try to neutralize its effects by increasing their hold over those who are bound to control the firms – shareholders and governments. Especially in the latter area it happens that employers are only too willing to accept workers' claims so as to enforce their own demands over governmental agencies, as for example is the case with the unending disputes between heads of boards of nationalized industries and their governments about the principle of profitability of their respective industries (railways and public transport, mining, postal services, etc.).

Socio-economic Organization and the Limits of Workers' Self-management

One could rightly argue that the managers and administrators in industry are merely agents of the institutional and social order they act within. The clash between the principle of workers' self-government and the rights of managers who, rightly or wrongly, are in power to control the firm is thus inevitable as long as the demands of employees are at odds with the interests of those groups which decide about the targets the managers have to pursue, whether or not these groups rely on private property or incorporate the unlimited power of the state.

In the Western world, the extension of workers' demands beyond certain limits is self-defeating because of the market forces that operate within capitalist societies. The system itself thus creates safeguards against excessive claims and under the circumstances the workers are by no means eager to transform privately owned factories into co-operatives, even if they are strong enough to do so. Even nationalization does not appear in many cases to be a good solution for satisfying workers' demands, since the private sector has proved in recent decades much more generous to its employees than have the state-owned industries. And once we take a closer look at the public sector with its low wages, overtime work and strenuous jobs the implementation of the programme of industrial democracy seems much more distant here than it does in more prosperous industries.

On top of that, state-owned industries are too closely integrated into the whole of the national economy to allow any substantial increase in the interference of employees in the running of these institutions. It is in these industries that the old distinction between what, how and in what conditions to produce seems to be directly linked with the differentiation between the subjects of decision-making (consumers, technologists and workers), as pointed out by British socialists. The workers are supposed to have their say (if at all) about the conditions in which they perform their duties. The decisions about what and how to produce are left, however, to outside factors – the government having a final say on behalf of the community. It is assumed that the employees, regarded as a part of that community, cannot unilaterally enforce their interests at the expense of their fellow citizens. The state comes forward as a power supposed to maintain the balance between the occupational groups (and the interest groups in general) and society as a whole.

Robert Dahl, analysing the attitude of the Labour Party to workers' control, summarized the reasons for which Labour-supported workers' participation in private industries and opposed it in nationalized industries in the following way:

1. Trade unions must maintain their complete independence to perform their basic function of representing the workers' interests. This independence would be compromised if their representatives were on the board of control.
2. Members of the governing body cannot at the same time answer to the workers of an industry as their representatives and bear responsibility to the minister for its administration. To attempt to lay such a double duty on them may well result in making the governing body in a sense a negotiating committee, in which the workers' representative will be in an ambiguous position.
3. Parliament, representing the community in general, must have ultimate control over policy, secured through a responsible minister and a board accountable to the minister.[4]

These are arguments that cannot be dismissed by referring to the rightist deviation of Labour Party leaders or by reminding ourselves of the vested interests of the private sector, which tends to manipulate the state and the state-controlled industries for the benefit of capital. Whatever the interest is that the state tries to protect, be it those of a small group or of the community as a whole, there is always a problem of how to safeguard that interest against the pressure of one organization or one occupational sector. The principle of self-government, as long as it protects the particular interest of any group – the church, the army or the professions, for example, as well as different sections of employees – must thus clash with the rule of representative government, unless it is confined to boundaries imposed by well-defined legal institutions, accepted as fair and legitimate by the parties concerned.

In this case, however, it is not the institutional framework but the actual balance of social forces that really matters. Representative democracy defined as 'institutional arrangement for arriving at political decisions in which individuals acquire the power to decide by means of a competitive struggle for the people's vote'[5] is dead for purely technical reasons. Planning many years ahead, the high costs involved in capital investment, the cumulative effects of technological, economic or organizational change all make it virtually impossible to renegotiate any substantial issues once they have been implemented. Far-reaching, large-scale and long-term decision-making seems incompatible with selective control, *ex-post* bargaining and periodical revisions of current policies. It is at the very source, from the very beginning and in all aspects that the interest groups have to take part in governmental processes, be it deciding about wages, motorways, research and development, new industrial investments, housing projects or international agreements.

We come, however, at this very point to the main dilemma posed by the contradictions of capitalist societies. How can the workers accept the view that no section of the population should enforce its own will upon society as a whole while at the same time they may easily find that the interests of big business are being promoted without much respect for their own demands? How can one appeal to common values in a system in which maximization of profits remains the main target of economic activities?

One might point to the principle of representative government as the answer to these problems; the trouble is, however, that the political forms of representative democracy are less and less satisfactory from the point of view of different groups whose interests are never properly fought for through the mechanisms of general elections and party competition. Participative democracy thus means an attempt to break through the existing limitations of the political system, to enforce issues which might never be solved without direct action being taken. In that respect the workers of one particular area of the country or of one particular trade might never see their demands satisfied by any party claiming a majority vote, since the majority is not necessarily concerned with the plight of a tiny part of the working population. For the sake of their sectional interests the workers who expect redundancies might start an occupational strike, or the employees of a dying industry might try to take over control of it; one could hardly argue, however, that faced by the indifference of the larger community they have any other alternatives if they are to defend their interests.

It is for that very reason that pressure for direct action and for workers' control cannot be dismissed by referring to the requirements of social and economic equilibrium. In a system based on contradictions and adopting the existing balance of power as the ultimate principle of pragmatic solution, no political party can expect those who can improve their position not to press for it at the expense of other groups in society. Any government which appeals on behalf of the common interest for moderation and restraint of excessive demands is bound to fail in those attempts unless it applies similar discipline to the privileged minorities. At the same time the whole economic framework becomes more 'decisional' than it ever was, i.e. the situation of all groups is determined more and more by the economic and social policy adopted by the government. Efforts to influence decisions must thus increase – the focus of the power game is shifted from the industrial to the governmental level and the parties involved are more and more concerned with administrative technicalities, which seem to have a far-reaching influence on their strategic position in top decision-making.

Industrial democracy at that level then becomes a weapon of the workers in the general competition for the benefits of participation in governmental schemes, an instrument for enforcing those demands which cannot be presented as political issues subject to electoral campaigns and which are none the less of major importance for the majority of wage earners in different industries. To believe that parliaments and political parties resorting to legal institutions and traditional customs are able to solve the problem is sheer hypocrisy and is less and less acceptable to radicals both of the left and the right.

Workers' Self-management and the Socialist Order

All the dreams of the advocates of industrial democracy concentrate on the victory of socialism, seen as the fulfilment of the perfect society. And yet the greatest challenge to all democratic institutions was caused by the emergence of the communist system, which not only eradicated every sort of workers' autonomy but imposed upon wage-earners a harsh administration supported by ideological manipulation and police supervision. The fate of workers' opposition in the early 1920s in the Soviet Union, the enforced incorporation of the left-wing socialists into the Communist Party and the 'nationalization' of trade unions marked the development of the communist order, in which behind a screen of slogans about the dictatorship of the proletariat the power of political, administration and managerial *élites* was enforced upon the masses.

The almost complete divorce of communism from democracy brings many a socialist to a point where he is ready to agree to the capitalist order if only to avoid the alternative system of suppression of all democratic institutions in the course of imposing centralized planning and state controlled economy.

We face nowadays a situation in which two alternatives are available: on the one hand a system with too much planning, too much centralized decision-making, too great a concentration of power; and on the other, a system with too little planning, facing unsolvable dilemmas of market economy and unable to resist the pressures of private interests which are the vehicles of its dynamic development. In which case, we have to ask again: is it possible to dispense with the latter without opting for the former? Is the equation 'full socialism = totalitarianism' really the only one to be accepted as true?

This is the context within which we have to discuss the dominant issues of the modern world within the framework of the socialist idea. There is no escape from the questions raised above. Whatever the problem we are interested in – social planning, private ownership, tax systems or social welfare – it has to be related to the basic choice between the limitations of the past or the new constraints of the brave new world as depicted in communist rule.

The resulting philosophy of retreat and conciliation is best reflected in H. A. Clegg's conclusive remarks presented in his book *A New Approach to Industrial Democracy*, where we read:

'Public ownership may have profound effects on the management of industry, but if the essence of democracy is opposition, then changes in management cannot be of primary importance to industrial democracy . . . Earlier generations of socialists thought that it would be possible to improve upon the political institutions of a capitalist democracy. Modern socialists fear that the changes that were then proposed might, if applied, have accomplished the destruction of democracy, not its improvement . . . Similarly the syndicalists, the industrial unionists, the guild socialists and even supporters of joint control all thought they had a means of creating a far better order in industry than capitalism could ever offer. Now we think we know better. Their proposals would not have led to an industrial democracy. On the contrary they would have undermined the existing institutions of industrial democracy, already developed under capitalism.'[6]

This is a rather extreme viewpoint, and therefore gives a pretty clear presentation of the major problem, in contrast to much pseudo-progressive phraseology which tries to confuse the issue. Illuminating in this respect is the following remark, also by Clegg:

'There have been two schools of democrats, the one seeking to interpret democracy passively, as a means of ensuring as far as possible that governments act according to the wishes of the people and the other arguing that democracy must mean more than that, must mean the active participation of the people in the work of government. The first school have replied that "active participation" slips so easily into the assumption of a common purpose, and hence to some mystical general will. Then those whose actions and ideas seem contrary to "the general will" are regarded as evil and soon suppressed as disrupters of the common purpose. So that the last state of the democracy of active participation is indistinguishable from totalitarianism.'[7]

Clegg seems to dismiss the arguments of those who assert that, whether we want it or not, we are entering an era of organizational totalitarianism, the source of which is not participative democracy, but the progressive development of large-scale hierarchies in which the old principles of representation and parliamentary control become less and less effective. C. W. Mills was one of the first to signal this danger in his book *Power Elite*. Since then many studies have raised the same point and the events of the late 1960s seemed to corroborate this view of the crisis of representative democracy in the Western world. It is, however, in the communist countries that the issue is most salient.

The main point about participative democracy is deeply embedded in the assessment of the communist experiences which – whether we admit it or not – did not create a very convincing alternative to the present capitalist regimes. Those who are deeply dissatisfied with modern capitalism stop short at the question: is life under communist rule so much better as to allow the communists to take over power here?

The most devastating and yet unavoidable experience of communist revolution was the centralization of power, the impact of which was completely ignored by the revolutionary leaders. Political centralism was only part of the story. There was also economic centralism which, combined with full command over military and police forces, gave those in power an absolute dominance over society as a whole.

Concentration of power is the magic formula which brought about the failure of the socialist idea in its communist shape. This concentration of power took a very special form: on the one hand it meant the exclusion of all political forces and institutions which could not be controlled by the communists, i.e. the disarmament of society, and on the other it consisted in the progressive centralization of social administration so as to give full control to those at the top; thirdly, there was the process of changing the very social structure so as to make it fully adjusted to the absolute rule of the party *élite*, and there was the additional constant trend towards ensuring the maintenance of complete dominance over the masses by improving methods of total supervision. increasing terror and refining ideological monopoly.

The naïve belief that one can maintain democratic institutions within the party while getting rid of political democracy in society was doomed to failure and the old guard of communists was the first to learn the lesson.

All movements in communist countries which aimed at curtailing the power of the ruling *élites* were accompanied by demands for restoring workers' organizations and, where they could develop beyond the stage of political claims, workers' councils and workers' direct action became the main pillars of resistance and attack against party and state bureaucracy. The Polish 'October' of 1956, the Hungarian uprising in the same year and the December 1970 events in Poland developed along these lines. And the only country which managed to counteract the establishment of the Stalinist model – Yugoslavia – adopted the system of workers' representation as the major bulwark against the revival of totalitarian power.

When looked at from that angle, industrial democracy seems in the communist countries to be much more a political device than a for-

mula of economic organization. The very idea of workers' self-management, including the weapon of industrial action, is opposed to the
centralized power of the state. As long as the nature of the communist
leviathan consists in concentrating all power in the few hands of those
who are located at the top of the monstrous organizational hierarchy,
incorporating all institutions and associations into the system of the
party state and monopolizing all instruments of coercive control, the
idea of workers' organizations must be explosive and defy that system.
The whole balance of power remains unchallenged only as long as
society has no way of opposing the absolute rule of organizational
élites, who do their best to prevent any free associations and destroy all
attempts at creating any self-governing bodies that are not subject to
institutional supervision and are able to defend themselves if challenged
by the state.

A careful analysis of the 'revolutionary demands' forwarded by the
democratic opposition in the People's Republic reveals the same overall pattern. The demand is for the rotation of administrators and functionaries in their offices, elections starting virtually in the lowest
ranks, pluralism and freedom of decision-making for all sorts of participative bodies such as trade unions, youth organizations or co-operatives, wider use of referenda and, above all, self-management in
productive units, which implies workers' power not merely in the
economic but primarily in the political field. There is also invariably
put forward a claim for unrestricted information and all sorts of social
supervision over institutions which represent the system of organized
force – the police, in the first place. In this context participative democracy becomes a living formula of institutionalized safeguards against
centralized power, a way of exercising influence and maintaining the
control of rank and file citizens over structures which by their very
nature tend to subject individuals to their unchallenged dictatorship.
Ideas about forms of exercising political influence over organizational
systems are vague and must remain vague as long as there is no chance
of transforming them into mass action. Yet it is more than ever clear
that the general trend works in favour of and towards participative
democracy, as opposed to the traditional forms in which members of
society enjoy the dubious rights of electing the government once in a
while and face again the imminent danger of seeing the pseudo-
representative institutions converted into the organized power of those
who 'by general consent' may gain control over society as a whole.

The argument about incompatibility of the non-capitalist order with any sort of democracy is irrelevant for people living in the communist countries. For them, there is no way back towards 'de-nationalization' and the restoration of private economy, and yet the authoritarian structures have to be opposed despite the most elaborate contentions about the totalitarian nature of the system.

When examining the political experience of communist countries, there is no point, however, in concentrating on the workers as the only social group which are supposed to exercise their power over organized structures. Secondly there is no reason to limit participative democracy to production units, since modern societies are organized in all possible dimensions and hence all sorts of social control are needed. And in the third place we have to be aware that the new system engenders new contradictions which go beyond those between private owners and those who work for them. There is a growing danger of the dissociation of functionaries and experts from those whom they are supposed to serve. The very fact that every organization resembles one-party rule much more than a democratic system brings us to the issue of who should control those at the top, who are meant to exercise democratic control on behalf of rank and file members.

Briefly, I reject the claim that industrial democracy is the main issue of democratic reform and emphasize that it is but a part of the system of democratic participation. It is by concentrating on the system and not on one or other aspect of it that we can make a decisive step in clarifying a programme for the future.

Conclusions

In all discussions about industrial democracy one problem invariably emerges – that of the relationship between the ideology of social change and the organized form in which the change is implemented. It has become usual for those who generate ideas related to the future shape of society to fight for them by joining political parties, secret societies or urban guerillas. As a result of their 'activism' we face a situation in which either organized movements disregard the masses to follow the lead of the most radical thinkers or less 'radical' intellectuals try to adjust themselves to the institutionalized strategies of mass movements and avoid any theoretical issues which seem too controversial and unacceptable to their would-be supporters.

In the former case the idea of participative democracy is converted into what could be called mock-democracy or 'manipulative democracy' since the *avant-garde* does not seriously expect any direct consensus of rank and file citizens to back their programme; in the latter case the outlook of the most backward and lukewarm allies determines the ideological perspectives on industrial democracy.

What can be said with certainty is that a programme of industrial democracy can be incorporated into different ideological contexts as a response to various pressures and different social needs.

Whether we call ourselves communists, socialists or syndicalists there is so far one common denominator among all these standpoints – a commitment to ideas and concepts which belong to the past and which were generated in the nineteenth century as the answer to the evils of free-competitive capitalist society. Once we admit that we face nowadays a period of transition from that free-competitive capitalism to state control, interventionism and macro-economic planning the whole social and political perspective has to be thoroughly revised. There is no point then in arguing for or against socialism on grounds of central planning or State control, since most people are for planning and control in one way or another. The real question is about what kind of socialism we are aiming at, what kind of interventionism, centralized control and state planning we are prepared to accept.

In the long run, participative democracy, incorporated in the system of workers' self-management and elsewhere, could be regarded as a safeguard against the organized power of the state by making the workers and rank and file employees in general independent of organizational *élites* and able to resist them if necessary.

It is at that level that a new controversy is bound to loom large. The bureaucrat who used to be regarded as a mere tool of the privileged minorities has been converted into an arbitrary master located in well-organized structures which supply him with tools for controlling other people while co-ordinating their activities. Those who are better educated, better trained and better acquainted with the world of emerging bureaucracies tend to associate with them whether they approve of them or not. Intellectuals may advocate progressive social change and at the same time many of them are inclined to support that kind of change which deprives the masses of any say, while increasing their own power within the organization that employs them. Students may press for immediate revolution and yet welcome a programme implementing revolutionary change that deprives the workers of any influence while increasing the hold of the administrators and functionaries over them. Professional men criticize a system which gives the right to govern society to big business and the *élites* linked with it, and at the same time approve the view that those who hold organizational offices are fully entitled to exercise arbitrary rule over those placed in subordinate positions.

The controversy over industrial democracy at that level cuts across the basic division between those who are for socialism and a planned economy and those who are against them. Post-capitalist societies seem to generate in that respect new problems which are not easily answered within the traditional framework of social theory. Where should one look for reasonable suggestions? Can we expect to find them in the writings of the anarchists and syndicalists or in Marx's studies? I do not think any of these is to be relied upon, and the sooner we face the fact that we deal with a theory in the making the more chance we have of solving the problems involved.

17

COMMENT ON MARIA HIRSZOWICZ'S PAPER

Franz Marek

Any contribution in French inevitably raises epistemological problems.* The basic terms employed by Mrs Hirszowicz raise difficulties when used in French and English in different ways. For example the term 'autogestion' in French is translated into English in several differing ways, such as 'self-government' and 'self-management'. For a French activist this idiomatic language rather blurs the distinction between the perspectives of workers' control and the direction of the framework of a profit-based economy. The same preoccupation, not merely linguistic, is raised when we speak in English of terms like 'industrial democracy', 'social control of production', 'workers' control'. These concepts are not used in French, nor does 'co-partnership', which corresponds to 'Mitbestimmung' in German. Finally, participation: 'participation' in France has purely Gaullist overtones, an idea according to which de Gaulle was aiming at participation of the workers in the ownership and profits of firms, not at all in any increase in workers' power.

We can overcome this difficulty, which is not just a linguistic one, by bringing what has happened in the past history of the workers' movement and struggle into the present discussions in France, Italy and more and more in Germany.

In general one talks of Marx's analysis of the Paris Commune as the self-government of producers (*Selbstregierung der Prodizenten*) which he saw as the final discovery by the producing classes of how to govern in the context of the abolition of the state. Lenin and the protagonists of the October Revolution drew on this interpretation of the Commune by Marx, considering the soviets of workers and peasants as a higher form of direct democracy, starting from the places of production

* This paper was delivered in French.

and constituting power as a network of producing communes. The soviets, Antonio Gramsci concluded, are the organs of the producers not of the wage-earners, and this producers' democracy, according to Gramsci, opens a new era in the history of humanity. But the evolution of the Soviet Union soon rid the word 'soviet' of its original meaning. There are today Soviet diplomacy, Soviet dancers, Soviet ballet and a Soviet circus, but there are no soviets in the original sense of the word as organs of producers' power.

Mrs Hirszowicz's contribution cites a phrase of Clegg, who concludes ironically that the final stage of democratic participation by the workers is totalitarianism. But just the opposite has happened: the abolition of the soviets as organs of producers' democracy has contributed to the changing of the working class from a class 'for itself' to a class 'in itself'. The effect was so profound and the idea of a democracy of producers was so deeply buried in oblivion that Jaurès Medvedev, discussing the problems of democracy in the Soviet Union, did not go back to the idea of soviets. He rejects even the Yugoslav variant of self-management, and yet the merit of this variant is to restore the idea of the producers' democracy. This was the only serious attempt to revive what is called the lesson of the Paris Commune.

It is at this point that the question raised by Mrs Hirszowicz in her paper must be discussed. How can one explain the fact that the entire debate on worker's control, producers' democracy and democratic councils has been resurrected in the late 1960s and early 1970s?

To answer this question, one cannot stress enough the importance of the events of May 1968 in France and even more of those of the 'hot Autumn' of 1969 in Italy. They showed, it seems to me, that we are living in Europe at a time when the crisis of authority, the political and moral crisis of the bourgeois way of life, coincides with a serious crisis in the workers' movement. Revolt, in the first case, which is against a representative democracy that is more and more a formality, empty of reason, is the cause of this new resurgence of regionalism and nationalism; against a democracy which stops at the factory gates, the place where most people spend most of their active lives and most of their energy. This democracy gives no answer to the question: production for whom and for what? There is discontent too about the fact that technical development is aimed not at making work easier but at drawing maximum profit from wage-earners. And revolt, in the second case, which is against the bureaucratic paternalism of the workers' movement, against the watering down of the demands of the base through a pyramidical hierarchy of traditional organizations, party or union. This is the importance of the *assembleia operaia* at Pirelli and other enterprises, an assembly of Italian workers directly electing a workers' council – always revocable, reproducing in that too one of the lessons of the Paris Commune. Again, therefore, the transcending of the quantitative demands of the union to qualitative ones coming from the increased power of the workers in the factory. Moreover this re-birth of the idea of direct democracy of the producers finds its literary expression in the renewed interest in the works of Korsch, Pannekoek and others.

Mrs Hirszowicz's paper rightly presents some questions raised not only in the discussion but also in practice. In fact it is a very frequent phenomenon that the workers protest against the appalling monotony of the assembly line by acts of sabotage, increasing absenteeism and job-changing. In some workshops 80 per cent of non-specialized workers leave and are replaced by others because they cannot tolerate the terrible rhythm of the assembly line.

The hope of management that it can solve this problem by employ-ing immigrant workers is not always fulfilled, as shown by the wildcat strikes in France, Belgium and Italy, where people from the south come to Milan and Turin as immigrants, for these immigrant workers have sometimes been in the forefront of the fight. There are thus com-plaints by management, as Hirszowicz's paper reports, that the workers show a certain apathy and lack of interest in the schemes introduced by management to enlarge the influence of wage-earners.

Experiences are not always the same, however. For example, the very different experiment at Volvo in Sweden, where the idea of replacing the assembly-line by group-work, leaving a certain initiative and control to the workers, has had very positive results.

The problem lies elsewhere. There is a difference between a con-cession which makes work more interesting in the interests of the management, and achievements won in a struggle to enlarge workers' power; between a co-partnership giving a few places to union leaders on administrative councils, and workers' deputies elected in plenary meetings and revocable any time. Galbraith saw clearly the main question: 'Labour has won limited authority over his pay and working conditions, but not over the enterprise' (*The New Industrial State*, p. 69.)

Let me add in passing that I do not believe one can generalize the statement of the paper that all kinds of apathy amongst wage-earners are worse in nationalized than in private industry. Here, too, experiences differ. For example, that of Austria, where 60 per cent of large enterprises are nationalized, would tend to prove the contrary. Similarly in Italy, where the monetary agreements negotiated in the nationalized steel industry go far beyond anything achieved in private enterprise. The quotations from Dahl mentioned in the paper reflect rather the ambiguous situation of the unions and governmental parties and underline once again the difference between co-partnership and workers' control.

A few words about another argument which is rightly emphasized and can be carried further: workers are not sufficiently competent to control management, and it would be utopian to think of 100 per cent control by workers. I do not want to brush aside their argument but it reminds me of the words of Tocqueville who said that we should leave delicate questions of foreign affairs to the aristocrats.

I cannot treat the problem comprehensively here, but I would like to make two remarks which might facilitate discussion, without giving a solution. One historical comment that seems to me interesting and which I hope will not prove me wrong: in Czechoslovakia in 1968 the workers' councils changed their character with the June Law, by which they could elect and revoke their directors, decide on their position and on the statutes governing the factories. The workers elected technicians as 70 per cent of their representatives. They wanted to replace the bureaucrats, appointed not on ability but on position and for political reasons, with men who knew something. The principles of the right of election and of revocability gave them a certain assurance and confidence.

A second point seems to me more important. It is necessary to consider qualitative demands for workers' control in the contact of the non-utopian struggle, linked with opposition to hierarchical factory structure and differentiation between workers and bosses, for new relationships between the school and production, indeed, a new society which would have for its slogan the saying invented by the Italian workers, and which should be prominent in discussion about socialism: a society not only for living better, but for living differently. I have already discussed one aspect of this orientation which I find in the recent agreement between the metal-workers and the Italian government. After five months of struggle, and a demonstration of 300,000 metal workers in Rome, an agreement was reached which anticipated a single system of remuneration for workers and employers, 150 hours for permanent education and an equal bonus for all.

It seems to me, therefore, that it is in terms of autogestion that we must consider these grave problems of the competence of the wage-earners to control management, the acuteness of which I cannot deny. This obliges me, finally, to make some remarks about autogestion in Yugoslavia. The Marxist critic attacks bourgeois representative democracy for stopping at the factory entrance, but the Yugoslavian experience shows that if autogestion – i.e. self-management – stops at the factory exit it will be greatly retarded and create the danger that the workers will again be subjected to a layer of technocrats and bureaucrats. Even the important principles of revocability and reprobation lose their impact. And the further problems of the relations between workers' power in the factory and the general interest, which must find expression in the politics of investment, a programme of planning and a decisiveness in directing the affairs of the community, these problems – and here I agree with Mrs Hirszowicz – remain unresolved both theoretically and in practice.

The slogan of the Proudhonian anarchists, 'The factory for the workers', which is very dear to some leftists in France and Italy, is not a solution, as can be shown by the banal example of workers in a tobacco factory, or producing alcoholic drinks, who would be very interested in increasing the amount they produce although this would not at all be in the interests of the community. Moreover, we must have a different understanding of some types of enterprise. It is true, as Mrs Hirszowicz says, that while we speak of producers' democracy, we can no longer call only the manual worker a producer. But the Yugoslavian experiment shows that, if 'autogestion' puts factories, banks and joint stock companies on the same level, the factories and workers will be exploited. The Yugoslavian experiment remains the only one of the existing 'socialist' societies to use a system – about which I am not very enthusiastic – which has revived this idea of producers' democracy.

To finish, I will make a short autocritical remark, following the lesson Mr Harrington has given us. This problem of workers' control and direct democracy is now the main point of all discussions of the Western workers' movements, at least on the continent. The question that comes to mind is not 'What is wrong with the socialist idea?', but rather 'What is wrong with the reality in the East and the West that it does not correspond to the socialist idea?' I agree with Mrs Hirszowicz's conclusion, that we will not find the solution to these questions ready-made in the works of previous thinkers.

18

THE FUTURE OF SOCIALISM IN THE ADVANCED DEMOCRACIES

Richard Lowenthal

The purpose of this essay is to discuss the political chances of socialist movements in industrially advanced, democratic societies. It does not deal with the problems of 'socialist' states under communist one-party rule, nor with those of 'socialist' movements seeking to transform countries still wrestling with the problems of modernization. Even within the industrially advanced democracies, I shall only try to deal with movements which, for all their differences in programme and strategy, have a minimum of common outlook with regard to the direction in which they seek to transform society and the kind of means they envisage – an outlook based, I believe, on a common origin.

The common direction of all socialist movements, it seems to me, is the goal of a social order founded on more social and economic *equality*, higher social and economic *security*, and greater emphasis on *community values* than are produced by the spontaneous development of an industrial economy under the profit motive. The common denominator of the means all these movements envisage for approaching that goal is that they seek some form of effective *social control* over the dynamics of that economy.

Three Types of Socialist Movements

Three main types of movements falling under this broad definition exist in modern societies today. They are distinguished not only by different emphasis and elaboration with regard to various aspects of the goal, but – more relevant for their political chances – by different strategies for achieving it.

1. The *communists* believe that the socialist ideal can become reality only in a society without social classes and without state power; that the road to that goal must pass through the nationalization or collecti-

vization of all means of production (hence through the destruction of the basis of livelihood of all classes defined by their private ownership of means of production, which demands repeated revolutionary upheavals); and that this achievement requires a concentration of dictatorial state power in the hands of their party for a considerable period. Even where they work patiently within the framework of liberal-democratic institutions, their ultimate concept of social control is therefore not democratic control in this framework, but monopolistic control by their own centralistic party.*

2. The *Social Democrats* regard a classless and stateless society as utopian in the sense of being strictly impossible in modern technological conditions. They consider the preservation of individual liberties as equally important with the socialist goal itself, and a pluralistic democracy as a precondition both for the defence of individual liberties and for effective social control. They therefore reject a programme of total nationalization and collectivization that could be imposed only by a revolutionary dictatorship and seek to exercise social control of the economic system in the direction of the socialist goal by reforms within the framework of political democracy such as the use of techniques for economic planning, the expansion of public enterprise, of social security and of workers' participation in management, and educational measures aimed at equality of opportunity and at a transformation of social values. They, too, need governmental power for this programme, but they will seek it only in democratic conditions where the continued existence of rival parties makes it precarious and impermanent.

3. The various currents of the New Left share with the communists the goal of a classless and stateless society and the critique of pluralistic democracy as a mere disguise of capitalist class rule. They tend, however, to distrust any dictatorship of a centralistic party as an obstacle to the goal of effective social control and to the 'withering away' of the

---

* In the last few years, the official statements issued by some West European communist parties, particularly in the context of electoral alliances with non-communists, have no longer conformed to the 'classic' concept of the 'Dictatorship of the Proletariat' as a single-party state used here. There are cases where this may still have to be regarded as a mere tactical disguise; that applies particularly to the French communists in view of their unchanged 'Bolshevik' internal party structure. But where there are serious indications of a genuine revision of the Leninist model in favour of a theoretical commitment to pluralistic democracy, arrived at after an inner-party discussion, as in the case of the Italian communists, we may indeed be faced with the beginning of a transformation of a communist party into a party that is becoming social democratic in principle, however militant it may remain.

state, and look to the revolutionary-democratic activity of the masses both as a means for the overthrow of the capitalist order and as the political form of the new order to which they aspire. Accordingly, they are not necessarily committed to the nationalization or collectivization of the property of all small producers, and their revolutionary strategy is not primarily directed to the seizure of the commanding heights of state power. Instead, they concentrate on mobilizing the masses both for material demands and for the conquest of 'direct democratic', i.e. plebiscitary, control of the organs of public administration, management, education and opinion; in this way, they seek to combine the struggle for legal reforms with the escalation of extra-legal conflicts involving all the institutions they regard as bastions of the physical, economic or ideological power of the ruling class. By means of this dual strategy, they hope gradually to take over the levers for manipulating the consciousness of the masses, to paralyse the levers of state power and to disorganize the functioning of the capitalist economy to the point when the generalization of conflicts will finally produce the collapse of the old political and social order and thus open the way for a new society without exploitation and oppression.

The Transformation of Social Problems

An attempt to judge the political chances of these three types of socialist movements demands an analysis of the principal problems causing social discontent in industrially advanced societies, and of the adequacy of the different strategies for dealing with these problems. In seeking to sketch the outlines of such an analysis, I shall start from the salient change produced in recent decades by the successful solution of some formerly central problems of those societies and the rise of others.

From the time of Karl Marx to the 1930s, the most powerful single cause of mass discontent in modern industrial societies was the cyclical development of uncontrolled capitalist economies in general and the recurrence of mass unemployment in particular. Closely linked with economic instability were the phenomena of mass poverty and social insecurity. These were felt most acutely by the industrial working class, but they also afflicted the ranks of the small independent producers in constant danger of ruin, as well as the distributive trades and their employees. During the same period, which coincided with the heyday of the nation-states and colonial empires, the 'imperialist' conflicts between the major powers were visibly motivated in part by economic rivalries for markets, raw materials, and spheres of capital investment;

so that the two world wars appeared in many eyes as due mainly to the influence of profit-seeking private interests on government policies. Accordingly, the classical socialist mass movements of both the social democratic and the communist type appealed primarily to the industrial working class. Their immediate programmes concentrated – along with the defence or expansion of democracy (according to the situation) – on achieving steady economic growth, full and stable employment, comprehensive social security and international peace and co-operation by planned control of the economic process, with the help of such measures of nationalization (or other forms of state intervention) as each party thought necessary and possible.

Under the impact of the world economic crisis of 1929–32 and of World War II and its aftermath, many of these problems have been solved or greatly reduced in importance in the leading Western industrial societies and in Japan – without revolutionary changes in the structure of ownership and under democratic political regimes. Techniques for achieving steady economic growth with high or near-full employment – first tried out towards the end of the Depression by the Swedish Social Democrats, the German National Socialists and the American New Deal, then spread by the requirements of rearmament and a war economy – have been generalized throughout the advanced democratic countries in the post-war period and proved largely independent from war or war-like conditions. The resulting economic affluence has combined with democratic pressures to make possible considerable, if uneven, expansions of social security in the same countries. It has also ended working class poverty as a mass phenomenon. The same transformation of the economic system has enabled the dismantling of the colonial empires to take place without the expected reduction of the living standards of the metropolitan masses, which have in fact resumed their rise. Finally, economic rivalries among the democratic industrial countries have not, of course, disappeared. But they have greatly lost in virulence owing both to common prosperity, to increasing economic interpenetration and to the perception of a common political interest in resisting the pressure of the communist powers. This has been most striking in the development of supra-national economic institutions in Western Europe.

As a result of these developments, most of the classical socialist movements in the advanced democracies have been increasingly 'deradicalized' in their practice and (to a lesser extent) in their ideology. The social democrats have played a leading role in the post-war transformation of Britain; but they have been most persistently success-ful in the Scandinavian countries where they were least committed to demands for nationalization and concentrated most exclusively on employment policy, social security, and redistributive reform. In West Germany, they achieved a growing share of governmental power only after a sharp break with the ideological remnants of doctrinaire tradi-tions. In France and Italy, where the communists traditionally consti-tuted the leading party of the working class, they have evolved (after the short period of the anti-fascist post-war coalitions) from violent opposition in 1948-9 to verbally radical, but practically reformist, opposition of a type similar to the pre-1914 social democrats during the 1950s and early 1960s. More recently they have made increasing efforts to become acceptable partners for a government coalition including assurances that they would respect the rules of the democratic game even if in power.

New Factors of Popular Discontent

Since the middle 1960s, however, new factors of popular discontent with the political, economic, and social functioning of the 'capitalist democracies' have become increasingly effective, and have begun once again to transform the political scene.

1. Possibly of only transitory importance, but probably responsible for the timing of the change, has been the widespread revival of belief in a link between capitalist interest and war among intellectuals and the youth which started from the revulsion against the US intervention in Viet Nam. It was this experience which gave a new plausibility to the fear that the East–West conflict with its attendant arms race was bound to lead to the horrors of actual war, and to the 'explanation' of the entire conflict by the machinations of the 'military–industrial complex' or by the class interests of the capitalists in general. Thus the universal desire for peace was once again turned into a motivation for radical anti-capitalism.

2. Most powerful among the new factors is probably the cultural revolt of an important part of the young generation against the 'affluent society' itself – the rebellion against its cult of the consumer's most marginal material enjoyments, its spirit of competitive achievement, and the emptiness of its leisure activities which results from the evident lack of a common purpose. In linking the spiritual emptiness from which they suffer with the predominance of the profit motive and of competition in the market, the rebels devalue the productive achieve-

ments of the modern societies and look for an alternative in a socialist community of sacrifice. On that basis, they bitterly reject all authorities which accept the prevailing values, and direct their revolt not only against capitalist ownership but against every form of established authority or 'domination'.

3. Closest to the traditional motivations for mass discontent is the apparent revival of the 'class struggle' in the advanced democracies in the context of accelerating inflation, and the emergence of stubborn, marginal, but by no means negligible pockets of poverty. The solution of the problem of maintaining high employment and steady economic growth has created the new, hitherto unsolved, problem of combining this achievement with monetary stability and trade union freedom. True, many experts regard a moderate rate of inflation as an acceptable price for assuring employment and freedom. But to keep it moderate requires a degree of restraint from both unions and employers that is difficult to ensure in conditions of full political and organizational freedom and in a climate of otherwise unrestrained materialism. In turn, accelerating inflation may not only bring competitive disadvantage for whichever country runs ahead of others, but above all spells social disadvantage for the mass of small savers as well as the recipients of fixed salaries, social insurance rents and welfare payments, which include precisely the most persistent pockets of real poverty. The result is a spreading conviction that the mechanism of 'the system' permits advantages to one group – a strong craft union, say, or a mass union, or the recipients of social benefits – only at the expense of another, and that restraint in such conditions is not meritorious but stupid.

4. However, the problem likely to prove ultimately decisive for the fate of 'the system', and of any socialist alternative, is that of the physical and biological limits to economic growth. This problem has for some time attracted widespread attention in the form of the fear of a 'poisoned environment'; but it also includes the increasingly unmanageable ugliness and traffic chaos in our overcrowded cities, and the aspect of a possible exhaustion of raw material and energy resources is clearly even more vital. In the short run, the call for protection of the environment against pollution and for attention to urban problems is a powerful reinforcement for the old socialist argument that private economic activity may cause heavy social costs that do not appear in the calculations of the individual entrepreneur, and that social control of investment decisions is therefore necessary. It thus strengthens the demand for more public control of the direction – as distinct

from the volume – of investment put forward on other social and cultural grounds. In the long run, the current debate about a suggested need to slow down the growth of output, and also of the human population, drastically or even to zero raises the question of the survival of the very type of industrial society we have known so far – a type that has been fundamentally geared to the assumption of growth both in the 'capitalist' and in the communist-governed economies.

All the new factors of popular discontent that have made themselves felt in the 'capitalist' democracies in recent years favour at first sight a revival of the strength and militancy of socialist movements, because they clearly reinforce the call for a greater emphasis on community values at the expense of the profit motive and of other forms of material self-interest, and for a corresponding strengthening of social control. The opposition of community values to the material egotism of individuals and groups lies at the core of the cultural revolt of the young. A similar shift in the balance of motivations from self-interest to community interest is increasingly regarded as a precondition for stopping accelerated inflation without resort either to a return to mass unemployment or to a suppression of trade union freedom. But obviously such a shift cannot be achieved by any amount of preaching while the dynamism of the economy remains based on the unrestrained pursuit of profit.

The relevance of capitalism to war and the armament race may well prove far more limited than is assumed in the mythology of the radical left, as both the poverty of its economic arguments and the recent policies of the conservative Nixon-Kissinger administration in the US indicate. But as Cold War tensions abate, the conflicts of economic interest among the advanced capitalist democracies are gaining in importance as obstacles to stable international cooperation, even though they continue to be far less virulent than comparable conflicts among communist states. Above all, an adjustment of industrial societies to the awareness of limits of growth seems inconceivable without extensive qualitative controls of the direction of investment, designed to ensure the primacy of the survival of the community over the free pursuit of profit by each particular enterprise.

Strength and Weakness of the 'New Left'

Of the three main types of socialist movements existing today, the 'New Left' is most naturally attuned to these new factors of social discontent. Indeed, it is the direct expression of the fact that many young people have come to reject a value system centred on material consumption, private gain and economic growth, as well as the need for efforts, sacrifices and discipline to achieve those goals. Within a few years, various movements of the New Left have been remarkably successful in transforming the climate of public discussion, undermining established authority, gaining influence on many educational institutions and weakening the organs of state power in a number of advanced democratic societies. They have also, by the example of militant actions of a new type and by organized work within the 'established' left-wing parties and trade unions, begun to influence the policy of the latter in the direction of shattering the reformist consensus of the previous period. In France, the student revolt of May 1968 became the occasion of mass strikes that forced a more militant wage policy on the communist-led trade unions and through them on the Communist Party. In Italy, a similar result was achieved by the gradual impact of 'wildcat strikes' frequently led by younger workers under the influence of radical splinter groups. In West Germany and Scandinavia, organized left-wing factions have developed in the social democratic parties due to the systematic work of younger activists representing the resurgence of ideology. New Left activity has thus converged with the inflationary tendencies of the system itself to restore a measure of working class militancy in Western Europe, even though the movement first arose outside the industrial working class.

Yet although New Left actions have frequently scored successes both for their immediate tactical objectives and for their strategic goal of transforming public consciousness, the movements of this type continue to lack the organizational and programmatic coherence which would qualify them as candidates for winning state power in their own right. Indeed, a profound distrust of every form of state power and an emphasis on 'mass action' from below continue to be characteristic not only of their psychology and behaviour, but of whatever strategic political concepts they have so far developed. Yet effective social control of advanced industrial economies is not seriously conceivable without the use of the co-ordinated coercive power of the state. Any attempt to replace it in this function by piecemeal activities from below – by means of strikes, factory occupations, workers' control, boycotts, etc. – must necessarily increase the tendency toward economic chaos in general the more successful it is in detail. It therefore risks producing not a socialist new order, but a fascist backlash, in the light of which all the partial revolts, so purposefully escalated yet ultimately without purpose, would turn out to have been stages of a Long March into total defeat.

It follows that the New Left movements cannot by themselves bring about a political victory for 'socialism' in their present form. Their impact on its chances will ultimately depend either on their evolution into new parties with a clearer concept of the road to power, or – more likely and more immediately – on the influence of their ideas and tactics on the established social democratic and communist parties.

Difficulties of a Social-Democratic Solution

Will the social democratic parties be able to harness the new forces of popular discontent for an attractive programme of extending social control by democratic reforms? Such a development is conceivable, because these parties are showing themselves, after a period of complacent ideological stagnation shattered by New Left criticism, increasingly open to new ideas, and because some of the new issues have a much broader potential appeal to the electorate than mere class issues. But any strategy for extending state control of the economy by peaceful democratic reform must in present conditions face at least three major difficulties.

The first difficulty is that a more comprehensive policy of state control of the economy is not compatible with a one-sided policy of re-distribution in favour of the industrial working class, either in substance or in tactics – and the 'left' currents in the social democratic and the trade union movement are committed to both. A more effective qualitative control of the direction of investment, and even more an effort to slow down economic growth, is bound to be bitterly resisted by most of the capitalist owners and most of the 'leisure class' accustomed to indulge in competitive consumption of luxury goods. It can only be justified by a decisive appeal to community values such as health, urban renewal, care for the poor, and ultimately to long-term survival; and it can only be achieved with the support of broad strata of middle class intellectuals, technicians, and employees and of such receivers of fixed incomes as the civil servants, the small savers, and the publicly-supported poor. The support of these strata cannot be won – and the argument for more control not be credibly sustained – by a party whose special ties to the unions cause it to satisfy wage demands at the price of accelerated inflation, or to gear a redistributive tax policy exclusively to the interests of the industrial workers. As the industrial working class is a declining minority in all advanced countries, one-sided, militant redistribution in its favour is a recipe for political crisis ending possibly in revolution, but more likely in fascist reaction – certainly not for sustained democratic reform.

The second major difficulty concerns the very nature of any policy of controlling the direction and/or slowing down the pace of economic growth. The great achievement of the first major advance towards social control of capitalist economies has been the assurance of reasonably stable employment at a high level by means of steady economic growth. It was a growth that was uneven only inasmuch as technological innovations and new needs produced sudden spurts of demand for some goods and a falling-off for others.

The recognition that the rapid growth of certain lines of production may cause harm to the environment out of all proportion to their usefulness to individual buyers, or that it tends quickly to exhaust resources that may be needed for more vital purposes for many years to come, does not make these lines automatically unprofitable. It depends on a judgment about their social importance or harmfulness that is different from that expressed by monetary demand on the market in the absence of qualitative controls. It can therefore only be made effective by specific measures which either change the data for the market or directly interfere with it by administrative orders. The same applies *a fortiori* to a distinction between technological innovations that tend to save or to waste scarce raw materials, to economize or to use up city space, to permit the long-term satisfaction of basic needs with less goods or to stimulate the need for more.

But apart from the inherent difficulty of winning acceptance for such qualitative controls (which may well be opposed by many consumers in the interest of variety and freedom of choice as well as by capitalist producers in search of profits), their overall effect is likely to slow down the average pace of economic growth in the advanced industrial countries, as may indeed be inevitable if the approach of resource exhaustion is to be avoided – and this is bound to affect the level of employment in several ways, because employment largely depends on investment. On one side, the decision to stop investment for growth in certain directions is bound to create pockets of unemployment that can only be absorbed gradually by the retraining of workers and the relocation of alternative industries. On the other hand, such absorption will only be possible to the extent that overall growth continues. In a market economy, that can only be assured if there are always one or more particular lines of investment in new 'growth industries' that provide the basis for the profit expectations of other investors and hence the impetus for the whole movement. In short, planning for high and stable employment in a limited growth economy poses problems which, while not insoluble, are inherently far more complicated than planning for stimulation of maximum growth. While at first sight each particular problem can be handled most easily by imposing particular measures of restriction or stimulation, the proliferation of such measures threatens to produce a loss of flexibility and efficiency and a consequent impoverishment in the manner familiar from war economies or from administrative planning of the Soviet type.

Now I do believe that *some* such loss of consumer satisfaction due to increased controls is indeed a preferable alternative to an uncontrolled race towards increasing destruction of the environment and exhaustion of resources; and it may therefore have to be accepted as an inescapable part of any realistic 'socialist' programme for the coming period. But the difficulty of striking the right balance and of preparing a co-ordinated set of measures that will be both effective and democratically acceptable is surely obvious.

The third major difficulty lies in the narrow limits of any purely national policy of controlling economic growth. This is familiar from the present problem of keeping the employment- and growth-stimulating policies of different countries in step in conditions of national sovereignty over monetary policy. Any country that temporarily adopts deflationary measures may gain a competitive advantage in foreign trade, or may compel its competitors to deflate as well at the expense of full employment. But while this has proved manageable in a context of universal commitment to steady growth, a major policy reversal in favour of a long-term slow-down could clearly not be carried through in a national context. The risks of widening technological gaps opening between nations accustomed to close economic co-operation and leading to the creation of new trade barriers between them, need only be mentioned to show that a slow-down policy could only be carried out by agreement among the leading industrial nations of the world – hence after a victory of the control programme in most of them. A socialist policy in this field can only be international. Moreover, the implications of a slow-down of growth for armaments policy raise the question of its feasibility in a world divided by long-term conflict between rival power groups.

In addition to these three major difficulties of extending social control over the economy by democratic structural reforms within the advanced societies, there is the enormous problem of their impact on the Third World. The poor and underdeveloped countries with rapidly increasing populations constitute the majority of mankind. These countries cannot, and should not, be expected to slow down their (often all-too-slow) economic growth, on which the attainment of a tolerable standard of living for their masses depends. No politically and humanly conceivable redistribution between the 'rich' and the 'poor' countries could possibly enable them to dispense with such growth. Moreover, they may well feel that a slowdown of economic growth in the advanced countries would further reduce their chances of obtaining adequate outlets for their exports and sufficient aid for their own economic development.

Above all, no long-term equilibrium on this planet is now conceivable without a slow-down and probably an end to the growth of population, which concerns those countries in the first place. Even apart from the fundamental difficulty for any government to control a growth that depends, after all, on the most private enterprise that exists, many of the governments concerned may well be ideologically reluctant to stop the growth of what they regard as a power resource in the long run. But this is, I must note, not really a special difficulty for a social democratic solution of the problems of the modern societies, but a general difficulty for any solution.

The Dilemma of Western Communism

At first glance, most of the major difficulties of extending state control by democratic reform appear to favour the *communist* alternative. Fundamentally opposed as they are to the regimes of the advanced democracies, the communists will find it easy to exploit the new popular revulsion against war and the 'anti-communist' Cold War. They have merely to return to their tradition of class struggle in order to support the new trade union militancy against any appeals for restraint or 'concerted action', while denouncing the acceleration of inflation and ascribing it to the machinations of the monopolies and, more generally, to the capitalist system founded on private profits. They are also free to advocate both nationalization and increasingly detailed planning as in harmony with their doctrine and with the model of the Soviet Union. Thus they have a good chance of influencing the activism of the New Left (including those of its currents that operate in other socialist parties) by offering it a way of combining anti-capitalist

233

and anti-government militancy with a power-oriented political strategy.

But the communists in the advanced democracies can do this only at a price – that of abandoning their efforts of recent years to become 'democratically respectable' in order to qualify for membership in a government majority. These efforts have long shaped their political strategy in Italy and have lately increasingly influenced it in France. It was precisely this strategy which made them potentially useful to Soviet foreign policy in a climate of *détente*, and formed the basis of the compromise under which Moscow tolerated a measure of criticism on their part so long as they maintained a general pro-Soviet orientation. A return to the pursuit of militancy without regard for the functioning of 'the system' would necessarily isolate the communists from their potential democratic partners. While it might bring them short-term successes among sections of the working class, it would cause – for the reasons I have mentioned in discussing the problems of social democracy – bitter resentment among large sections of the middle classes and the recipients of fixed incomes. This would not only deprive them of any chance of winning a democratic majority on their own; it would also ensure that, if they succeeded in creating a major crisis of the democratic system, the hopes of most of the victims of that crisis would not turn to them, but rather to some kind of authoritarian or fascist alternative. The same would apply *a fortiori* if the communists' unwillingness to adopt a strategy of unrestrained militancy led to the growth of a militant mass party of New Left outlook in one country or another.

Whether the communists decide to continue the pursuit of democratic respectability or to opt for a return to 'revolutionary' militancy, they will thus be faced with the same dilemma as the social democrats – between a narrow concentration on their traditional working class basis or the winning of a broad majority for social transformation. Moreover, the dilemma of the national limits of social control will haunt the communists in the special form of the familiar limitations of public confidence in them, owing to their persistent basic orientation to the model of an outside power. Only if we assume that a communist party came to power in an advanced industrial country in spite of these difficulties (which has never happened yet), would it then have a decisive advantage over any social democratic government in *maintaining* power in spite of the difficulties of transition. It could (and would) suspend the operation of democracy and ruthlessly pursue its programme of social and economic transformation. Whether such a system of dictatorial state control of the economy could be described as *social control* in the sense of our initial working definition of 'socialism' is, of course, the subject of a well-worn controversy.

New Forces making for Socialism

Our tentative exploration of the political chances of socialism in modern societies has obviously raised more questions than it could answer. One broad result, however, seems to be clear. The historical forces pressing for a socialist transformation of industrial societies are today of a radically different kind from what they appeared to be in the view of socialist thinkers of the nineteenth and the first half of the twentieth century.

Karl Marx believed that socialism would win when the capitalist relations of production had become a fetter on the further development of the productive forces. Lenin saw the imperialist stage of capitalism as characterized by 'parasitic stagnation', and concluded that the time was ripe for socialist revolution on an international scale. The actual development of the capitalist economies, particularly since their partial transformation by public policies of high employment and steady growth, has completely refuted them. The growth of the productive forces in the advanced societies has in recent decades accelerated to a pace never dreamt of by either the prophets of socialism or the critics of capitalism.

What has happened, however, is that under the impulse of the profit motive, the forces of destruction have grown along with the forces of production – not only in the familiar sense of the increasing destructiveness of modern weapons, but of the destructive impact of modern industrial technology on the environment and the natural resources – until they now threaten to outpace the latter. It looks as if the acceleration of technical progress under the profit system is tending to destroy its own material foundation. The call for socialism is thus turning from a cry for 'liberating the productive forces from the fetters of capitalist ownership' into a cry for taming the uncontrolled growth of these forces promoted by the profit motive, so as to control its destructive effects.

But if this is so, it does not only mean that the forces pressing for socialism have changed their character. It means that the basic relation between material progress and human values, on which the development of modern societies has been based, has to be rethought, and with it the relation of individual freedom and social survival. The nineteenth century in the West was dominated by a growing conviction that material progress was the foundation of all human progress. It was a conviction that has spread from the West into all countries in the process of modernization, and of which the Marxian interpretation of history was perhaps the most comprehensive expression. That view has now become demonstrably outdated. Socialism can no longer be conceived as *assuring* a new unfolding of the human personality *on the basis* of unheard-of material progress, but must be seen as dependent on a change in the order of human values *at the expense* of the primacy of material progress.

Moreover, this change also affects the social value attached by the liberal tradition to the free pursuit of individual and group interests. Only extreme economic liberalism of the Manchester type has ever held that this freedom could or should be unlimited. But a far broader and more powerful tradition has argued, ever since the late eighteenth century, that given a common framework of moral and institutional 'rules of the game', the free pursuit of these interests by individuals and groups was a dynamic force of incomparable power for the common welfare. This view was based on the experience of the process of modernization in the West and was economically expressed in Adam Smith's doctrine of the 'hidden hand'. In a different form it also underlies the historical optimism of Hegel's 'cunning of reason' and even of the Marxian dialectic of the class struggle. In all these philosophies, men are shown to contribute ultimately to the common good, even if often unwittingly, by the pursuit of their selfish interests. (By contrast, Lenin's teaching that the purpose of history can only be fulfilled by imposing the leadership of an *élite* in possession of the correct consciousness is in radical opposition to this materialist optimism of the modern West.)

Now, just as the dominant influence of those optimistic philosophies expressed the hopes aroused by the dynamics of material progress that the unique freedom of individual action in Western societies had unleashed, so the growing realization of the self-destructive potential of those dynamics is bound to raise doubt about the very core of modern Western optimism – the expectation to see individual freedom and social necessity reconciled by the course of history. For if history has now reached a stage where the free pursuit of individual self-interest tends to clash with the requirements of social survival, then the reconciliation is, to say the least, neither as assured in the present order as liberal optimism, nor as certain in a future socialist order as Marxist optimism proclaimed. The question is rather whether, in the light of our present predicament, such a reconciliation will turn out to be impossible – or merely very difficult. It is on the answer to that question that the political chances of socialism in modern societies will ultimately depend.

To see this, one has merely to recall that all forms of the socialist idea known in the West are based on some kind of synthesis of liberal individualist values and community values, just as are all modern Western forms of the democratic idea. Obviously, belief in the fundamental incompatibility of both kinds of values leads to fascist or anarchist conclusions, according to one's choice. The very concept of social control as understood in Western socialism implies a political framework permitting an effective control and change of the rulers by the citizenry. All modern experience (and particularly the experience of the communist single-party states) has shown this to be possible only in democracy of a liberal, pluralistic type. If the necessities of social survival are in conflict not only with a particular, narrowly selfish interpretation of individual freedom and a particular type of economic institution geared to that interpretation, but with the fundamental rights of the autonomous, self-improving individual developed in cenr turies of Western history, then there can be no future either fo- socialism as defined here or for Western democracy. Indeed, on these terms there could be no future for Western civilization, only a choice between its decay in late Roman anarchy or its petrifaction in the bureaucratic stagnation of a new Byzantine despotism. But if, as I believe, the basic individualist values are neither in pre-established harmony nor in ineradicable conflict with the social necessities of our time, then the task of socialists in advanced societies is to reinterpret these values in a manner compatible with the present necessities of social survival, to devise appropriate economic institutions, and to win a growing majority of democratic opinion for both.

Clearly, the political success of socialism in that sense could only be achieved in the face of enormous difficulties, and it would be very far from ushering in a utopian paradise. It would merely ensure survival for a humanity threatened by self-destruction, for our form of democracy – and for our civilization.

19

THE THEORY AND IDEOLOGY
OF SOCIALISM

Gilles Martinet

Theoretically, we are supposed to be discussing both the theory and the ideology of socialism.

Theory and ideology are often so closely tied up with each other that it is difficult to distinguish between them. Nevertheless, this is what must be done if we wish to do away with the confusion that characterizes most discussions about socialism.

The objective of the theoretical or scientific approach is knowledge. The ideological approach inclines to the creation of a system of representation capable of inspiring and guiding action. No great collective movement is, in fact. conceivable without emotional motivations, without moral imperatives, without simplifying myths, in short without an ideology. Some political men claim, to be sure, that their actions are not based on any ideological preoccupation. But you need only read their speeches to realize that what they mean by this is only new ideologies which are too subversive or too subtle for them, and that they are, in fact, repeating all the themes of traditional ideologies – patriotism, family or free enterprise.

Man needs ideology as he needs oxygen. But at the same time, he has a need to accumulate an increasingly wide range of knowledge, to attain an ever higher degree of lucidity. Our world is dominated, in large measure, by the accentuation of the contradiction between the extraordinary progress of the sciences and the much slower evolution of the ideologies. The tendency to lay down as of now objectives technically and socially still out of reach, a tendency that may be observed particularly among the young, merely represents an attempt to make up for this time lag by accomplishing an ideological leap into the future in the absence of a political leap.

Nowhere else does this contradiction manifest itself with so much

THE THEORY AND IDEOLOGY OF SOCIALISM

force and significance as among the advocates of socialist revolution. This can be explained not only by the fact that the movements they have formed are at the origin of the principal political transformations of our time but also by the fact that these movements have from the very first been imbued with high theoretical ambitions. I know perfectly well that most of the social democratic parties, like some libertarian and spontaneist groups, have rejected what for a long time was called scientific socialism, that is to say Marxism. But all the communist and left-socialist tendencies continue to believe in it. In their discussions and polemics, they never fail to question the scientific character of the theses of their adversaries. And when they condemn one or another experiment it is because it deviates, or supposedly deviates, from the theory. Who is faithful to Marx's idea of socialism and who is not? That seems to be the question.

This way of looking at problems has naturally provoked diametrically opposed reactions. Why encumber oneself, some people ask, with a theory which is over a century old? Does not the divorce between theory and reality simply mean that Marx's ideas were utopian? So the baby is thrown out with the bathwater, for not only genuinely outworn theses but also concepts which are still valid are rejected.

Was Marx a scientist or a utopian? Was he a theoretician or an ideologist? Why not admit that he was both?

The work of the theoretician marks a decisive turning-point in the history of the human sciences, in so far as it has placed the relationship between man and his work at the centre of social analysis and the relationship between power and classes at the centre of political analysis. It will be objected that much of this work has become obsolete. But for me this is not the important point. I do not belong to that category of pious Marxists for whom any criticism of Marx's work constitutes a sacrilegious act. I do, however, consider that Marx's basic approach – man and work, power and classes – is no less essentially pertinent to the study of societies in transition than it is to the study of capitalist societies. This of course on one condition, that we be not limited solely to the concepts formulated by Marx and that we are able to invent new ones which may throw light on phenomena such as mutual exploitation, new trade relationships or new forms of nationalism.

There is also the political theory whose ambition it was to promote the rapid rise of the new working class movement, to exalt its ardour and to steer its action towards the conquest of power. Here, Marx was the ideologist rather than the scientist. The great weakness of most of

239

those people who claim to be Marxists is that they refuse to recognize this. They constantly confuse the logical inductions that Marx drew from his analysis of the mechanisms of capitalist society with the more or less rash extrapolations he indulged in based on certain political episodes or in the heat of certain polemics.

This is very well illustrated by Marx's attitude towards the Paris Commune. He was well aware of the real situation which had existed in France and he knew to what degree the Jacobin and libertarian tendencies had won out over all the others. But as soon as the event had finished, he only wanted to retain what he thought represented a promise for the future. The reality of the Commune interested him much less than the use he could make of it. I admit that I admire the audacity with which Marx carried out this formidable historical kidnapping. I admire much less those who, a century later, regard his distortions and his extrapolations as scientific fact. The Communards had taken the Convention of 1793 as a model, that is to say the election of an Assembly disposing of both legislative and executive power. However, according to legend, they had at least found the way to put into practice the dictatorship of the proletariat. The Communards had decreed that no government official would earn over 6,000 francs per year, that is to say more than four times the salary of a worker at that time. But as legend has it, they did not tolerate that the salary of any government official be superior to that of a worker's salary. And so on.

This legend is not a purely French legend nor a purely European one. It has become a universal legend. For example, think of some of the episodes that occurred during the Chinese cultural revolution such as the ephemeral commune of Shanghai in 1967. This is a classic example of how a historical myth develops, a process comparable to that of all the national myths that weigh down our political debates in Europe as in America and in Asia.

During the 1950s and at the beginning of the 1960s, that is to say during a period marked both by the development of the techno-structure in the capitalist countries, and by the relative discredit of Stalinism in the so-called socialist countries, some people thought that the power of attraction of these myths was going to diminish and that we would witness the end of ideologies. This was an error of analysis which the ideological behaviour of the new generations was soon to reveal.

The problem for the socialist movement is not to free itself of ideologies. It could not even if it wanted to. The problem is how to fill the enormous gap that has been created between the ideological vision it continues to claim for itself and the real possibilities for transformation that a study of the so-called socialist societies brings out.

The ideas having preceded the experiences, it was natural to consider the experiences in the light of the ideas, in other words to judge the different forms of communism – for from now on there are several different kinds of communism – in the name of communism. But this leads only to an impasse. According to some, the wide gulf that exists between the predictions and the reality proves that Marxism should be dropped as an out-of-date and archaic doctrine. Others are determined to prove that only special historical circumstances, the economic backwardness of Russia and then of China and the pressure of world capitalism, explain why the predictions of Marx and Lenin have not yet been realized. On every side, the final analysis leads back to the thesis which was in each case its point of departure.

Therefore, it is necessary to reverse the order of the factors and to start an examination of communism with a concrete analysis of the different forms of communism. To be sure, each experience develops within a well-defined historical and national context. The fact that there may be not one or two but fourteen experiences makes it possible for us, however, to go further than a purely historical analysis (which remains indispensable in my opinion) and to undertake a structural study of those societies which in the first two-thirds of the twentieth century have attempted to carry out the collective appropriation of the means of production. We can thus go beyond the descriptive stage and arrive at a valid theory of socialist development and its contradictions, a theory that concerns not only the economically backward countries but the most highly industrialized countries as well.

I will have occasion to return to certain aspects of this socialist development during our later discussions. I will merely emphasize here a point concerning the relationships between the new theory of social development (whose bases are just beginning to be laid) and present-day ideologies of the socialist movement.

In the first text addressed to us by the organizers of the Tokyo seminar two themes were advanced: the theme of equality and the theme of self-government or worker–management in industry. These two themes do in fact play a very important role in contemporary socialist ideologies. They are already old themes but themes which have known periods of relative eclipse, then periods of resurgence.

For this reason, we may have the impression that the same ideas have continued to influence men since the last century. This impression is not entirely false. There does exist an ideological heritage that the socialist generations hand down to each other and whose earliest origins go back to the European eighteenth century, the century of light. But this impression is to be distrusted. For each time an idea is revived, that idea does not have the same content, in so far as the ideological tendencies behind it are not sociologically the same.

Take for example the evolution of the idea of self-government in industry in a country like France. At the beginning of the century, it was an idea very widespread among militants of the trade union movement. That was the time when more or less anarchistic revolutionary tendencies dominated this movement, which was essentially a movement made up of skilled workers. The problem for these workers was to run the business in place of the employers and to organize society on the basis of a free association of producing communities. Thus, they believed that only those who had a thorough knowledge of their trade could be revolutionaries. It goes without saying that this was the ideology of workers in small enterprises, in workshops of medium size, that posed only relatively simple technical problems. Hence, the leaders of the French trade unions regarded the development of large-scale mechanical industries as a catastrophe. The unskilled workers recruited by this kind of industry could not be revolutionaries because they were not capable of managing it in place of the employers.

Between the two world wars and during the twenty years following the second one, the workers' movement was very little concerned with self-government in industry. The objective then was nationalization and planification. For a little less than ten years now, however, and above all since the events of May 1968, we have seen the theme of self-government reappear. It is most prevalent in Christian leftist circles. It affects certain sectors of the working class (on the one hand, highly skilled workers, and on the other hand, workers of peasant origin) and certain groups of the intelligentsia and the sub-intelligentsia (more sensitive, actually, to egalitarian demands than to demands for self-government) but it is of particular and primary concern to the technician groups.

It is significant that during the events of May 1968 the problems of management were really posed only in those enterprises which included a high percentage of technicians and managers: electronic factories, chemical enterprises, research departments, architectural offices and medical laboratories. This phenomenon must be compared with what we see in Yugoslavia where the workers' councils include an increasingly large proportion of technicians, and with what we have been able to ascertain in Czechoslovakia during the brief experience of the Prague springtime.

These observations are obviously very schematic. They require many additions and it would be necessary, among other things, to take into account the generation phenomenon which is superimposed on the social phenomena. But this is not the important point. What is important is that the self-government ideologies are not put forth by those who uphold them as emanating from intellectual milieus or from technicians but as ideologies which are specifically worker ideologies. It is the working class which is supposed to want equality and self-government.

As I have said, such tendencies have existed or still exist in a marginal way within the trade union movement. But it is impossible to say that today they characterize this movement as a whole.

When Tito's government granted them self-government, the Yugoslav workers imposed a certain levelling of the wage scale for two years. After this period wage differentials again became very pronounced. Later on, the workers took an interest in certain aspects of self-government: those most directly related to specific working conditions such as recruitment, work pace, employment guarantees and wages. The problems of general management such as investment, manufacturing processes and markets were almost always left to the directors or to the technicians who were members of the workers' council. Therefore, most of the advocates of self-government in Western Europe do not like to see the Yugoslav example evoked. They feel that it worked out in the way it did because Yugoslavia was still a backward country. In fact, they tremble at the idea of questioning the dogma according to which the working class is destined to exercise for a certain period, that period which precedes the advent of a communist society, the role of ruling class.

This is without any doubt the most noteworthy ideological stumbling-block of our time. Not a single one of the revolutions which have occurred during the last fifty years have brought the working class to power. Everywhere, the real working class has been replaced by a 'historical' working class, which is none other than the Communist Party and its bureaucratic apparatus. Everywhere, the wage earning system exists. Everywhere, surplus value is extracted from the surplus labour-time of the workers. Nowhere do the latter have control over the utilization of this surplus value. The monopoly of its distribution belongs to a social class which enjoys considerable privileges. But we pretend to believe that this is only the result of a series of deviations and betrayals, of a sombre bureaucratic plot. And even when the growing role of the technicians is acknowledged and when we emphasize the necessity of forging a historical block made up of the forces capable of bringing socialism into being, we specify that this block must be formed around and under the control of the working class. We add, in a conciliatory spirit, that technicians, bureaucrats and workers are members of the same wage-earning class. This is quite true in a way. But it does not allow for consideration of the conflicts that develop within this class itself.

No one can deny the political importance of the workers' movement. Its role is already considerable in the capitalist countries, and would no doubt be still greater in the so-called socialist countries if the social class in power in these countries would just tolerate the existence of an autonomous trade union movement. Ota Šik had some very accurate things to say about this subject at the time of the Prague springtime. But this does not mean that the working class can change into a ruling class. It is by no means obvious that the elimination of the workers as a class, which is one of the objectives of socialism, will result from power passing into the hands of the working class.

This naturally goes against Marx's teaching. To begin with, he maintained that the proletariat was a revolutionary class and a universal class, that is to say, bearer of the values of humanity because of its impoverishment within the framework of capitalist society. Its essential humanity is all the greater since capitalist society refuses to recognize in it anything human whatsoever. Marx later substituted an economic analysis for this purely philosophical analysis. The bourgeoisie-proletariat conflict was then superimposed on the contradiction between the productive forces and the production relationship: the capitalist system is condemned and the proletariat, assimilated to the productive forces, becomes the agent of the inevitable transformation. In thus assimilating the proletariat to the productive forces, Marx accomplished a sort of logical masterstroke. But the flaw was difficult to distinguish so long as the real experience had not occurred. Today, we can no longer speak of the power of the working class but only of the power of those who govern in its name.

Any theory of socialist development must take this reality into account.

It will no doubt be pointed out that what I have been saying calls into question one of the most exalting and unifying myths used by the socialist movement. It will also be pointed out that I emphasize the need for ideological motivations and thus the need for myths. I do not deny this. But there are creative utopias and sterile utopias.

In our time, which is in the true sense of the word a time of transition (i.e. a time in which we can already do without private capital but not without the production relationships and the economic mechanisms created by capitalism), the self-government utopias, when they are not confined to the narow framework of enterprise, and the egalitarian utopias, when they go beyond the single problem of remuneration, are creative utopias in so far as they open the way to an evolution which in the long run can really lead to the establishment of new relationships between men. The worker utopias are, on the other hand, dangerous in that they mask the survival of certain forms of exploitation and, in a more general way, hide the reality of the social contradictions which inevitably stamp the first phase of socialism. Any democratic system implies the recognition of antagonistic forces existing within a given society. Socialism cannot escape from this rule without suffering, as in the case of many countries, the cruel weight of censorship and police.

I do not know if these thoughts have corresponded to the preoccupations of the organizers of this seminar. I have wanted above all to underline the importance of methodological questions, to distinguish clearly between theoretical and ideological reasoning, which is of the highest importance since these two steps are often linked together and too often confused one with the other. Socialist theory must be fundamentally renewed in the light of experience and among socialist ideologies there are some that must be dropped and others, on the contrary, into which we must breathe new life. Here, I am naturally speaking as an advocate of socialist transformation. But I think that everyone has understood this.

20

EPILOGUE

Stuart Hampshire

The conference was intended to be a discussion among socialists of the shortcomings of socialist theory and of the relation of these shortcomings to socialist practice.

The intention was largely realized, I think, at least in the discussion, if not in all the papers submitted to the conference. It turned out that socialist theory usually meant Marxism and some forms of Marxist revisionism. Socialist practice usually, but not always, meant the policies of communist parties, whether in government, as in the Soviet Union and Eastern Europe, or aspiring to government, as elsewhere in Europe.

My own impression of the discussion, and of the papers that were its basis, is a personal reaction, and I know that the impression is in no way representative or typical. Taking the conference as a whole, I even suspect that my conclusions were exceptional and eccentric. We had different links to socialism, different national experiences, different philosophical training, different party allegiances; there was no reason to expect convergence of opinions. There was reason to hope for clarification and correction of one's opinions, and this happened in my case.

I had in recent years been led to the conclusion, partly by philosophical arguments, that theories of human nature and development in the nineteenth century had started from a false premiss. The premiss is most strongly and famously stated in various forms in Hegel; but it comes from Christian doctrine, from the system of belief which the young Hegel confronted and which he thought that his philosophy would absorb. Christianity is the religion that associated salvation with history, and which recognized that this was its peculiarity. Even if there is not a Second Coming to be expected, at least there is a Resurrection. Salvation is not necessarily, or primarily, a mode of existence, a way of being in the world; nor is it a way of viewing the world. It can enter into a possible narrative of events, as something that happens at a certain time, just as death happens at a certain time, whether the death of an individual or of a nation or of a civilization. Hegel, Saint-Simon, Marx, and the positivist philosophers, Comte and Herbert Spencer, agree at one point: that their philosophies, which are to replace orthodox Christian dogma, describe a historical destiny, a path to salvation at the due time. They reject Christian teaching with their suggestion that the salvation comes about through a social change and not primarily through a direct change in the soul of the individual.

The false premiss, as I now believe, is the linking of the idea of salvation with the idea of a great historical event. One can understand, even if one does not accept, the idea that individual men may be regenerated by a conversion that leaves them with a faith in God and with a faith in a set of moral commands which they believe to be God's commands. When this happens they will be saved, and for them the kingdom of ends will be realized. This seems to me a false, though familiar, belief. Similarly, one can understand, even if one does not accept, the idea that there are discoverable laws of social change and that men can to some extent reconstruct the social order in accordance with a plan, and to that extent rationally. This may be true and also it may be false. We do not yet know; the evidence is not in, and we cannot tell. Triumphing over orthodox Christianity, Hegel linked salvation to self-conscious social and political reconstruction in a culmination of history which is to be expected soon; and Marx followed him in this third way.

I would now argue, though I will not argue here, that socialists and political thinkers generally ought to discard this historical and social variant of a theodicy, and that they should recognize the absolute contingency of the existence of the species and of its future development. By 'contingency' I mean the opposite of the necessity which a comparatively simple and comparatively precise and entirely general law, such as the law of gravitation, confers on a case which falls precisely under it. The contingency is of the kind that a doctor recognizes, in some comparatively well developed branch of medicine, when he advises an individual patient on his probable progress towards health. The survival of the species is far from certain, and depends upon a complex combination of many favouring factors. The species came into existence in the first place as the outcome of a complex combination of many favouring factors. Similarly, the development of any one, or any set, of human societies towards a more desired social organization depends, at best, upon the favourable trends in the societies not being cancelled by external events which are harmful and not predicted. Many independent variables – demographic, technological, social, accidents of heredity, of climate – would need to be integrated in a single calculation if a definite and rational computation of future trends were ever to be made. Within this calculation the trends that lead towards a future nuclear war, and the trends that make such a war less and less likely, would be put side by side and judged. A doctor often needs to make such distinctions of trends within an organism and to make also a concluding judgement. If human societies are studied by the various social sciences in this general setting, one may discard the assumption that there is a special evolutionary process at work in human development, alongside the evolution by national selection to which every species is liable.

Throughout the discussions at the conference, and in reading most of the papers submitted, I thought that the perspective that adaptations of Marxism provided was a false perspective. I had the idea that we were being superstitious, like men still talking about alchemy when chemistry was already proving to be a different science with uncertain prospects. Like alchemy, Marxism had performed an immense service in the development of knowledge, with new connections perceived which helped to give the social sciences an ambitious programme and many lines of successful inquiry. The analogy with alchemy, the sense of an old dream, was most vivid when the conference discussed nationalism, the most powerful and interesting phenomenon in contemporary politics. No interpretative scheme, or framework of rational argument, was offered or, it seemed, could easily be offered within traditional socialist thought. One peered into a huge gulf of ignorance, in which could be seen, floating in the general darkness, a few scattered strands of sociology and social anthropology and a few historical studies of the phenomenon, but no coherent and solid structure. Several of the participants seemed to want to dismiss the problem as of no great theoretical significance. It seemed to me that a reasonable view would allow that one must be strictly empirical on such an issue and that one must acknowledge the facts without theory being available. The fact is that changes in economic organization, and in consequent social structures, do not seem to be correlated to the expected degree with variations in identification with a social group. Tribalism, Nationalism, exclusive attachment to a Church or to a linguistic group, do not significantly diminish as high technology and more intensive education develop. The point of theoretical interest should be: are all theories of the one-track development of social life, and of corresponding tastes and interests, founded on an illusion? Will the moral sciences, particularly social anthropology and psychology, gradually show much more complicated patterns of tradition and conformity and of sudden change?

For me socialism is not so much a theory as a set of moral injunctions, which seem to me clearly right and rationally justifiable: first, that the elimination of poverty ought to be the first priority of government after defence: secondly, that as great inequalities in wealth between different social groups lead to inequalities in power and in freedom of action, they are generally unjust and need to be redressed by governmental action; thirdly, that democratically elected governments ought to ensure that primary and basic human needs are given priority within the economic system, even if this involves some loss in the aggregate of goods and services which would otherwise be available. How these moral requirements are best realized, at particular times and places, and also both in general, are matters for the social sciences and also for a critical reading of history; after them also for personal experience and for worldly insight. At present socialism needs a variety of evidence, open minds with moral conviction, and distrust of all unitary theories. These were my possibly unrepresentative and untypical conclusions.

NOTES

CHAPTER 2 The Myth of Human Self-identity *Unity of Civil and Political Society in Socialist Thought*

1 Edward Abramowski, 'Etyka a rewolucja' in *Filozofia spoleczna* (wybór pism) (Warsaw, 1965), pp. 179–80.
2 L. Trotsky, *The Defence of Terrorism: A Reply to Karl Kautsky* (Labour Publishing Co., London, 1921), p. 126.
3 *Ibid.*, p. 125.
4 *Ibid.*, p. 130.
5 *Ibid.*, p. 131.

CHAPTER 5 Reflections on Equality

1 Crane Brinton, *Encyclopedia of the Social Sciences*, vol. 5 (Macmillan, New York, 1931), p. 574ff.
2 Ernst Troeltsch, *Aufsätze zur Geistesgeschichte und Religionssoziologie* 'Das stoisch-christliche Naturrecht und das moderne profane Naturrecht' (Aalen, 1966), pp. 174–6. Max Pohlenz, *Die Stoa: Geschichte einer geistigen Bewesung*, 2 vols (Göttingen, 1964), pp. 135–6. For a general survey see the suggestive book by A. P. D'Entrèves, *Natural Law: A Historical Survey* (Harper Torchbooks, New York, 1965). Cf. the penetrating study by Joachim Ritter, *Naturrecht bei Aristoteles* (Stuttgart, 1961). Cf. also Ernest Barker, in O. Gierke, *Natural Law and the Theory of Society*, Cambridge University Press, 1950), p. XXXV ff.

To the Stoics Nature was synonymous with Reason, and Reason was synonymous with God. They believed that the true city or polity of mankind was a single 'city of God', or cosmopolis (transcending the old historical and positive cities), and that all men were united, as reasonable creatures, in this city of God, which was also a city of Reason and of Nature. They believed that true laws was the law of this city – the law of Reason; the Law of Nature. According to the teaching of Zeno, the founder of Stoicism, men should not live in different cities, divided by separate rules of justice: they should consider all men fellow-citizens, and there should be one life and order, as of a flock on a common pasture feeding together under a common law. This common law (*koinos nomos*), which is the law universal and natural, may remind us of the *koiné* or *lingua franca* of the Hellenistic period. It is the legal corollary to Alexander's world-state. But the *koiné* was actual fact: the *koinos nomos* remained an aspiration. It was an ideal law which would only become actual if men were purely rational. Its principles were ideal principles. Among these ideal principles was that of equality. By nature, and as reasonable creatures, all human beings were equal. By nature the woman was equal to the man, and the slave to the master. This was the teaching of Zeno: and it was a teaching which had its effects, in later days in Rome.

3 See also *Mark* 8:33*ff*:

... he rebuked Peter, saying ... : thou savourest not the things of God, but the things that be of man ... For whosoever will save his life shall lose it; but whosoever shall lose his life for my sake and the gospel's shall save it.

For what shall it profit a man, if he shall gain the whole world, and lose his own soul?

Romans 2: 11: 'For there is no respect of persons with God.' See also *Mark* 10:17–26 and *Matthew* 19: 16–24.

4 Augustine, *De Civitate Dei*, XIX, Chapter XV.

5 Cf. C. H. McIlwain, *The Growth of Political Thought in the West* (New York, 1932), p. 325ff.

6 Heinrich A. Rommen, *The Natural Law: A Study in Legal and Social History and Philosophy* (Herder Book Co., St Louis and London, 1947).

7 Cf. the following works for a general orientation and bibliography: A. Aulard, *Histoire politique de la Révolution française* (Paris, 1905), pp. 1–48. Georges Lefebvre, 'La Révolution française' in *Peuples et Civilisations* (Paris, 1957), see Index under *Egalité*. See also the important book by Carl L. Becker, *The Declaration of Independence: A Study in the History of Political Ideas* (Vintage Books, New York, 1958).

8 Georg Jellinek, *Die Erklärung der Menschen- und Bürgerrechte* (Leipzig, 1904).

9 Marx, *Economic and Philosophic Manuscripts of 1844* (translated by Martin Milligan) (Foreign Languages Publishing House, Moscow, 1961), p. 123ff. (published in London by Lawrence and Wishart).

10 Karl Marx, *Selected Works*, vol. 2 (Lawrence and Wishart, 1942), p. 566.

11 Marx and Engels, *The Communist Manifesto* (Allen and Unwin, 1948), p. 35.

12 Max Weber, *Gesammelte Aufsätze zur Soziologie und Sozialpolitik* Tübingen, 1924), p. 511.

13 Max Weber, *Zur Lage der bürgerlichen Demokratie in Russland*, Archives of Social Science and Social Politics, vol. XXII, (Tübingen, 1906), p. 347.

14 Weber, *Gesammelte Aufsätze*, p. 497.

15 Karl Marx, *Selected Works*, vol. 2, p. 566.

16 Cf. Joan McDonald, *Rousseau and the French Revolution, 1762–1791* (Athlone Press, London, 1965). See Rousseau, Premiere version du *Contrat social*, in J.-J. Rousseau, *Political Writings*, vol. I, ed. C. E. Vaughan (Blackwell, 1962), p. 497, where we read:
> Si l'on recherche, en quoi consiste précisément ce plus grand bien de tous, qui doit être la base de tout système de la législation, on trouvera qu'il se réduit à ces deux objets principaux, [la *liberté* et l'*égalité*. La liberté parce que toute dépendance particulière est autant de force ôtée au corps de l'Etat; l'égalité parce que la liberté ne peut subsister sans elle].

Rousseau repeats this passage in the final version of the *Contrat Social*; cf. Rousseau, *Œuvres Completes*, vol. III (Pléiade edition, Paris, 1964), p. 391. The passage in brackets has been excerpted by Marx in his Kreuznach notebooks of 1843.

17 I should perhaps note in this context the surprisingly close affinity between neo-Confucian thought and Stoic ideas. Thus we read in Meng-Tseu, who lived and taught approximately at the same time, perhaps a little earlier, than the Stoic Isocrates:
> What is it which men possess which is common to all? It is what we call natural reason, natural equity. Holy men have merely been the first to discover, like Y-ya for flavours (tastes), what the hearts of all men possess equally. It is for this reason that natural reason and natural equity please our hearts, as flesh prepared from beasts fed on grass and corn pleases our taste.
>
> Meng-Tseu said: On Mount Nieouchan there were beautiful trees. But because these beautiful trees grew on the border of the great kingdom, they were cut down with axe and sickle. Can they still be called beautiful? Those trees which had grown day and night, watered by dew and rain, still grew new off-shoots and leaves. But cattle and sheep came there to graze, and harmed

them. This is why the mountain is as bare and denuded as it is now seen to be. Any man who sees it so denuded must think it has never borne forests of trees. Is this therefore the natural state of the mountain?

Although it may be this for man, is it not thoughts of humanity and equity which are preserved in his heart. In him, passions which have made him abandon his heart's good and noble thoughts, are like the axe and sickle for the mountain trees attacking them every day. Can his soul still be called beautiful (when it has lost its beauty)?

Meng-Tseu, *Les Livres sacrés de l'Orient*, ed. G. Pauthier (Paris, 1840), p. 182. The Couvreur edition of Mencius was unfortunately not available to me. From the Wilhelm edition of Mencius, I quote only the last paragraph, p. 134 (cf. Richard Wilhelm, ed., *Mong Dsi*(Jena, 1916)):

Und was das Herz anlangt: nur hier allein sollte es keine solche Übereinsteimmung geben? Was ist es nun worin die Herzen übereinstimmen? Es ist die Vernunft, es ist die Gerechtigkeit. Die Heiligen haben zuerst gefunden, werin unsere Herzen übereinstimmen, darum erfreut Vernunft und Gerechtigkeit ganz ebenso unser Herz, wie Mastfleisch unsern Gaumen erfeut.

The Analects of Confucius are conveniently read in Arthur Waley's admirable translation (Allen and Unwin, 1938). See also Henri Maspero and Etienne Balazs, *Histoire et Institutions de la Chine ancienne* (Paris, 1967).

18 Alexis de Tocqueville, *Recollections*, ed. J. P. Mayer and A. P. Kerr (Anchor Books, New York, 1971), Introduction, pp. xiv–xv.

19 Cf. J. P. Mayer, *Alexis de Tocqueville, Analytiker des Massenzeitalters* (Munich, 1972).

20 Alexis de Tocqueville, *Œuvres Complètes*, ed. J. P. Mayer, tome II: *L'Ancien Régime et la Révolution, fragments et notes inédites sur la révolution* (Gallimard, Paris, 1953), pp. 334–5.

21 Cf. *Philosophische Anthropologie heute*, by R. Rocek and Oscar Schatz (Munich, 1972), which has an important bibliography. See Also the valuable book by Jean Baudrillard, *La Société de Consommation* (Paris, 1970), where the *anomie* of our contemporary Western societies is convincingly analysed. In addition, consult the recent volumes: Roger Bastide, *Sociologie et Psychoanalyse* (Paris, 1972), Georges Balandier, *Sens et Puissance* (Paris, 1971); J. P. Mayer,

'Retrospect', in *Sociology of Film* (new edition, Arno Press, York, 1972), with bibliographical indications; Edouard Morot-Sir, *La Pensée française d'aujourd'hui* (Paris, 1971), a brilliant short book. Cf. also Lucien Febvre, *Combats pour l'histoire* (Paris, 1965), see particularly the essays on: 'Méthodes et solutions pratiques: Henri Wallon et la psychologie appliquée'; 'Une vue d'ensemble: Histoire et Psychologie'; and 'Comment reconstituer la vie affective d'autrefois? La Sensibilité et l'histoire', p. 201ff.

CHAPTER 6 Socialism and Equality

1 James S. Coleman, 'Equality of Opportunity and Equality of Results', *Harvard Educational Review*, 43 (February 1973), p. 137.

2 See p. 56.

3 Though equality is an objective central to socialism, socialists have not, in general, been very explicit about its content or the values on which it rests. I have (perhaps surprisingly) found the ideas of certain English egalitarians and socialists (Arnold, Morris, Tawney, Cole, Orwell) especially helpful.

4 Babeuf came perhaps the nearest to doing so, proclaiming, 'Let there be no other difference between people than that of age or sex. Since all have the same needs and the same faculties, let them henceforth have the same education and the same diet. They are content with the same sun and the same air for all; why should not the same portion and the same quality of nourishment not suffice for each of them?' *Manifeste des égaux* [1796] in M. Leroy, ed., *Les Précurseurs français du socialisme de Condorcet à Proudhon* (Editions du temps présent, Paris, 1948), pp. 67–8 (frons. S. Lukes).

5 See A. B. Atkinson, *Unequal Shares: Wealth in Britain* (Allen Lane, The Penguin Press, 1972), pp. 80ff.

6 H. Dalton, *Some Aspects of Inequality of Incomes in Modern Communities* (Routledge, 1925), cited in *ibid.*, p. 84.

7 Christopher Jencks *et al.*, *Inequality. A Reassessment of the Effects of Family and Schooling in America* (Allen Lane, The Penguin Press, 1974), pp. 9–10.

8 The argument which follows, spelling out the principle of equal respect, is taken from the present author's *Individualism* (Blackwell, 1973), Part III.

9 Condorcet, *Sketch for the Progress of the Human Mind* [1793], translated by June Barraclough (Weidenfeld and Nicolson, 1955), p. 184.

10 R. H. Tawney, *Equality*, 4th edition, 1952 (Allen and Unwin, 1931), p. 260.

11 *Ibid.*, p. 153.

12 William Godwin, *Enquiry Concerning Political Justice and its influence on Morals and Happiness* [1793], 3rd edition, vol. 1 (London, 1798) pp. 214–15.

13 William Morris, *Letters on Socialism* [1888] (privately printed, London, 1894), Letter I, p. 5.

14 *Op. cit.*, p. 254.

15 George Orwell, *Homage to Catalonia* (Secker and Warburg, 1938; Penguin edition, 1962), p. 66.

16 Bernard Williams, 'The Idea of Equality' in P. Laslett and W. G. Runciman, eds, *Philosophy, Politics and Society: Second Series* (Blackwell, 1962), pp. 117, 118.

17 *Ibid.*, pp. 119–20.

18 Friedrich A. Hayek, *Individualism, True and False* (Hodges, Figgis & Co., Dublin, and Blackwell, 1946), p. 24.

19 Tawney, *op. cit.*, p. 87.

20 *Op. cit.*, p. 135.

21 Matthew Arnold, 'Democracy' [1861] in Lionel Trilling, ed., *The Portable Matthew Arnold* (Viking Press, 1949), pp. 442–3.

22 *Op. cit.*, p. 49.

23 *Ibid.*, pp. 35–6.

24 *Ibid.*, p. 47.

25 *Ibid.*, p. 108.

26 C. A. R. Crosland, *The Future of Socialism* (Cape, 1956), pp. 150–1.

27 See J. H. Goldthorpe, 'Social Stratification in Industrial Society', reprinted in R. Bendix and S. M. Lipset, eds, *Class, Status and Power: Social Stratification in Comparative Perspective*, 2nd edition, (Routledge, 1967).

28 Frank Parkin, *Class, Inequality and Political Order* (MacGibbon and Kee, 1971), p. 39.

29 P. M. Blau and O. D. Duncan, *The American Occupational Structure* (John Wiley, New York, 1967), p. 7.

30 See H. F. Lydall, *The Structure of Earnings* (Oxford University Press, 1968).

31 Cited in David Lane, *The End of Inequality? Stratification under State Socialism* (Penguin Education, 1971), p. 81.

32 See, e.g. H. Gordon Skilling and Franklyn Griffiths, eds, *Interest Groups in Soviet Politics* (Princeton University Press, 1971).

33 P. J. D. Wiles and S. Markowski, 'Income Distribution under Communism and Capitalism: Some Facts about Poland, the UK, the USA and the USSR', *Soviet Studies*, 22 (1971), p. 344.

34 *Ibid.*, p. 353.

35 Atkinson, *op. cit.*

36 See John Westergaard and Henrietta Resler, *Class in Contemporary Britain* (Heinemann, forthcoming). I am grateful to the authors for their permission to read the text of this extremely valuable study in advance of publication.

37 Atkinson, *op. cit.*, pp. 37–8.

38 *Ibid.*, p. 251.

39 *Ibid.*, p. 77.

40 See Westergaard and Resler, *op. cit.*, and Parkin, *op. cit.*, pp. 125–6.

41 Parkin, *op. cit.*, p. 127.

42 See Goldthorpe, *art. cit.*, p. 653.

43 D. Wedderburn and C. Craig, 'Relative Deprivation in Work', paper presented at the British Association for the Advancement of Science (Exeter, 1969), cited in Parkin, *op. cit.* p. 26.

44 C. Kerr *et al.*, *Industrialism and Industrial Man* (Harvard University Press, 1960).

45 See Westergaard and Resler, *op. cit.* and the present author's *Power: a Radical View* (Macmillan, London, 1974), and 'Political Ritual and Social Integration', *Sociology* (forthcoming).

46 Lane, *op. cit.*, p. 69.

47 See Parkin, *op. cit.*, p. 144 and his article, 'Class Stratification in Socialist Societies', *British Journal of Sociology* (December 1969).

48 Lane, *op. cit.*, pp. 72–4.

49 Parkin, *op. cit.*, p. 146.

50 Parkin, *op. cit.*, p. 147, cf. Lane, *op. cit.*, p. 78.

51 Parkin, *op. cit.*, p. 149.

52 P. Machonin, 'Social Stratification in Contemporary Czechoslovakia', *American Journal of Sociology*, 75 (1970), pp. 725–41. For an English summary of Machonin and his associates' full-scale study of this subject, see Ernest Gellner, 'The Pluralist Anti-levellers of Prague', *European Journal of Sociology* tome XII (1971), pp. 312–25.

53 Wiles and Markowski, *art. cit.*, p. 344.

54 *Ibid.*

55 See Atkinson, *op. cit.*, p. 77 and Lydall, *op. cit.*

56 See Michalina Vaughan, 'Poland', in Margaret Scotford Archer and

Salvador Giner (eds), *Contemporary Europe. Class, Status and Power* (Weidenfeld and Nicolson, 1971).

57 Lane, *op. cit.*, pp. 129–37.

58 H. J. Eysenck, *The Inequality of Man* (Temple Smith, 1973), p. 224.

59 *Ibid.*, p. 270.

60 *Ibid.*, pp. 159, 224.

61 *Ibid.*, pp. 224.

62 R. Herrnstein, *IQ in the Meritocracy* (Allen Lane, The Penguin Press, 1973).

63 Arthur R. Jensen, *Educability and Group Differences* (Methuen, 1973), p. 363.

64 Jencks, *op. cit.*, p. 315.

65 *Ibid.*, p. 71.

66 *Op. cit.*, p. 111.

67 See Jencks, *op. cit.*, Appendix A.

68 See Jencks, *op. cit.*

69 *Ibid.*, Chapter 3, Part II.

70 *Ibid.*, p. 72.

71 K. Davis and W. E. Moore, 'Some Principles of Stratification' in Bendix and Lipset, *Class Status and Power* (see n. 27), p. 47.

72 *Ibid.*, p. 48.

73 *Ibid.*, p. 48.

74 See G. A. Huaco, 'The Functionalist Theory of Stratification: Two Decades of Controversy', *Inquiry*, 9 (Autumn 1966), pp. 215–40.

75 Ralf Dahrendorf, 'On the Origin of Social Inequality', in P. Laslett and W. G. Runciman, eds, *Philosophy, Politics and Society: Second Series* (Blackwell, 1962), p. 107.

76 *Ibid.*, p. 103.

77 *Ibid.*, p. 103.

78 *Ibid.*, p. 102.

79 Parkin, *op. cit.*, pp. 181–2.

80 *Ibid.*, p. 183.

81 *Ibid.*, p. 184.

CHAPTER 7 Socialism, Revolution and Violence

1 Gajo Petrović, 'Philosophy and Politics in Socialism', *Praxis*, 2–3 (1965); *Marx in the Mid-Twentieth Century* (Doubleday, 1967); 'Philosophy and Socialism', *Praxis*, 4 (1967).

CHAPTER 8 On the Development of Marxism towards Precision

1 Maurice Merleau–Ponty, *Humanismus und Terror*, II (Frankfurt, 1966), p. 33.
2 Lucien Sève, *Marxismus und Theorie der Persönlichkeit* (Frankfurt, 1972), p. 135.
3 Friedrich Engels to Joseph Bloch, 21 September 1890, in *Marx Engels Werke* (Dietz, Berlin, 1962), 37, p. 463.
4 Rossana Rossanda, 'Unsere Schwierigkeiten mit den Sozialistischen Ländern' in *Kursbuch* 30, (Berlin, December 1972).
5 Louis Althusser, *Pour Marx* (Penguin, 1972), p. 23.
6 Althusser, *Pour Marx*, p. 238.
7 Louis Althusser, Etienne Balibar *et al.*, *Das Kapital lesen* (Hamburg, 1972), p. 339.
8 Karl Marx, *Grundisse der Kritik der politischen Oekonomie* in *Marx Engels Werke* (Dietz, Berlin, 1962), p. 176.
9 Karl Marx, *Manuskripte*, I, 3, pp. 106–7.
10 Quoted in Adam Schaff, *Marxismus und das menschliche Individuum* (Vienna, Frankfurt, Zurich), p. 117.
11 Friedrich Engels to Franz Mehring, London, 14 July 1893, *Marx Engels Werke*, Vol. 39 (Dietz, Berlin, 1962).
12 Peter Huchel, 'Psalm' in *Chausseen, Chausseen* (Frankfurt, 1963), p. 84.

CHAPTER 9 Socialism and the Working Class

1 S. M. Lipset, 'The Changing Class Structure and Contemporary European Politics', in S. R. Graubard, ed,. *A New Europe?* (Houghton Mifflin, 1964), p. 338.
2 There is a useful analysis of the limited degree of affluence even among American workers in Andrew Levison, 'The Divided Working Class', *The Nation* (1 May 1972), pp. 558–62.
3 John H. Goldthorpe, David Lockwood, Frank Bechhofer and Jennifer Platt, *The Affluent Worker*, 3 vols (Cambridge University Press, 1968–9).
4 Goldthorpe *et al.*, *The Affluent Worker*, vol. 3, p. 157.
5 *Ibid.*, p. 180.
6 Heinrich Popitz *et al.*, *Das Gesellschaftsbild des Arbeiters*) Mohr, Tübingen, 1957).
7 Horst Kern and Michael Schumann, *Industriearbeit und Arbeiterbewusstsein* (Frankfurt, Europäische Verlagsanstalt, 1970); Michael

Schumann *et al.*, *Am Beispiel der Septemberstreiks* (Europäische Verlagsanstalt, Frankfurt, 1971).

8 Andrée Andrieux and Jean Lignon, *L'ouvrier d'aujourd'hui* (Marcel Rivière, Paris, 1960).

9 Herbert Marcuse, *One-Dimensional Man* (Routledge, 1964), pp. 29, 31.

10 See especially Daniel Bell, 'Labor in the Post-Industrial Society', *Dissent* (Winter 1972), pp. 163–89.

11 David M. Gordon, in *Dissent* (Winter 1972), pp. 209–11.

12 See the works cited earlier, by Popitz *et al.* and by Andrieux and Lignon.

13 See, for example, Schumann *et al.*, *Am Beispiel der Septemberstreiks*.

14 Serge Mallet, 'Socialism and the New Working Class', *International Socialist Journal*, April 1965.

15 See his earlier work, *La nouvelle class ouvière* (Editions du Seuil, Paris, 1963), which reports studies of three modern enterprises in France.

16 Alain Touraine, *The Post-Industrial Society* (Random House, 1971).

17 *Ibid.*, p. 18.

18 Michael Schumann, *Am Beispiel der Septemberstreiks*.

19 Tom Bottomore 'The Class Structure in Western Europe', in Margaret Scotford Archer and Salvador Giner, eds, *Contemporary Europe: Class, Status and Power* (Weidenfeld and Nicolson, 1971), especially pp. 404–5.

20 Albrecht Wellmer, *Critical Theory of Society* (Herder and Herder, New York, 1971), pp. 121–2.

CHAPTER 10 Socialism and The Nation

1 We have to bypass here the specific problems relating to the national question that exist and have long existed in Czechoslovakia and Yugoslavia. Although these problems are pertinent to our topic, especially in the case of Yugoslavia, there are so many specific factors involved (e.g. the complex relationships between Croatia and Slovenia with Serbia after World War II) that we cannot treat them in a paper such as this.

2 'The presuppositions of socialism and the tasks of the Social Democrats', English edition under the title, *Evolutionary Socialism: A Criticism and Affirmation* (Independent Labour Party, London, 1909).

3 This quote is taken from Helga Grebing, *Geschichte der deutschen*

Arbeiterbewegung, 3rd edition (dtv, Munich, 1972), p. 138 – a book to which I am greatly indebted for its stimulating perspective.

4 Cf. Leszek Kolakowski, *Der evolutionäre Geist* (Kohlhammer, Stuttgart, 1973), especially pp. 46ff.

CHAPTER 11 Socialism and Nationalism

1 H. Seton-Watson, *Nationalism and Communism* (Methuen, 1964), p. 3.
2 H. Kahn, *The Idea of Nationalism: A Study in Its Origins and Background*, 2nd edition (MacMillan, New York 1961), p. 330.
3 P. F. Sugar, 'External and Domestic Roots of Eastern European Nationalism' in P. F. Sugar and I. J. Lederer, eds, *Nationalism in Eastern Europe* (University of Washington Press, 1969), p. 8.
4 E. H. Carr, *Nationalism and After* (Macmillan, 1945), p. 33.
5 Carr, *Nationalism and After*, p. 21.
6 F. Palacký in *Národní noviny*, nos. 10 and 12 (1848), my translation.
7 Seton–Watson, *Nationalism and Communism*, p. 4.
8 A. Toynbee, *A Study of History* (Oxford University Press and Thames & Hudson, 1972), p. 34.
9 N. W. Heer, *Politics and History in the Soviet Union* (MIT Press, 1971), p. 10.
10 On the fluctuations in the treatment of nationalism by the communist parties, see also M. Djilas, 'Jugoslawiens Krise – eine Krise der Partei', *Die Zeit* (28 July 1972), p. 48.
11 B. Ward, *Nationalism and Ideology* (Hamish Hamilton, 1967), p. 101.

CHAPTER 12 Leisure as the Means of Production

1 George Lichtheim, *Marxism in Modern France* (Columbia University Press, 1966), p. 122.
2 *Ibid.*, p. 147.
3 *Das Kapital*, vol. I, in *Marx Engels Werke* (Berlin: Dietz Verlag, 1962), vol. XXIII, p. 447.
4 *Grundrisse der Kritik der Politische Oekonomie* (Dietz, Berlin, 1953).
5 *Marx Engels Werke*, XXV, p. 828.
6 Robert Blauner, *Alienation and Freedom* (University of Chicago Press, 1964), Chapter VI, 'The Chemical Operator: Control over Automated Technology'.
7 Daniel Bell in *The End of Ideology*, New Revised Edition (Collier Books, New York, 1961), pp. 270–1.

8 I have detailed an analysis of the Revolution in my *Socialism*, (Saturday Review Press, New York; 1972), Chapter VIII, and will not repeat it here.

9 V. I. Lenin, 'The Immediate Tasks of the Soviet Government', in *Collected Works* (Progress Publishers, Moscow, 1965), vol. XXVII, p. 259.

10 These brief and sketchy references to East German philosophical trends are deeply indebted to Peter C. Ludz's brilliant summary of them in *The Changing Party Elite in East Germany* (MIT Press, 1972), 'Major Trends of Change and Inertia in the Ideological System', Chapter IV.

11 *Ibid.*, p. 407.

12 Oskar Lange, 'The Computer and the Market', in C. H. Feinstein, ed., *Socialism, Capitalism And Economic Growth* (Cambridge University Press, 1967), p. 158.

13 'Technology and the American Economy', Report of the National Commission on Technology, Automation and Economic Progress (Washington; Government Printing Office, 1966), p. 2.

14 Bureau of the Census, *The American Almanac: The Statistical Abstract of the United States* (Grosset and Dunlap, 1973), pp. 217 and 225.

15 Rex Hardesty, 'The Changing American Workforce', *Free Trade Union News* (January 1973).

16 'Work in America', Report of a Special Task Force to the Secretary of Health, Education and Welfare (mimeo) (December 1972), pp. 12 and 17.

17 Quoted in 'Democratizing the Work Place', by Irving Bluestone, Vice-President, United Automobile Workers (UAW, mimeo) (22 June 1972), p. 16.

18 'Work in America', Chapter IV, 'The Redesign of Jobs'.

19 Herman Kahn and Anthony J. Wiener, *The Year 2000* (Macmillan, New York, 1967), p. 195.

20 Marcuse in Erich Fromm, ed., *Socialist Humanism* (Doubleday, 1965), p. 101.

CHAPTER 14 Socialism and Ownership

1 E. Kardelj, 'Protivrečnosti društvene svojine u savremenoj socijalist-ičkoj praksi', in *Teorija i Praksa Samoupravljanja u Jugoslaviji* (Radnička Štampa, Belgrade, 1972).

2 S. Kavčič, 'Razvojne možnosti Slovenije', *Teorija in Praksa* (1968).
3 O. Lange, *On the Economic Theory of Socialism* (University of Minnesota Press, 1948), p. 125.

CHAPTER 15 Socialism and Ownership

REFERENCES

Brus, W. ed., *Ekonomia Polityczna Socjalizmu*, 3rd edition (Warsaw, 1967).
Brus, W., *The Market in a Socialist Economy* (Routledge, 1972).
Brus, W., *Il sistema politico e la proprietà sociale nel socialismo* (Rome, 1973) (forthcoming).
Debreu, G., *The Theory of Value* (Wiley, 1959).
Dobb, M. H., 'The Entrepreneur Myth', *Economica*, no. 10 (February 1924).
Dobb, M. H., *Capitalist Enterprise and Social Progress* (Routledge, 1925).
Dobb, M. H., 'A Note on Saving and Investment in the Socialist Economy', *Economic Journal* (1938).
Dobb, M. H., *Argument on Socialism* (Lawrence and Wishart, 1966).
Dobb, M. H., *Socialist Planning: Some Problems* (Lawrence and Wishart, 1970).
Goodwin, R. M., *Elementary Economics from the Higher Standpoint* (Cambridge University Press, 1970).
Gray, J., 'The Chinese Model', *L'Est*, no. 2 (1971); also in A. Nove, D. M. Nuti, eds, *Socialist Economics* (1972).
Guevara, Che, 'Man and Socialism in Cuba' (1965); also in B. Silverman, ed., *Man and Socialism in Cuba* (1971).
Horvat, B., *An Essay in Yugoslav Society*, IASP (1969).
Keynes, J. M., 'Am I a Liberal?' (1925), in *Essays in Persuasion* (Macmillan, London, 1931).
Keynes, J. M., 'The End of Laissez-faire' (1926), in *Essays in Persuasion*; *The General Theory of Employment, Interest and Money* (Macmillan, London; Harcourt Brace, New York, 1936).
Kuron, J. and Modzelewski, K., 'An Open Letter to the Party', *International Socialism* (1968).
Lange, O., 'The Political Economy of Socialism' (1958), in *Papers in Economics and Sociology* (Warsaw, 1970).
Lenin, V. I., 'The Impending Catastrophe and How to Combat it' (1917), *Collected Works*, vol. 25 (Lawrence and Wishart, 1923).

Lenin, V. I., 'Left-wing Childishness and Petty Bourgeois Mentality' (1918), *Collected Works*, vol. 27.

Lenin, V. I., 'On Co-operation' (1923), *Collected Works*, vol. 33.

Mao Tse-tung, *How to Handle Contradictions among the People* (Communist Party of Great Britain, 1958).

Marx, K. and Engels, F., *The Communist Manifesto* (1848).

Marx, K., *Capital*, vol. I (1867).

Morishima, M., *Marx's Economies* (Cambridge University Press, 1973).

Nuti, D. M., 'On Incomes Policy', *Science and Society* (Fall 1969).

Nuti, D. M., 'Contra la ganancia', *Economia y Desarrollo* (Havana, 1972).

Nuti, D. M., 'The Transformation of Labour Values into Production Prices and the Marxian Theory of Exploitation', *Ekonomista* (1973a).

Nuti, D. M., 'The Political Economy of Socialism – Orthodoxy and Change in Polish Texts', *Soviet Studies* (1973b).

Robinson, J., *Notes from China* (Blackwell, 1964).

Rowthorn, R. E., 'The Reduction of Complex to Simple Labour' (mimeo) (1973).

Schumpeter, J. A., *Capitalism, Socialism and Democracy* (Allen and Unwin, 1943).

Schweitzer, A., 'Profits under Nazi Planning', *Quarterly Journal of Economics* (November 1946).

Sirc, L. *Economic Devolution in Eastern Europe* (Longman, 1969).

CHAPTER 16 Industrial Democracy, Self-management and Social Control of Production

1 C. A. R. Crosland, 'What the Worker Wants', *Encounter* (February 1959).

2 Blumberg, *Industrial Democracy* (Constable, 1968).

3 T. Burns and G. M. Stalker, *The Management of Innovation* (Tavistock Press, 1961).

4 Robert Dahl, 'Workers' Control of Industry and the British Labor Party,' *American Political Science Review* (October 1947).

5 J. Schumpeter, *Capitalism, Socialism and Democracy*, p. 269.

6 H. A. Clegg, *A New Approach to Industrial Democracy* (Blackwell, 1960), p. 29.

7 H. A. Clegg, 'Industrial Democracy and Nationalisation' (1951), in W. E. J. McCarthy (ed.), *Trade Unions* (Penguin, 1972), p. 84.

NOTES ON THE CONTRIBUTORS

TOM BOTTOMORE, b. 1920. Professor of Sociology at the University of Sussex. Taught at the London School of Economics and Simon Fraser University, Vancouver. President, British Sociological Association (1969–71). Vice-President of the International Sociological Association since 1970. Author of many studies on Marxism, sociological theory and social stratification.

WLODZIMIERZ BRUS, b. 1921 in Plock, Poland. Senior Research Fellow of St Antony's College, Oxford. Formerly Professor of Political Economy at Warsaw University (expelled for political reasons in 1968). Vice-Chairman of the Polish Economic Council (1957–63). Visiting Professor at the Universities of Rome, Glasgow and Louvain. Author of several books on general economic theory and on the economic problems of socialism.

STUART HAMPSHIRE, b. 1914. Warden of Wadham College, Oxford. Educated at Oxford. Formerly Professor of Philosophy at University College, London and Princeton University. Author of a number of books on the philosophy of mind, social philosophy and the history of philosophy.

MICHAEL HARRINGTON, b. 1928 in St Louis, Missouri. Professor at Queen's College, City University of New York. Studied in Chicago. Formerly National Chairman of the Young Socialist League (1954–7) and the Socialist Party (1968–72). Chairman, Democratic Socialist Organizing Committee (1973——). Author of books on contemporary American social and political life and on the theory of socialism.

MARIA HIRSZOWICZ, b. 1925 in Poland. Lecturer in Sociology at the University of Reading. Formerly Professor at Warsaw University (expelled in 1968 for political reasons). Author of many books on the sociology of organization, the sociology of power and industrial relations.

LESZEK KOLAKOWSKI, b. 1927 in Radom, Poland. Senior Research Fellow at All Souls College, Oxford. Formerly Professor of the History of Philosophy at the University of Warsaw (expelled in 1968 for political reasons). Visiting Professor at McGill University, Montreal and University of California at Berkeley. Author of books on the history of philosophy, the history of religion, and the philosophy of culture.

VLADIMIR V. KUSIN, b. 1929 in Czechoslovakia. Senior editor of ABSEES and member of the Institute of Soviet and East European Studies at the University of Glasgow. Studied history and political science at Charles University in Prague. Has published several studies on recent Czechoslovak history, in particular *The Intellectual Origins of the Prague Spring* and *Political Grouping in the Czechoslovak Reform Movement*.

RICHARD LOWENTHAL has been since 1961 Professor at the Free University, Berlin and at various times Guest Professor at Columbia University. Fellow of the Centre for Advanced Study in Behavioural Science at Stanford University. Visiting Fellow of All Souls, Oxford. He is author of *Beyond Capitalism* (1947) and *World Communism: The Disintegration of a Secular Faith* (1964) and has contributed to volumes and periodicals published in many countries.

STEVEN LUKES, b. 1941. Sociologist. Studied at Oxford. Now a Fellow and Tutor in Sociology and Politics at Balliol College, Oxford. Among his publications are *Emile Durkheim* (1973), *Individualism* (1973) and *Power: A Radical View* (1974).

PETER C. LUDZ, b. 1931. Professor of Political Science at the University of Munich, West Germany, since 1973. Studied in Munich, Mainz, Berlin, Paris. Formerly Professor at the Free University in Berlin and University of Bielefeld. Senior Research Fellow at Columbia University, New York. Has written many studies on the political sociology of Eastern Europe, especially East Germany.

FRANZ MAREK, b. 1913. Political leader and author of many studies on the history of Marxism and on political theory. Member of the Central Committee (1945–70) and Political Bureau (1948–69) of the Austrian Communist Party. Editor of the *Wiener Tagebuch*.

GILLES HENRI MARTINET has been since 1965 National Secretaire Adjoint of the PSU and administrator of *Le Nouvel Observateur*. He is the author of *Le Marxisme de Notre Temps* (1962).

J. P. MAYER, b. 1903. Professor at Reading University and Director of the Tocqueville Research Centre at Reading. Published Marx's early manuscripts and is editing Tocqueville's works. Author of books on the history of political thought, on Tocqueville and Max Weber.

DOMENICO MARIO NUTI, b. 1937 in Arezzo, Italy. Fellow of King's College, Cambridge. Assistant Lecturer in Economics at the University of Cambridge. Studied law and economics in Rome, Warsaw and Cambridge. Taught at the Universities of Rome, Bologna, Louvain. Author of several studies on the economic theory of production, investment and distribution and on the economics of Eastern Europe.

GAJO PETROVIC, b. 1927 in Karlovac, Yugoslavia. Professor of Philosophy at the University of Zagreb. Editor-in-chief of the journal *Praxis* since 1964. Studied in Zagreb, Leningrad, Moscow. Has published several books on Marxist philosophy and on British analytical philosophy.

FRITZ J. RADDATZ, b. 1931 in Berlin. Professor at the Technische Universität in Hannover. Director of the Der Spiegel Institute for International Research. Studied in Berlin. Has published numerous works on the theory of literature and on contemporary German literature.

LJUBO SIRC, b. 1920 in Yugoslavia. Senior Lecturer in Political Economy at the University of Glasgow. Studied in Ljubljana and Fribourg (Switzerland). Has written many studies on economic development in Eastern Europe and on international trade and finance.

CHARLES TAYLOR, b. 1931. Professor of Political Science and Philosophy at McGill University, Montreal, Canada. Member of Federal Executive of the New Democratic Party of Canada. Studied in Montreal and Oxford. Author of studies on the philosophy of mind and the history of philosophy.

Participants in the Reading Conference who did not contribute papers:

ROBERT CECIL. Reader in Contemporary German History and Deputy Chairman of the Graduate School of Contemporary European Studies at the University of Reading.

G. A. COHEN. Lecturer in Philosophy at University College, London.

KLAUS H. HENNING. Lecturer in Economics at the University of Reading.

ERIC HOBSBAWM. Professor of Economic and Social History at Birkbeck College, University of London.

WALTER KENDALL. Senior Research Fellow at Nuffield College, Oxford.

MICHAEL STEWART. Reader in Political Economy at University College, London.

INDEX